Teaching Developmentally Disabled Children:

The **ME** Book

Teaching Developmentally Disabled Children

The **ME** Book

by

O. Ivar Lovaas, Ph.D.

Department of Psychology
University of California, Los Angeles

with
Andrea Ackerman, Ph.D.,
Dean Alexander, Ph.D.,
Paula Firestone, M.A.,
Marlyn Perkins, Ph.D., and
Douglas B. Young, Ph.D.
and with contributions by
Edward G. Carr, Ph.D. and
Crighton Newsom, Ph.D.

Printed in the United States of America

Library of Congress Cataloging in Publication Data

Lovaas, O. Ivar.
Teaching developmentally disabled children.

Includes bibliographies and index.
1. Developmentally disabled children—United States—Addresses, essays, lectures.
2. Developmentally disabled children—Education. 3. Developmentally disabled children—Care and treatment—Addresses, essays, lectures. 4. Children—Management. 5. Parenting—United States. I. Title.
HQ773.6.L68   371.91′6   80-26047
ISBN 0-936104-78-3 (previously 0-8391-1567-9)

pro·ed
An International Publisher
8700 Shoal Creek Boulevard
Austin, Texas 78757-6897
800/897-3202 Fax 800/397-7633
Order online at http://www.proedinc.com

17 18 19 20 21 22 23 24   04 03 02 01 00 99

CONTENTS

CO-AUTHORS AND CONTRIBUTORS

Andrea Ackerman, Ph.D.
Department of Psychology
University of California at Los Angeles
Los Angeles, California 90024

Dean D. Alexander, Ph.D.
Department of Psychology
Claremont Graduate School
Claremont, California 91711

Edward G. Carr, Ph.D.
State University of New York at Stony Brook
and
Suffolk Child Development Center
Stony Brook, New York 11794

Paula Firestone, M.A.
Department of Psychology
University of California at Los Angeles
Los Angeles, California 90024

Crighton Newsom, Ph.D.
Research Coordinator
Suffolk Child Development Center
State University of New York at Stony Brook
Stony Brook, New York 11794

Marlyn Perkins, Ph.D.
Department of Education
Educational Psychology Division
University of California at Santa Barbara
Santa Barbara, California 93105

Douglas B. Young, Ph.D.
Private Practice
Los Angeles Psychosocial Center
6331 Hollywood Boulevard
Suite 1000
Los Angeles, California 90024

PREFACE

This book contains a set of programs that were started many years ago in an attempt to provide help for parents and teachers in dealing with their developmentally disabled children. One of the parents called these programs the "Me Book," for this is really a book for the child. As a result of following the programs presented in this book, the child does become more of a person, an individual, more of a "me." So, we adopted the subtitle *The Me Book*.

The book evolved and developed out of our experiences in working with developmentally disabled children. A description of these experiences will clarify our approach, for they formed the basis of our teaching philosophy. We hope that this explanation of our teaching philosophy will help clarify our position, so that it will seem less arbitrary and perhaps be less objectionable to those persons holding different views. Let us begin by relating the mistakes we made, because sometimes one can learn a great deal from mistakes.

In 1964, we institutionalized a group of children with severe developmental disabilities and began to formulate teaching programs designed to help them overcome atavistic and tantrum behaviors, to help them develop language, to improve their play and social interactions, and to build the other kinds of behavioral skills that these children needed in order to function better in less restrictive environments. This book contains revisions of many of the teaching programs which were initiated at that time.

A more complete summary of our early treatment successes and failures have been presented elsewhere (Lovaas, O. I., Koegel, R. L., Simmons, J. Q., and Long, J. S. Some generalization and follow-up measures on autistic children in behavior therapy. *Journal of Applied Behavior Analysis*, 1973, 6, 131-165). The main findings and implications are summarized below.

Certain positive aspects of our teaching programs became apparent quite soon. For example, we could help the children quickly overcome many of their undesirable and interfering behaviors, such as their tantrums, their bizarre ritualistic behaviors, and their self-injurious behaviors. We were also able to teach them some very complex behaviors, such as language, which many had thought would prove too difficult for these children to grasp. The procedures were very time-consuming, but they were effective, for all the children did learn, although some learned more than others.

The first serious mistake we made in this program was to treat the children within an institutional (hospital or clinic) environment. The changes we created in the child's behaviors did not generalize, or transfer, to the rest of the child's environment, such as his home or school. However, we were successful when we made special efforts to bring about generalization. These special efforts involved working out the treatment and educational programming in these other environments, which brought us to question the necessity or desirability of using a hospital as a teaching and learning environment. Our goal was to help these children to live and function in the real world, and not in an artificial setting, such as an institution.

We had hospitalized the children in the first place because we still held the old view we had been taught that children like those with whom we worked were "ill" due to either psychological or organic reasons. That is, it was thought that they had experienced either inadequate parenting or had suffered from some organic brain damage. It seemed to follow, then, that since they were "ill" they needed "treatment," ideally in a "hospital." Given our background, it made sense at the time; it was an easy mistake to make. We decided, then, to change the place of treatment from the institution to the child's natural environment; that is, we began to treat him in his home and school.

The second major mistake we made was to isolate the parents from their child's treatment. We thought it quite appropriate that professional persons such as ourselves should play the major role in the treatment program, with a smaller role being assigned to the parents and the child's teachers. The children's problems were very complex, we felt, and only the most educated persons could help. The children needed *professional* intervention. There were several major problems associated with this decision. First, the children needed a great deal of treatment time in order to show improvement and there were so many such children that there were simply not enough professional persons available to meet the treatment needs. Second, if the parents didn't know exactly what their child's treatment program consisted of, what we were doing, why we were doing it, and what the final goals were, then they wouldn't be able to help their child maintain the gains made in therapy, and the child would regress. We realized our errors, and changed our approach to teaching the child's parents and teachers exactly how we had taught the children. The child's treatment was placed in the hands of the adults in his natural, everyday community. The parents and teachers became the child's primary therapists, and we became their consultants.

In retrospect, this new development made good sense. If a child's behavior is influenced by the environment in which he lives and learns, and since a child's environment is composed of several different settings (such as school, home, and neighborhood) then it follows that the child's *total* environment should be arranged to become therapeutic and educational, if the child is to make maximal gains in treatment.

A third major mistake was to expect a "breakthrough." We were expecting a sudden step forward, that possibly somehow we would hit upon some central cognitive, emotional, or social event inside the child's mind that would help him make a sudden and major leap ahead. Traditional conceptions are filled with such promises. Such a leap would have been so gratifying, and it would have made our work so much easier. It never happened. Instead, progress followed a slow, step-by-step upward progression, with only a few and minor spurts ahead. We learned to settle down for hard work. Persons who work with developmentally disabled children may take some comforts in Charles Darwin's basic hypothesis: *Natura non facit saltum* (Nature does not make leaps). (Actually, anyone who has been a parent also may become impressed with how slow *normal* children develop: it takes 9 months to be born, a whole year to learn how to walk, and a full 2 years before even minimal speech is occurring. And the infant is practicing literally 12 to 14 hours a day, 7 days a week, and takes no vacation!)

There were several other developments that emerged as we moved away from the traditional disease model of service delivery. We broke down the large hypothetical constructs of "autism," "aphasia," "retardation," etc. into more manageable components or behaviors. We didn't offer *treatment* for autism or schizophrenia; instead we were *teaching* the children specific behaviors such as language, play, and affection. These teaching programs were "interchangeable" across diagnostic categories in the sense that what we had learned about teaching language to retarded children could just as easily be applied to teaching language to aphasic or autistic children. The whole diagnostic enterprise became increasingly irrelevant.

One of the most gratifying aspects of our project centered around the development of specific intervention techniques. For years, many professionals had felt extremely uncomfortable when confronted with questions from parents or teachers concerning how to deal with specific behavioral problems: How do you toilet train? How do you help the mute child speak? How do you help an aggressive child become more friendly? At last, we had found some concrete answers to those questions. Perhaps the former lack of answers to these questions was the reason for postulating internal problems as the cause for the child's problems in the first place. If the problems were internal and hidden, then no one, except trained professionals, could work on them. Perhaps such isolation helped prolong our ignorance.

Rather than viewing the child as ill or diseased, we came to view him as "different"—different in the sense that the average or common environment, which does so well for the average child, does not fit the needs nor provide the structure necessary to be a good teaching/learning environment for these exceptional children. Our task was, then, to construct a special environment, one in which the disabled child could learn. We chose to deviate from the average environment only as much as was absolutely necessary to make it a suitable learning environment for our children. We did this for two reasons: first, it would make it easier to return the child to his community later on, and second, the common environment has been developing over thousands of years, and it does possess some educational wisdom, even though this is not always apparent. We chose, therefore, to teach the children, whenever possible, as normal parents teach their normal children.

To summarize and state some implications:

1. The place of intervention was changed from the institution to the child's natural, everyday community.
2. The locus of intervention was changed from treatment to teaching.
3. Teaching was placed in the hands of the child's teachers and parents.
4. Autism, retardation, brain damage, and other diagnostic categories were broken down into smaller and more manageable units of behavior such as language, play, and self-help skills. These behaviors cut across diagnostic categories.
5. Diagnostic testing became de-emphasized.

These were the main developments. There were several others, and many of these occurred in other parts of the country, sometimes independent of theoretical orientation. For example, institutionalization became de-emphasized by almost all professionals. Gestaltists and existentialists also rejected the disease model and associated diagnosis. Some developments were quite independent of theoretical orientations—for example, the more new knowledge we gained, the more democratic the process became. That is, the consumers, or the parents, had a greater part in determining the kinds of services to be delivered. It would be interesting to speculate on all that has happened, but space does not permit.

The most important steps in behavioral teaching centered on breaking down the large and rather general problem of "disability" into more manageable and separate behavioral units, and to relate these behaviors to more manipulable environmental variables. Such analysis and systematic manipulation appears to have greatly facilitated scientific inquiry, which is a key to progress in education and psychology. We can see the beginning of *cumulative* knowledge. Since such an analysis is still in its beginning stages, this manual can best serve to establish both a helping and a working relationship between students and persons with developmental disabilities, where much more has to be investigated and learned in order for us to become truly successful teachers. When we do find out how to successfully teach, we will then have the tools and skills necessary to help developmentally disabled persons become functioning members of society; there will be no more retarded persons.

This short history may seem rather arbitrary and unfair to those who are trying to understand and help developmentally disabled persons from the point of view of dealing with internal dysfunction or damage, the related diagnosis, and the subsequent treatment. Perhaps the issue of "Who is right?" can be clarified if we examine two different strategies for gathering information. One can characterize research efforts as being largely deductive or largely inductive. Some investigators make generalizations (inferences about underlying dysfunction) after examining relatively few data, while others prefer to accumulate much more information or data before they feel they can justify a general theoretical statement. A former teacher of mine (Professor Ben McKeever at the University of Washington) divided researchers into two groups, *shaft sinkers* and *pyramid builders*. A shaft sinker works in relative isolation, he moves from one area to another, sinking shafts and hoping that he will strike a well of knowledge. When he does, a great number of problems will be solved at the same time. On the other hand, a pyramid builder feels that knowledge can best be gained by several persons working together, where each piece of information is sought to compliment or strengthen other pieces of information, where higher levels are built after lower levels are secured, and so on. He may not know exactly how the pyramid will look when it is finished, but he may have some general idea when he starts. Personality theorists, psychopathologists, and the like would be shaft sinkers, behaviorists would be pyramid builders. So far, the shaft sinkers haven't struck oil yet. The behaviorists have more going for them; the foundation of a pyramid under construction is more substantial and more reassuring than a dry well. In the future, perhaps, there will be a successful shaft sinker. The definition of a genius is one who finds the well with relatively little prior knowledge. And many a pyramid builder may just be a pebble piler in disguise. In any case, there is no *a priori* right or wrong way of making hypotheses about nature. My apology to all potential shaft sinkers.

Let us express our gratitude to the large number of students who have helped develop the programs presented in this book. These were students at UCLA who were enrolled in Psychology 170 A "Introduction to Behavior Modification," and Psychology 170 B "Behavior Modification Laboratory." They were dedicated to helping the less fortunate, they were flexible and open-minded, intelligent and creative, and, in general, all the good things one associates with the kinds of persons we all would like to work with. Many thanks to our colleagues in the Department of Psychology at UCLA, for their willingness to overlook some problems and reinforce the main efforts. We also want to thank the Staff at Camarillo State Hospital in Camarillo, California, for their help in facilitating the research which underlies many of the teaching programs in this book. Thanks also to Drs. Barbara Andersen and Crighton Newsom for their editorial comments. Very special thanks for the support of the National Institute of Mental Health (Grants MH 32803 and MH 1140) and particularly to Dr. Morris Parloff for his kind guidance. Finally, we want to thank Kristen Hannum for guiding and organizing the preparation of this manuscript, a very difficult job at times.

To Beth, Mike and Marty, Rick, Pam, Billy, Chuck, Bill, Dean, Jimmy, Leslie, Bruce, Eric, Scott, and all the other children who followed them, and their dear parents, for all their help and guidance.

INTRODUCTION

This book is intended for teachers and parents to help developmentally disabled persons learn to live more meaningful lives. It should be helpful for persons retarded in behavioral development, be it as a result of mental retardation, brain damage, autism, severe aphasia, severe emotional disorder, childhood schizophrenia, or any other of a number of disorders. Although most of the programs were developed with children and youth, they can be used for persons of any age.

Developmentally disabled persons often share a number of common characteristics. They typically score within the retarded range of intellectual functioning on IQ tests. Developmentally disabled persons often need to learn some of the most basic aspects of living, including eating, toileting, and dressing. Some persons do not know how to play, and others need to learn to get along with peers and to develop friendships. They often need help in developing their language. Some individuals are mute, while others can talk but cannot express themselves well. Almost all developmentally disabled persons need help with school. Older persons with developmental disabilities need to learn to spend their leisure time more effectively. This book presents a set of teaching programs designed to help persons lessen or overcome these behavioral deficiencies.

In addition to needing help with acquiring new behaviors, many developmentally disabled persons also need to unlearn certain maladaptive behaviors, such as throwing tantrums when frustrated and spending hours alone in seemingly meaningless ritualistic play. Our programs help parents and teachers better understand these problem behaviors and teach children and students to better manage their behaviors. Through this help students should become easier to handle at school and able to fit in their community. They should become happier persons.

Throughout this book we refer to developmentally disabled or behaviorally retarded (delayed) persons as students or children. We often use the term *child* in referring to the students even though some of the "children" we worked with were actually adults. Perhaps *child-like* would have been a better term. Caregivers, such as parents, teachers, speech therapists, psychiatric technicians, nurses, and psychologists, who work with developmentally disabled persons are called parents or teachers. When pronouns are needed in our discussion of developmentally disabled persons, we have selected the mascu-

1

line form to avoid awkward double pronoun constructions and to reflect the fact most of these students are male.

OUR TEACHING PHILOSOPHY

We created a special teaching environment that resembled the normal or average environment as much as possible. The following general statements underlie our teaching philosophy:

1. All living organisms show variability in their behaviors. Charles Darwin was the first to recognize the importance of such variability for the purpose of survival of the species. We can regard developmentally disabled persons as instances of such variability. Behavioral variability (deviance) is not considered to be symptomatic of underlying mental illness or disease, and therefore requiring its own unique form of treatment. Although many developmentally disabled individuals suffer from serious organic brain damage, it has not been to the educational advantage of developmentally disabled individuals to be treated as mentally ill. Laws of learning apply to individuals with deviant organic structure as they do to individuals with less deviant structure.

2. The average environment treats the *average* person best, apparently because the average environment was selected and/or shaped by the average person. Persons at either extreme do not learn well from the average environment because that environment has not been constructed for them.

3. Special education and psychology may help those who deviate from the average by creating and constructing special teaching environments in which the deviant may learn.

4. This special environment should differ as little as possible from the average environment because 1) the appropriateness of the average environment, implicit in the process of "natural selection" and its development over thousands of years, is not to be lightly dismissed, and 2) one of the primary goals of education for developmentally disabled persons is to help them function more adequately in their *natural* environment. The smaller the difference between the special therapeutic/educational environment constructed for the child and the average environment to which, it is hoped, he will return, the easier the transition.

We employed rewards and punishment analogous to those used with normal children in creating the special teaching environment. We taught the children at home, not in hospitals or clinics, because children live and learn in homes. Parents and teachers were taught the programs because they care for and teach children. Our programs present a set of teaching steps, very similar to those employed with normal children, but certain features are temporarily exaggerated and the teaching process is slowed down. Our procedures can be taught to and used by anyone.

In this book we share our experiences of the last 18 years in helping developmentally disabled persons learn to behave in a more normal way. The book is written with as few technical terms as possible. It is intended to help parents and teachers who have little or no background in modern learning theory or behavior modification, which is the basic conceptual system underlying our teaching programs. Although the teaching steps are presented in everyday language, and parents and teachers learn about behavior modification by carrying out the various programs, we recommend certain introductory texts on learning theory and behavior modification that present more theoretical and research information. (See the recommended reading list at the end of Unit I.) A better understanding of the foundations of our programs can be gained by reading one or more of these texts along with this teaching manual. Understanding the basic theory helps teachers and parents become more creative in developing their

Introduction

own programs. There are even several published teaching manuals that deal with problems similar to the ones addressed in this manual. Bernal's (1978) review of these manuals can help you select the appropriate one.

WORDS OF CAUTION

Some words of caution about our treatment/teaching philosophy are in order before we describe our teaching programs. First, no one approach will solve all the problems of developmentally disabled persons. Rather, the persons who try to help these individuals need to draw upon a variety of concepts and teaching techniques. For example, each client will have somewhat different needs and the context within which he functions will be different. Procedures that work particularly well for an affectionate and frightened blind child may be somewhat different from those that work for an aggressive, autistic child. What works well in treating a child in his family in his natural community may not work equally well for an institutionalized adult. The "teacher-therapist-parent" has to be flexible, innovative, and able to draw upon a variety of techniques and procedures.

We do know now that certain basic processes work for all persons and that a working knowledge of these processes is essential for providing effective help. One such procedure, or principle, used for providing help is the *pleasure-pain principle,* which is infinitely better understood today than when first proposed by the Greeks. This principle was renamed *learning by trial and error,* and later called *The Law of Effect* and *instrumental learning.* Today most persons refer to this principle as *operant conditioning* and the application of that principle as *behavior modification* or *applied behavior analysis.* In psychology and education, operant conditioning may well be like the principle of gravity in physics. We all know about gravity, but you need to know it in detail to transport a person to the moon. Likewise, with operant learning, we observe it and use it every day, but to work the principle effectively with developmentally disabled persons requires more than superficial knowledge. It is hoped that this teaching manual will help you learn to use the principle of operant learning more effectively, but keep in mind that, just as a physicist needs to know more than the laws of gravity to transport a person to the moon, you need to know more than the laws of operant behavior to move a person to more adequate functioning.

We have limited ourselves to the use of operant learning in devising our programs for teaching developmentally disabled persons. We recognize the considerable investment that other professionals have made in other approaches and hope that no one is upset or angered by the focus of this book.

GUIDING PRINCIPLES

To help you in implementing our teaching programs, six guiding principles, which transcend the specific techniques involved in the programs, have been identified.

1. *All persons who consistently interact with developmentally disabled persons have to learn to be teachers.* To keep your child in his natural community as long as possible you must become an effective teacher. Primarily, this is for his own protection since living in an environment that is the least restrictive, most natural one will optimize his learning experiences. But it also serves to protect you, as a parent or teacher, against the hurt of separation or against the trauma of giving up your child to persons or processes you don't understand or over which you have limited control. By

learning our teaching procedures you will be exposed to the best help that professionals can offer you and your child at the present time. When you have the best information, you can make the best decisions; others don't have to make decisions for you.

2. *Set small goals in the beginning so that both you and your child will be rewarded. Find pleasure in small steps forward.* You should be pleased at reaching a set of smaller goals, rather than hoping and struggling for some often unattainable and absolute ideal of normalcy or overall excellence. This book teaches you to identify and reach smaller, quite attainable goals. You still can anticipate normalcy and excellence in some areas, but you should not expect it in all. This does not mean that you will become an unhappy parent or teacher. Often the happiest people are those who curb their ambitions a bit, those individuals who work for a set of smaller goals that can be attained within a reasonable amount of time. Remember, excellence is relative; there will always be more to learn, so it is important to find pleasure in reachable goals.

3. *Be prepared for much hard work. Protect yourself from burn-out by forming a "teaching team."* If you take your teaching seriously, if you do all the one-to-one teaching yourself, you may burn out after 1 or 2 years. Be prepared for hard work; developmentally disabled persons often have to be taught everything in the smallest detail. Many do not respond in the beginning, and you have to be extremely patient. Get some help to prevent burn-out. Hire assistants and form a "teaching team." The ideal teaching team probably numbers between four and eight people, each working about four to eight hours per week. If your child gets from 20 to 60 hours of one-on-one teaching per week, he will probably get as much instruction as he can handle. It is critical that teaching be carried out everywhere—at home, at school, as many hours a day as possible. Everybody has to teach, and everybody has to teach in a consistent manner, at least in the beginning.

    This manual should help you become a good teacher and shows you how to use your assistants effectively. After only 2 or 3 hours of instruction, your assistants should be of help to you. They learn what you have learned from the program, and then they do most of the work with your child. You are the expert; you are the consultant. Assistants can be parents, teachers, normal siblings, or high school and college students. (There are some amazingly good high school and college students who will work for little money, if not for free.)

    Choose your assistants through "job interviews." That is, have the prospective assistant interact with your child. If you like the way he handles himself "on the spot," and if he seems easy to instruct, you probably will have a good worker. Expect your assistants to stay on the job for 6 months to a couple of years; they come and go, you have to stay. If you have a large group of assistants, assign specific responsibilities (and authorities) to different persons. For example, one person becomes the expert at constructing programs for building some aspect of language, another person leads the group in building play skills, one works on dressing and self-help, one is the liaison between the parents and the teacher, and so on. Each person works in every program, but each program has only one person in charge. You are in charge of the entire program.

    Have a weekly "staff meeting" for 1 hour to discuss what has been done in the past week and to lay plans for the following week. Each person should work with the child in front of everyone else during staff meetings to get feedback, positive or negative, regarding teaching methods. Such weekly supervision is important. During the first 2 or 3 months, it perhaps is best to have assistants work in pairs so that they can better identify each other's mistakes and note superior procedures. If a team member doesn't agree to this and feels so "senior" and experienced that he wants to do it his own way, or so sensitive that he can't stand criticism, then let that person go before he hurts your program. If you are a teacher, hope that the child's parents will be open to feedback as you are. If you are a parent, hope that you are welcomed to the child's school. If the teacher does not welcome you to the child's class, consult with the school principal and perhaps consider changing teachers or schools.

4. *Have your child work for what he wants; make him responsible.* Developmentally disabled persons have to work particularly hard. Their work is to learn, your job is to teach. The responsibility is shared. With responsibility, the developmentally disabled individual takes on dignity and "acquires" certain basic rights as a person. No one has the right to be taken care of, no matter how retarded he is. So, put your child to work; his work is to learn.

5. *Try not to be frightened or feel guilty by the child's emotional outbursts or withdrawal. You are the boss, you make the decisions.* Almost all persons, including the retarded and especially the autistic and emotionally disturbed, want it differently. Sometimes they will become so angry that they act out aggressively against themselves, the furniture, or you. They scare you. Or they will withdraw and make you feel guilty. They may try to frighten you into quitting. Don't let them do that because it will hurt *them* in the long run. They have no right to act bizarrely, many professional opinions notwithstanding. On the contrary, you have a right to expect decent behavior from your children. If you work hard for your child, he should be grateful, work hard, and show affection to you in return. You have to teach him that, and the programs in this book help you do so.

   Keep in mind that sometimes it is the child who is particularly aggressive or who looks very bizarre when you make demands of him who will progress well in the program; he is responding. The child who is not bothered by demands often moves more slowly in our programs. Your child's basic humanity is showing when he screams and slaps himself or strikes out at you. But you have to stop that behavior and teach him better ways to cope with his frustrations.

6. *Begin by making the child's appearance as normal as possible.* Before you begin teaching, make your child look as normal as possible. For example, don't let him get too fat. Many disabled persons look like big balloons and just the sight of them invites ridicule and isolation. You may want to consult a dietician for help. Similarly, dress your child nicely in clothes that fit and look like clothes his peers are wearing. (Have his siblings pick out his clothes, if you don't know what is "in.") Don't let him wear peculiar clothing. Help him wash his face, like his normal peers do, to reduce skin problems. Give him a nice haircut; have his hair styled if you can afford it. All too often retarded persons become socially excluded immediately on the basis of their appearance.

HOW THE BOOK IS ORGANIZED

Unit I introduces certain basic teaching principles that center on how to present instructions, how to break down teaching material to manageable components, how to select rewards and punishments, how to use them in teaching, etc. Problem behaviors of developmentally disabled persons, how to record them, and what to do about them are also discussed.

   Unit II presents various programs for helping the child get ready to learn. These programs start out with the most simple tasks, such as how to teach a child to sit in a chair, how to help him attend to his teacher, and how to better manage disruptive behaviors. Steps for helping to generalize learning are also discussed.

Unit III teaches the beginnings of language, such as teaching the child to follow simple instructions and commands, how to identify similarities (matching), and the early steps in helping the child to imitate the behaviors of others. This unit also introduces teaching programs for early play skills.

Unit IV presents programs for building self-help skills, such as appropriate eating, dressing, and toileting.

Unit V deals with intermediate language, including teaching the child to follow more complicated instructions, to verbally describe certain basic aspects of his environment, and to ask for things. This unit also presents a program for teaching signing (manual communication) to those persons who have problems with learning verbal language. It also contains a program for helping persons overcome echolalic and psychotic (inappropriate) language.

Unit VI deals with advanced language, including the building of elementary sentences, and presents programs for teaching abstract language (prepositions, pronouns, color, form, etc.).

Unit VII presents programs on how to help developmentally disabled persons adjust to the community, such as going to a restaurant or a supermarket. There is a chapter on how to teach a developmentally disabled person to learn by observing others learn, which deals with his understanding of feelings and emotions. There are programs on how to teach him to become more spontaneous and to develop his imagination. Other chapters include advice to teachers who work in classroom settings, and review some common mistakes in behavioral teaching and present certain precautions.

The book is arranged from the easy to the complex. Certain sections of this book will be difficult to understand, but other parts will be easy. The beginning is always the hardest. Once you are halfway through this book, having taught your child or student the first dozen programs, you will begin to feel like an expert, a person with confidence. But have patience in the beginning with both yourself and your child. The programs are laid out in a developmental sequence, such that the early programs should be started before the later ones. Once a program is started, and the child shows some beginning mastery, subsequent programs may be introduced so that they overlap with the earlier ones. Most of the programs are continuous (that is, they have no meaningful ending point). Thus, in the beginning, a child may be on three or four programs (for example, during the first months he may be on programs for reducing tantrums, sitting properly, establishing eye-to-face contact, and developing nonverbal imitation), while a year later he may be on 30 or 40 concurrent programs.

The early programs are laid out in considerable step-by-step detail. Such great detail may seem redundant in some places, but we judged it best to be careful and safe. Later programs, such as those in Unit VII, are presented with minimal procedural detail, and require familiarity with the teaching steps outlined in earlier chapters to be administered.

The parent or teacher should become familiar with the whole book in order to select a particular combination of programs for a particular child. For example, there are programs in Unit VII that may be applicable even early in teaching. We recommend starting with the programs in Unit II, and establishing a solid base before going on to subsequent programs.

After working through most of the programs in this book, a teacher should have a "feel" for how to teach using behavioral procedures, and should be able to construct teaching programs. The programs we describe can serve as a basis for instructing a developmentally disabled person in everything that he needs to learn.

The book is supplemented by videotapes depicting examples of most of the programs we describe. (For information on how to obtain these tapes, please write to University Park Press.) The book and the tapes should be used jointly, for the best results. The tapes show how the lessons are paced, the close interaction between adult and child, the way in which rewards are given, the subtleties of certain instructions, and many other details that can only be shown visually. We strongly recommend that you view these videotapes. Each tape is about 20 minutes long. They are organized as follows:

Tape 1: *Getting Ready to Learn*—covers early control (as in teaching the child to eat, look, control tantrums, and pay attention), examples of how to build nonverbal imitation, match-to-sample, and beginnings of receptive language. Tape 1 deals with material covered in Units I and II and parts of Unit III in the book.

Tape 2: *Early Language*—shows steps in teaching verbal imitation and how to teach the child to identify objects and behaviors, to label objects and body parts, and to make verbal demands. Tape 2 corresponds to the last part of Unit III and most of Unit V in the book.

Tape 3: *Basic Self-Help Skills*—shows examples of programs for bedmaking, tooth-brushing, shaving, putting on cosmetics, and other personal/homemaking skills. Certain household chores are also depicted, such as vacuuming, setting the table, and preparing food. Tape 3 corresponds to Unit IV in the book.

Tape 4: *Advanced Language*—corresponds to Unit VI in the book. It deals with teaching abstract language, such as pronouns, prepositions, shapes, and time, and certain "cognitive" tasks such as seeking information and becoming more spontaneous.

Tape 5: *Expanding World*—corresponds to Unit VII in the book and shows programs on formal school-type tasks, cause and effect relationships, feelings, pretending and imagining, and observational learning. It also reviews some of the more common mistakes in behavioral teaching.

Good luck!

REFERENCE

Bernal, M. E., & North, J. A. A survey of parent training manuals. *Journal of Applied Behavior Analysis*, 1978, *11*, 533-544.

UNIT I

BASIC INFORMATION

Unit I is an introduction, and in a sense a summary, of how to teach. Chapter 1 introduces several techniques for increasing and decreasing different aspects of your child's behavior. You want to teach your child to listen *more*, to talk *more*, and to take *more* care of his personal needs. We define certain techniques, like rewards, that will *increase* some of your child's behaviors if used correctly. There are other things you will wish your child would do less, or not at all, such as wetting his bed, being physically too active, or getting too angry. We introduce and define certain procedures, like ignoring or punishing, in order to *decrease* such behaviors.

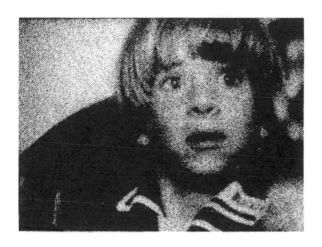

Keep in mind that when we introduce and define terms, such as *rewards* and *punishments* in Chapter 1, it is just an introduction. These terms are used again and again throughout the book. If you don't see exactly how they are applied after reading Chapter 1, don't worry. You will have a much better understanding of these terms and concepts after you have worked through the first three or four chapters, and you will understand them like an expert after you have finished the book.

Chapter 2 discusses the use of physical punishment. It is a controversial process, capable of causing much harm if used incorrectly, but having benefits when properly used.

Chapter 3 presents some of the behavior characteristics of developmentally disabled persons. You need to recognize and try to understand these problem behaviors if you are to work with these people effectively. Not all developmentally disabled persons show these problems, but many do. For example, we discuss how developmentally disabled persons can become very angry and hard to manage at times, or that they can be very inattentive. We present certain techniques to help overcome these problems or to work around them. Chapter 4 describes methods of recording behavior. Unit I, then, consists of an introduction of teaching techniques and problems to overcome.

9

CHAPTER 1

HOW TO DO IT

This chapter examines the basic processes involved in teaching your child new behaviors and in shaping, or changing, existing behaviors. Many terms and concepts used in our teaching programs are defined, discussed, and explained by everyday examples. Rewards, punishments, overcorrection, shaping, and prompting are only a few of the concepts that must be understood before you can teach the programs to your child. These terms and others are defined in more detail within the context of the actual teaching programs but are presented here so that you can begin to become familiar with them.

SELECTING REWARDS

Positive Rewards

Usually, when a child does something correct, you reward him. You say, "Here's 25¢ for a candy bar," "You can stay up later tonight," "Have a bite of ice cream," or something similar to these statements. That is, you give him something he wants. Adults reward children, particularly when they are young, in this direct, positive way. In the beginning, the rewards may be quite noticeable and concrete, like ice cream and kisses. As the child develops, the rewards usually become more subtle, as when they are conveyed by just a glance or some other minimal recognition of the person's behavior. Many teachers feel that certain behaviors may themselves become rewarding, and that extrinsic rewards, like food and social praise, are not necessary to maintain the behavior. But, in the beginning, it pays to exaggerate the rewards for a particular behavior, just to be on the safe side. These rewards are called *positives*.

When you reward developmentally disabled persons be very emphatic and loud—exclaim a very loud "Good," "Fine," or "You're great." If there is an audience, have them clap or give lots of hugs, kisses, and strokes. We typically use food rewards in addition to the words of encouragement and praise. For example, you can create hundreds of rewards for good behavior by cutting a child's meal into many small pieces (i.e., portions about the size of half a sugar cube, one very small swallow of liquid, one quick lick off a caramel sucker, etc.). Mealtime becomes a good time to begin to teach.

The more familiar you become with the person you are to teach, the more you will learn about the kinds of rewards that will work for that individual. For example, some persons are very responsive to verbal approval (such as "Good" and "Fine"), while others are indifferent to such statements. A few persons may even seem bothered or punished by social approval (you tell them "Good," and they stop behaving, as if they were punished). You have to try different kinds of approval and see what works best. We have found that *activity* is quite rewarding for all of our students. There seems to exist a need for activity, just as there is a need for food and water. Notice how people like to move around, run, jiggle their feet, and so on. Children love recess in school, where they can run around and yell for 10 minutes. In fact, for most children recess is the best time they have all day. We therefore try to "program" different kinds of activity as a reward for correct behavior. For example, you may want to let your child get out of the chair for 5 seconds as a reward for sitting quietly and working well. Incidentally, if you want to teach your child to sit properly in a chair, don't let him get out of the chair if he behaves inappropriately because this permission to get up may function as a reward for inappropriate behavior. Many children have favorite objects they are attached to, such as a blanket, a stick, or a doll. While you are teaching you may want to use the object as a reward by taking it away and then returning it to the child to hold (for 5 seconds) after he has behaved in a desirable way. Almost anything your child wants—be it food, verbal approval, activity, or favorite objects—can be used as a reward, and the more rewards you have to offer your child, the more effective you will be as a teacher.

Some of the more basic rewards that you can consider using include:

Tastes or small bites of different kinds of food
Small sips of liquid
Kissing, hugging, tickling, stroking, fondling
Verbal approval like "Good," "Swell," and "Great"
Activities like jumping, running, stretching, rolling, laughing
Listening to music
Colorful and varied visual displays

Reward your child a little each time in order to avoid early satiation. For example, don't give him a whole caramel sucker, but rather just a 1-second lick on that sucker, or give him one small swallow of juice, 3 to 4 seconds of kissing or music, 5 seconds of jumping up and down, etc. By being so stingy you can make your rewards work for a long time so that your child will work hard for them for several hours a day. A reward needs to last for only a few (3 to 5) seconds in the beginning. And remember, a variety of rewards is important in order to avoid satiation. Positive rewards, or "positives," as we sometimes call them, are referred to as "positive reinforcers" in the technical literature. We use these terms interchangeably.

Escaping Negatives

Another kind of reward is to *escape from negatives.* Typically, a normal child will feel anxious about failure; his being correct *reduces* his anxiety or discomfort. However, some developmentally retarded children do not feel such anxiety and tension about being wrong. They often appear content and happy with themselves and the world as it is, even though they are considerably behind their peers and may someday face institutionalization. In such cases a teacher may try to make them a little upset and uneasy about being wrong by either withholding positive rewards or disapproving of their behavior by, for example, loudly exclaiming "No!" This is done to increase the children's motivation to learn and, therefore, to help them reduce future problems. When a child is uneasy about being wrong and then is finally right, it can mean to him: "Relax, I am doing all right." Being right is rewarding because it reduces apprehension and other negatives. In the technical literature, this kind of rewarding process is referred to as "negative reinforcement," since a behavior is reinforced (that is, strengthened) by the removal of something negative.

By becoming firm with your child, and perhaps making him a little upset or scared by yelling at him or hitting his bottom, your social rewards (saying "Good" and your kisses and hugs) become almost immediately more important and effective for him. It is as if he appreciates you more, once you have shown him that you also can be angry with him.

Contrast Between Positives and Negatives

It is critical that the contrast between positives and negatives be as strong as possible, particularly in the early stages of teaching. If your "Good" sounds like your "No," or if your "happy" face looks like your "angry" face, you probably won't be able to teach much to developmentally retarded children. Later, they will learn the informational value of "Good" and "No," and you won't have to be so loud.

Typically, we use positives (like food and kisses) when we work to teach the child something *new*. We use escape from negatives to help maintain what the child already has learned. That is, if we are sure that he knows what we are asking him to do (because he does it when he is hungry and we feed him for being correct), then we are very disapproving and stern with him if he does not act correctly when asked at another time. His reward, then, becomes escaping our disapproval.

Some children are quite anxious at the beginning of training and they are bothered when they are wrong. We have found that such children are easier to work with. Much of their reward is to learn to master their anxiety. Such children are more motivated than the placid ones and are easier to teach. A mild disapproval can be of major impact and you therefore must be careful. It might serve to motivate the child to exaggerate the differences between positive rewards for appropriate behavior and firm reprimands for mistakes; this is perhaps the main way of teaching the child the differences between the two kinds of consequences.

Reward Schedules

In addition to the two basic kinds of rewards (getting positives, escaping negatives), you need to keep in mind that the rewards have to be *immediate*. As soon as the correct behavior occurs, *within a second* the child should be rewarded. His behavior and your reward should occur almost concurrently. As you progress with the programs, you may be able to delay your reward.

You will get maximum use of your rewards if you use them economically. In the beginning, when the child doesn't know what to do and you have to teach him everything, you may have to reward him *every* time he is correct. Later, as he shows some mastery and you are more interested in maintaining or preserving what he has already learned, shift away from continuous rewarding to partial rewarding. Only reward him once in a while. Technically, this is referred to as placing the child on a *partial schedule* of reward, and the operation is called *thinning the schedule*. How "thin" you can make the reward schedule depends on many variables, and differs between children and tasks. Thin the schedule and look for *schedule strain;* if his behavior falls apart or begins to fluctuate widely, "thicken" the schedule, that is, reward him more often. Once you have recovered his behavior, start thinning again.

Another important point to remember is that as soon as possible, shift away from food rewards to rewards that are as normal and natural as possible, such as social rewards, like "Good" or "Right." The child will let you know when to shift; if you discontinue food rewards and the child's behavior begins to fall apart, go back to food, recover his behavior, and then start shifting again.

Individual Differences in Rewards

When you begin to learn more about a child, you will find a large range of unexpected and idiosyncratic events that give him great pleasure and that can be used as rewards. Parents usually know these specific events and can save a teacher months of hard work by sharing their knowledge with the teacher. For example, children who are very fond of music may be rewarded for correct behavior by being allowed to listen to a favorite piece of music for a few seconds. Children can be rewarded by holding a favorite object for a few seconds. Children who like to be alone can be left alone as a reward. The list goes on as rewards for behaviors vary for each child.

A hug and a kiss on the cheek may be very rewarding to one child but may be "punishing" to another (they might even whine and grimace when you kiss them). So, if you kiss and hug a child who doesn't want it, it probably doesn't help him learn. On the other hand, almost every child likes to eat, so you can be more sure about what you are doing when you use food rewards. (A few children don't like to eat when you feed them, particularly not when you feed them as a reward for their being correct. Perhaps they don't like to give you that much control over them, or they don't like to give you the pleasure of rewarding them. You may have to "work through" this resistance, to feed and reward him anyway, because most children will eventually accept your rewards (and your being the boss) if you persist.)

It is also surprising to find a few children who are quite rewarded by your being angry and saying, "No." They smile and seem to work hard to get you upset. Be careful that you are not rewarding a child when you get angry and say "No." We will say more about that later.

EXTRINSIC AND INTRINSIC REWARDS

Extrinsic rewards are controlled by others. It is wise to use such rewards in the early stages of learning, because you obtain more control over the learning process and most children can be motivated to learn by such extrinsic rewards. There is another set of rewards, intrinsic rewards, which are very significant, probably crucial for a really successful outcome. These are the rewards that the child experiences as intrinsic to performing the task. Some children show that the task is rewarding for them from the beginning, others learn to find intrinsic rewards after exposure to the task, and still others never find the task rewarding by itself, but need to rely on extrinsic rewards. We shall talk more about intrinsic rewards in later chapters but one example will help to illustrate the meaning of intrinsic rewards. Some children don't talk at all, they are mute in the beginning, and to teach them to talk you may need extrinsic rewards, such as food and approval. When the child vocalizes, he gets food. Now what will happen is that some previously mute children, a few months or a year into such an extrinsically motivated "talking" program (such as verbal imitation training discussed in Chapter 10), will start to talk without apparent extrinsic reinforcement. They become *echolalic,* that is, they will begin to echo whatever you say, much the same as young, normal children do for a while, whether you reward them or not. In this program, *matching* (when the child sounds like an adult) apparently becomes the reward for talking. The child is matching and apparently matching is rewarding to him. The teacher can drop the extrinsic (food or praise) reward.

Intrinsic rewards take over when the teaching goes right, but in the beginning you may use extrinsic rewards, to get your child going. Some children may not like to talk, even after considerable training on your part. For such children, specific extrinsic rewards, like food and activities, may have to be programmed contingent on their talking "forever," which, of course, makes the verbal language program cumbersome and rather impractical. We discuss this transition between extrinsic and intrinsic rewards at several places in this book.

Summary Comments about Rewards

We have made the following points so far:

1. *Getting positives* and *escaping negatives* are both rewards. A reward is any event that, after being given contingent on behavior, serves to increase that behavior.
2. Food and activity are biological or primary rewards. Praise and approval are social rewards.
3. *Extrinsic rewards* are controlled by others in the child's environment. *Intrinsic rewards* are those aspects of a certain task or behavior that the child finds enjoyable. The child controls intrinsic rewards.
4. It is important to *reward immediately;* that is, as soon as the child does the desired behavior, you should reward him at once.
5. There are large *individual differences* among children as to what they find rewarding. It is important to determine for each child rewards he finds pleasing and rewards he does not.
6. *Partial reward schedules* are necessary in order to maintain behavior that has been acquired and in order to avoid satiation on rewards.

ACQUISITION AND EXTINCTION

When your child is getting rewards for his behavior and he is learning, he is on *acquisition* and his desired behavior should be getting stronger. Suppose you suddenly decided not to reward him anymore. He behaves as before, but you act as if you did not notice the behavior, as if his behavior had no noticeable effect on you. This is called placing the behavior on *extinction*. For example, you have strenuously taught the child some desirable behavior by using several explicit rewards. You now send the child home (or to school as the case may be) and he receives no explicit reward. The behavior you so carefully built is now "on extinction"; it will go away because it is no longer being rewarded. "Working through" a tantrum is a good example of extinction. Your child may scream and kick, but you go about your business as if the behavior is not occurring. Almost certainly, the tantrum will disappear. Extinction, then, is a powerful, although time-consuming and demanding, method to get rid of a behavior. Extinction is described more in the next chapter.

PUNISHMENT

Punishment is used to stop or decrease behavior. Parents of normal children often use punishment, probably because it sometimes helps them deal with their children. If you are going to use punishment, let there be no uncertainty in the child's mind that you mean business. Some of the kinds of punishment you can use are discussed below.

Aversives

One method of punishment is to do something to the child that "hurts", for example, a swat on the behind, or a loud, sharp "No!" These punishments are called *aversives*. For some children "No" is all you have to say; they stop whatever it is they are doing. For other children a verbal reprimand just will not work; but a swat on the behind is almost always effective, if it is hard enough so it "smarts" (practice on your friends to get some idea of how hard you hit). The advantage of swats that are strong and given correctly is that you don't have to use too many. If you only verbally disapprove, you may end up yelling a lot, which is unpleasant for everyone and gives you less opportunity to show affection. Sometimes you can get caught in a real "fight" with a child when you escalate aversives. You hit harder, but the child just becomes more and more stubborn. If that happens, immediately back off, and try something else. Just as adults are clever in finding different things that are rewarding to a child, a good adult will find forms of discipline that are less dramatic than physical punishment. Try something the child does not like to do as punishment. For example, some children dislike athletics, so you can program athletics (like sit-ups or running around the block) contingent on the undesirable behavior. Washing dishes is punishing for some, as is being lifted off the floor.

When you work in schools or hospitals, or when your child is an adult, physical punishment may be inappropriate or illegal. But you will probably find out that to be maximally effective as a teacher, you have to be quite firm at times, and this may even include physical punishment. We discuss this issue in some detail at the end of this chapter and in several other parts of the book.

Time-Out: Taking Away Positives

In addition to, and sometimes instead of, using aversives like a swat, or loudly yelling "No!" adults will punish a child by taking something away from him. Often this "taking away" can be simply accomplished by the teacher turning her face away from the child, or, a little more extensively, by placing the child in the corner of the room, and perhaps escalating to placing him in an "isolation room," that is, a quiet uninteresting room away from other activities. A common factor of these operations is that they signal to the child that there is a certain amount of time when he will not get positives. Therefore, these procedures have been called *time-out* (from positive rewards). The child may be placed in time-out for 3 to 5 minutes, the last 30 seconds of which he has to be quiet. If you take him out of time-out when he is throwing a tantrum, you may inadvertently be rewarding him for tantrums. Be careful, also, not to keep the child in time-out for more than 5 minutes at a time. On occasion, you may feel that you have to place him in time-out for longer periods, but the longer the periods, the less effective the procedure is as an educational tool because children need to be with you and to be taught appropriate behavior.

There are at least two problems associated with time-out. First, some children do not find time-out punishing. That is, they would rather be in time-out than with others; being with people and learning are not important to them. Placing a child in time-out under such circumstances will only make him worse. Second, time-out requires time away from the learning situation, which means that the child has less opportunity to learn new material.

There are no good data on which method of punishment works best, time-out or aversives, and there are also no good data on which has the most undesirable side effects. Perhaps physical aversives primarily produce anxiety, while time-out produces guilt. Some people would rather try to cope with anxiety than with guilt.

Rules for Using Punishment

Questions are often raised about how strict one should be, how much time-out to use, how long it should last, or where to put the child in time-out. Similar questions are made regarding physical punishment, how hard to hit, how long, etc. Here are some general rules regarding punishment, which will be elaborated in later sections:

1. If strong discipline, such as time-out and physical aversives, is going to work, its effectiveness should be evident almost immediately, sometimes after one minute, and certainly by the end of the day. You have to keep a record when you use strong discipline to make sure that the behavior you punish is decreasing. That is the only justification for using aversives.
2. The strength of the punishment that you use depends on the child's behavior and how that behavior is affected by punishment. If the behavior decreases with weak punishment, there is no need for stronger measures.
3. Our experience has shown that time-out exceeding 20 minutes is not helpful. Most of the time, isolation of about 5 minutes is ample. Remember to wait for the child to quiet down before you remove him from time-out, or to wait at least until he begins to quiet down. This is to ensure that you are rewarding and reinforcing quiet behavior.

   We have heard of persons who have used time-out lasting for several hours or even all day. It is difficult to see how that could be of any benefit to the child.
4. As for spankings and swats, only use as much force as is necessary to hurt a little bit and to cause some apprehension in the child. Practice on your friends so that you can be told how much is just "hard enough." Also have someone watch you when you punish your child to monitor you and to give you objective feedback.

   We have heard about children who have been hit or pinched so hard that their skin is dramatically discolored. It seems quite unnecessary to use such strong physical aversives.
5. Throughout your training and teaching programs remember to keep an accurate record (i.e., collect data). This will ensure that you will be able to tell just what effects you have had on your child's behavior. One can only use these kinds of disciplinary actions if they work. Record keeping is discussed in Chapter 4.

Rewards include getting positives and losing negatives. Punishment is the opposite—getting negatives and losing positives. Another relatively new procedure called *overcorrection* has been developed as a meaningful alternative to physical punishment, which is such a controversial issue at this time. Overcorrection is discussed below.

Overcorrection

Overcorrection is a procedure developed by Foxx and Azrin (1973) to help reduce aggressive, disruptive, and inappropriate behaviors in developmentally disabled persons. Overcorrection was developed as an alternative to punishment. Its success has been judged not only in terms of its effectiveness, but also in its minimization of the "negative properties" of punishment.

Perhaps it is easiest to introduce *overcorrection* by giving some examples of its use. Suppose your child repeatedly spills milk on the floor. To stop that from happening in the future, you might have him not only clean up the mess by himself but also mop most of the kitchen floor. Then you could have him practice carrying glasses of milk around. Any spills would have to be cleaned up "extra neat." Or, suppose your child deflated the tires on a neighbor's car as a Halloween prank. As a parent you might have your child re-inflate your neighbor's tires using a bicycle pump, and, for good measure, have the child spend the rest of the day pumping up tires. One of the main points in these examples is to emphasize that the person has to do something unpleasant as a consequence for the undesirable behavior, and this unpleasantness does not involve physical punishment.

Overcorrection sometimes has a component called *restitution,* which requires that the individual also restores the environment to an improved state. Examples of restitution are: requiring a child who tears a book to glue not only the pages of that book but many other books as well, and demanding that a child who throws objects pick up not only those objects but many other objects also. Sometimes a second component called *positive practice* is added to overcorrection. Positive practice occurs when the offender practices the appropriate behavior. The child who writes on walls would practice writing on paper, the child who tears books might be required to read books, and the child who throws objects might be taught a more appropriate way to display anger or might be taught to show a great deal of affection and concern for others.

Overcorrection is a procedure that combines many principles of behavior modification. Overcorrection involves time-out, which occurs when the student is removed from any opportunity to engage in reinforcing activities because he is restoring the environment and practicing the appropriate behavior. The procedure also involves *response cost,* where the student has to remove the original source of reinforcement, such as the marks on the wall. Punishment appears to be another component of overcorrection. For example, when used for toilet training, the child is given a shower when soiled. He may not like to shower (particularly not in the middle of the night, if he soiled at that time) or he may not like a lukewarm or cool shower. Essentially, he is forced to do something he doesn't like. Another teaching principle employed in overcorrection is the establishment of *appropriate stimulus control.* That is, the child is required to perform the appropriate behaviors while in the presence of appropriate cues. For example, the child who tears books may be taught more appropriate behaviors in the presence of books, such as reading them, looking at the pictures, or taking care of them. Therefore, the success of overcorrection might be in the combined use of several successful techniques.

The following guidelines should followed when using overcorrection:

1. The correction procedure should be related to the inappropriate behavior. For example, if the student has been tearing paper, then he may be taught to glue and fix paper. If he has been spilling food on the floor, then he is taught to clean the floor. The consequence somehow relates to the behavior.
2. A correction procedure should be applied immediately, that is, within seconds after the undesirable behavior has occurred.
3. Overcorrection should signal a time-out from all reinforcement. During the overcorrection procedure, show him no affection, don't give elaborate explanations, and don't let him eat or have the company of friends.
4. The offender should be the only person involved in the correction procedure. Don't make it a game, and don't let others do the work for him.
5. The environment should be completely restored to its original state.
6. Guidance should only be given if the child is unable or unwilling to do the overcorrection on his own. If he resists, you persist, and "push him" (physically move his hands and limbs) through the behavior. Use as much physical force as is necessary to make him complete the task.
7. An extended period of time (such as 20 minutes rather than 5) should be used for overcorrection. The longer the period the better.
8. An appropriate alternative behavior must be taught.

Overcorrection has in a short time become a very effective procedure for decreasing inappropriate behaviors, and you should be familiar with how it works. Note that it does consume a good deal of time, which may be better spent learning new behaviors. Notice, also, that when you have to move (prompt) the child physically in an act, you may have to exert considerable physical force to help him comply. You may at such times run the risk of bruising or physically hurting the child, or the child you are working with may be physically so big that you can't budge him. This is a serious drawback of certain forms of overcorrection.

Summary Comments about Punishment

We have made the following points so far:

1. *Getting aversives* and *losing positives* (time-out) are methods of punishment. Punishment is any event that, when it is given contingent on some behavior, serves to reduce the occurrence of that behavior.
2. There are individual differences among children in their responses to different kinds of punishment.
3. Overcorrection is a procedure used to decrease the occurrence of behavior by having the person do things he does not like to do. It has components added such as restitution and positive practice.

SHAPING BEHAVIOR

Selecting Target Behaviors

Once you have decided on the rewards and punishment you want to use, the next issue deals with what kinds of behaviors to teach, and how to teach them. The rule is to start with something simple because you want to be a successful teacher and you want your child to be a successful learner. Select some behavior goal for the child, which is called a *target behavior* or *target response*. The behaviors are then broken down into small units, or sections, each being taught separately. That way he may master the smaller units first, and then you help him put them together in a larger or more complex package later.

The target behavior for the following example is teaching your child to go to the toilet, a complex act that you break down into units of taking off the pants, sitting on the toilet, and eliminating. Each of these units may also be broken down into smaller units. For example, "taking off the pants," is a complex act itself that involves unbuttoning, unzipping, pulling down, etc. The point is to start with those elements of behavior with which he will be successful, so that you can reward him, for without rewards there is no learning. A good learning situation, then, is a situation where the teacher has broken down a complex behavior into units so simple that the child can be rewarded and can learn. If behaviors are rewarded, they will become stronger. That is why you have to simplify the task. If you give your child a task that is too difficult, he will not be receiving rewards, and he will not learn. Remember, also, that not only is a child who is rewarded learning new behaviors, but he is also happy. Rewards elicit happiness. Learning and happiness should go hand in hand. In summary, then, the first thing you do is pick a target behavior, then you break that behavior down into manageable components. The programs in this manual give step-by-step instructions on how to break complex behavior down into easier elements.

When the separate units are mastered, they are put together to form a complex response. The process whereby you "form" behaviors is called *shaping*. As the term *shaping* implies, you start with an approximation of the final target behavior (as when you have broken the target behavior into smaller elements). You reward these approximations to the target behavior and you slowly *shift your rewards* to only those behaviors that are close to the target behavior. That is, you only reward a behavior when it is a closer approximation to the target behavior than the previous behavior. Consider as an example teaching your child to say "mama." You may begin by breaking this word down into two sounds separated by a pause. You may further break down the two sounds into their component parts, teaching your child to first say "mm" and then "ah." The sound "mm" can also be broken down into two behaviors: pressing your lips together and vocalizing while your lips are together. You may initially reward the child for an approximation of the sound "mm"; that is, reward him when he closes his lips in preparation for making the sound, even if he does not yet vocalize (his "mm" is voiceless.) Once he is to the point that he closes his lips readily (perhaps in imitation of your closing your lips), you begin working on the second part of the behavior, that is, vocalizing. Perhaps it will be necessary to "prompt" him (see below). In any event, you reward him only after he closes his lips and vocalizes. Once he has that behavior, start rewarding him for saying "ah." Then put the two sounds together; "mah." When he can say "mah," then insist that he say the sound twice before he is rewarded; in this way you have built or *shaped* the behavior (saying "mama") using the technique of rewarding successive approximations of the target behavior. (Language training programs are presented in detail in Units III, V, and VI.) Shaping behavior is a bit like an art, which means that *every* step cannot be specified in advance. However, it can be learned, so that at the end of the "shaping exercises" given in this book you can expect to become a creative shaper. Some members of your teaching team will be better shapers than others; some have a knack for shaping. Watch them closely to see how they do it.

Prompts and Prompt Fading

When you teach you will find yourself "prompting" the child to help him exhibit the correct behaviors. In other words, you don't want to wait all day for the proper behavior to occur, so you *prompt* the behavior, that is, you manually or physically guide the child through the action. For example, you can't wait all day for your child to sit on the toilet, so you prompt him by picking him up and sitting him down on the toilet. You can't wait all day for him to urinate, so you prompt by giving him lots of things to drink during the day. You can't wait forever for the opportunity to reward him for vocalizing, so you tickle him to prompt his vocalization. Your child may never play patty-cake, so you prompt that behavior by moving his arms and hands through the motions, and then reward him. He may not like it, but you do it anyway. If he resists you too much, try another kind of prompt, and if he still struggles against you, voice your disapproval over his resistance, and give him ample rewards for compliance.

A good teacher is a person who is good at prompting the right responses and arranging the situation so that the child puts out "winning behaviors." There are a million ways to prompt a million behaviors, and if you are good at prompting, your child is on his way. He'll be learning because you and others will be able to reward him. Take a smile, for example. A child is doubly nice when he smiles. So you touch his belly button, or kiss his ear, or do whatever you do to get him to smile, and when he smiles, you reward him: "See everybody, how nice he smiles," applaud him, and give him food. "Have a sip of orange juice" (he drinks); "He is gorgeous, isn't he?" (you touch the child and he smiles again). "One more smile. Heavens, we are lucky today, would you like a piece of toast?" Loosen up a bit, and learn to do these interactions without a script. You have to become a "ham" in a way, which is not really all that difficult. It is often the spontaneous interactions that prompt the best behavior.

Once you can easily prompt a behavior, and you have had the opportunity to strengthen the behavior by rewarding it (say two to ten rewarded occurrences of the behavior), start *fading the prompt* in small, gradual steps. For example, if you have prompted a smile by tickling the child and have had the opportunity to reward the smile, gradually decrease the tickling so that he comes to smile more and more on his own, without too much prompting from you. But keep rewarding him for smiling. The rule is that you want him to exhibit the behavior, so you assist him through prompts. You also want him to start behaving on his own, so you fade the prompts by gradually removing your assistance, while continuing the rewards. It is particularly important to shift your rewards from prompted behavior to *un-prompted* behavior.

Giving Instructions

Instructions should be explicit and clear. That is, drop all the excess verbiage or "noise" in an instruction and get it down to essentials. If you want your child to sit down, don't say "Chris, dear, listen to me, what I am asking you is to please be a good boy and sit down on the chair for me." Just say "Sit." Say it loudly and clearly. Your child would never understand the instructions in our first sentence because there is just too much noise in it. If you are teaching him to identify (by pointing) red versus blue colors, don't say "Chris, look here, point to the blue color paper." Just say "Red" or "Blue." It is "red" or "blue" that he has to attend to. The rest of the words in the sentence are unnecessary, and could serve to obscure the relevant word.

Trials

A trial can be thought of as a single teaching unit. It starts with the teacher's instructions and ends with the child's response, or failure to respond. Failure to respond may be defined as no response within 3 to 5 seconds following the teacher's instructions. Rewards as well as prompts may be included in a trial. The time that elapses after the conclusion of one trial and the start of another (the between trial interval) may last anywhere from one-half second to several seconds. Depending on how elaborate the instructions are, how time-consuming the prompt is (if there are prompts), how long the response is and how long the reward takes (if there is one), a teacher may run anywhere from 1 to 20 or more trials per minute.

The instructions for the trials have to be paced or timed correctly. Koegel, Russo, and Rincover (1977) referred to this aspect of training as the *discrete trial procedure*. The intent is to present your instructions and the training material clearly, concisely, and discriminably, that is, in a neat little package with a definite start and a definite conclusion. Suppose you want your child to learn the receptive meaning of the word "doll." A poor approach to this teaching task would be to have the doll on the table while presenting your child with the confusing instructions, "Point to the doll, please," and repeating the instructions while your child is looking someplace else and isn't attending to you or the instructions or the doll. Instead, you should first get his attention. (Getting the child's attention is explained in Chapter 6.) Once you have his attention, immediately place the doll on the table, while at the same time saying, "Doll." Placing the doll, the *stimulus display,* clearly in his field of vision while saying "doll" helps him attend to the instructions being given. You may want to wait 2 to 3 seconds between each time you present him with the instructions and the stimulus display. Sometimes 2 seconds are too short; in other situations, they are too long. Some children on some tasks are "available" (open and attending to the teacher) when the teacher presents the instructions in relatively quick succession. At other times the child "drifts off" and you have to wait until he "comes back," or you have to prompt him to attend to you. Pacing of the presentation of your instructions is critical to learning (because it facilitates getting the child's attention), yet little systematic information is available to the teacher about such pacing and attention-building techniques at this time. One learns such pacing through experience in working with children.

Remember not to overwork the child. If he has been "in the chair" receiving formal instruction for 5 minutes, he should probably get up and move around to play for 1 minute. A five to one ratio of work to play may be ideal during a teaching session. You may want to arrange your day in alternating

2-hour blocks of teaching sessions and "free" play periods (this free play should also be educational). This would mean that the child would get as much as 6 hours of formal, in the chair, one-on-one teaching per day. You may want to increase the workload with older children.

SUMMARY OF "HOW TO DO IT"

It may be helpful to summarize what has been said so far about the important elements in a teaching situation. Remember, the terms in the following list will appear repeatedly throughout the book, and they will also be further defined as they come up again in different contexts. These are very abstract terms; their full meaning will become more apparent as you gain more experience in working with your child.

Rewards

1. *Getting positives* is rewarding. Positives may be food, activity, sensory stimulation, or social praise and approval.
2. *Escaping negatives* is also rewarding. The feeling of anxiety or fear is usually an unpleasant experience for a person; anything which would lead to a reduction in anxiety would be rewarding. Disapproval is an example of a social negative.
3. Immediate delivery
4. Reward schedules
5. Individual differences
6. Extrinsic and intrinsic rewards

Acquisition and Extinction

Punishment

1. *Getting negatives* is punishing. A negative may be a physical aversive, like a spanking, or it may be the performance of a task that the person doesn't like to do, such as washing dishes or doing sit-ups.
2. *Losing positives* is also punishing. Not being allowed to watch a favorite television show, or not getting a candy bar are examples of losing positives. *Time-out* is another example of this kind of punishment, for the person is isolated from the environment, and is therefore not receiving any rewards at all. *Overcorrection* may be another form of punishment.
3. Note that points 4, 5, and 6 from Rewards also apply to punishment.

Shaping Behavior

1. *Select target behaviors.* Break down the target response into its component parts. Reward approximations to the target response.
2. *Prompting and Prompt Fading*
   a. Help the behavior occur (as in physically guiding the child through the behavior).
   b. Gradually remove (fade) such assistance.
3. *Instructions*
   a. Make the instructions clear and concise.
   b. Pace them well; present them when the child is attending.
   c. Use the discrete trial procedure.
4. *Trials* start with the teacher's instructions, including any prompts, followed by the child's response or failure to respond, and the teacher's reward or punishment (if any).

CHAPTER 2

PHYSICAL PUNISHMENT

Punishment is a controversial intervention that has given rise to much debate and misinformation. One could write at length about the issues involved, but it is most appropriate for this book to limit the discussion of punishment to certain points that are of special significance to the developmentally disabled.

Punishment often means revenge ("an eye for an eye" attitude), which is inappropriate for any society, and particularly out of place when dealing with children. Punishment may also mean displaced aggression. Many parents will punish a child, not because of the child's behavior, but as an expression of their own anxiety over their failure to cope. That is, parents project their failures onto their children, and punish them. On a larger, social scale, punishment means oppression. History shows that every form of political tyranny has used massive aversive control, such as physical punishment. History also shows that people rise against such tyrants to rid themselves of punishment and oppression. Psychological theorists from Freud to Skinner speak strongly against punishment, claiming the effects of punishment are too detrimental to warrant its use.

On the other hand, if one asks parents of normal children if they use physical punishment, and if it helps them in handling their children, the great majority will answer "Yes" to both questions. Furthermore, research data from carefully controlled studies point to punishment as an effective and practical way of stopping undesirable behavior, and also suggest the side effects of punishment to be less undesirable than expected, often, in fact, to be desirable. There are several, quite thorough and objective reviews of punishment. We suggest a review article by Harris and Ersner-Hershfield (1978), "Behavioral suppression of seriously disruptive behavior in psychotic and retarded patients: A review of punishment and its alternatives." A good book on the subject of punishment is *Punishment: Its Effects on Human Behavior* (Axelrod and Apsche, 1980). You may also want to refer to the chapter on punishment by Azrin and Holz in *Operant Behavior: Areas of Research and Application (1966)*.

It will seem totally inappropriate to many people to even suggest the use of physical punishment with developmentally disabled persons. How can it even be suggested that an adult punish a mentally ill or retarded child? Even if punishment helps to raise a normal child, a sick and retarded child seems so helpless and vulnerable, so unable to benefit from the consequences of his behaviors.

Therefore, it may seem surprising that punishment has been used with some developmentally disabled children under certain circumstances and that when *used carefully* and *correctly*, it has been shown to help such children. Before we proceed further in this discussion, it may be helpful if we define the term *punishment* as it is used in the context of this book and give some examples of the behaviors of developmentally disabled persons that respond favorably to punishment. Keep in mind, also, that the use of punishment can only be maintained in an environment where one records data on its effects. That is, the question of whether or not to use punishment should be made on the basis of empirical data, that is, on the facts about its usefulness and failures.

Most often in the psychological learning literature, punishment is defined as an event, accompanying a behavior, that serves to decrease that behavior. At least two kinds of events serve that purpose: 1) the presentation of a physically aversive event, which may range anywhere from a spanking or a slap, to a stressful behavior, like hard physical exercises; and 2) the removal of a rewarding event, which may range anywhere from an adult turning her face away from a child, to placing the child in isolation (time-out). In both instances it is critical that the event be shown to decrease behavior. Some persons may find some or all of these events neutral or rewarding and, therefore, not punishing.

BEHAVIORS FOR WHICH ONE MAY CONSIDER USING PUNISHMENT

It is important to consider some problems that are particularly handicapping for the disabled child in order to formulate rules about whether or not to punish. One of the problems that faces parents and teachers of developmentally disabled children centers on what behaviors are so seriously maladaptive that they warrant the use of physical aversives. Self-destructiveness is one such behavior. To use an extreme example, we were recently asked to advise on the treatment of a severely self-destructive 10-year-old boy, who had been self-destructive since he was 2 years old. He has been institutionalized for most of his life because he could not be managed by his parents. He was retarded and he had "autistic features." A variety of interventions had been tried, including changing hospitals, using drugs in various amounts, psychotherapy, and prolonged periods in physical restraints, among others. His head and face were full of scar tissue from self-inflicted wounds, his ears were swollen to the size of tennis balls and filled with blood, he had broken his nose, he often damaged his knees by knocking them against his head, and he had lately been hitting his elbows against his sides and lower back so as to rupture his kidneys. If this behavior continued he would die.

Other children have certain problem behaviors that, although not life endangering, like self-destructive behavior, nevertheless seriously interfere with their own learning. These behaviors, too, may require extreme intervention measures, such as physical aversives. For example, many retarded and psychotic children will try feces smearing. In fact, most normal children try feces smearing at one time or another, but give it up. Some developmentally retarded persons, however, continue to smear their feces into adulthood. It is a horrible sight to see a 25-year-old adult smearing his own feces on his body, in his hair, and in his mouth. He will not die from feces smearing, but such behavior in most cases prevents the person from remaining at home with his parents. One can also be virtually certain that this person will not be very popular among the teaching personnel in an institution and will probably be moved to a less optimal ward. Yet, in all likelihood, aversives can be used to stop him from feces smearing, just as they can be used to stop self-injurious behaviors.

Some children are so aggressive that they pose a danger to other children. Particularly serious is the situation in which the life of a younger sibling is threatened. Few people know what tyrants some retarded or psychotic children can be or how their tyrannical behavior isolates them from normal environments. Teachers do not tolerate a great deal of aggressive behavior in their classrooms. If a child is too aggressive in public school, he may be dismissed from that school. Failure to keep a child in local schools can be disastrous. State hospitals are full of children who could have made it on the outside had it not been for the fact that they were allowed to develop self-defeating behaviors such as excessive aggression. Often, parents of such children have been aided by some well meaning, but probably misinformed, professional who was more concerned with defending abstract ideals about the perfect society (where no aversives exist), rather than helping persons cope with mundane, everyday practical problems of how to live with an angry, retarded individual.

The behaviors mentioned above—self-injurious behaviors, aggressive attacks on others, and other behaviors such as feces smearing, eating electrical cords, and running out in front of oncoming cars—are all behaviors that pose an immediate threat to the child's survival and most people would agree that, if necessary, aversives should be used to stop them.

For other sets of behaviors, the decision of whether or not to use physical punishment may seem less clear-cut, although these behaviors may be just as damaging to the child. For example, there is a group of behaviors, such as endless rocking, spinning, eye rolling, arm flapping, gazing, etc., that seem quite "addictive" to many children. Such behaviors are called *self-stimulatory* and seriously limit the child's response to what the teacher says and does. The child is "out of it" when he self-stimulates. You may attempt to suppress such behaviors by using punishment. These behaviors are discussed in the next chapter.

Disruptive or aberrant behaviors can also interfere with a child's development. For example, it is nice to go out to dinner once in a while as a family. In most restaurants, one is expected to behave reasonably well, sitting quietly and waiting to be served. Acting bizarrely, screaming, and so on, are usually not allowed. Such seriously disruptive behavior may necessitate strict disciplinary measures from the parent, such as a strong reprimand. The child will benefit from joining the family in eating out, going shopping, traveling, etc., and such discipline may be the most appropriate way to correct the child's maladaptive behavior.

SUMMARY COMMENTS ABOUT AVERSIVES

If an adult contemplates the use of aversives, important rules should be followed. These rules are spelled out in detail in later chapters and summarized below.

Explore alternatives. Make sure that alternatives have been tested as to their effectiveness. This is a difficult criterion to satisfy, but if one has tried to stop the undesirable behavior by other means for several weeks or months without an appreciable decrease in the disruptive behavior, then one should consider physical aversives. Alternatives might include: 1) giving him a different environment, such as placing him in another classroom, or having different adults or peers present, or 2) giving him more behavioral skills, such as teaching him alternative ways of expressing his wishes through better language in an enriched school curriculum, etc.

Build alternative behaviors. Never punish unless you can also teach the child some better way to express himself after you have stopped his disruptive behavior. Otherwise, the undesirable behavior will return shortly after you have stopped the active punishment. Think of punishment in this way: It serves to stop some disruptive behavior long enough so that the teacher or parent can build some constructive behavior to replace the interfering behavior. Technically speaking, the punishment prompts a pause in some disruptive behavior, and behavior during that pause (such as not behaving disruptively) is then rewarded.

Try nonphysical punishment first. That is, first try *extinction,* (not paying any attention to the behavior). Then try *time-out* (placing him in isolation contingent on the undesirable behavior), *overcorrection,* or other kinds of nonphysical aversives. Be extra careful that the child's disruptive behavior does not get some unintended payoff, like attention, sympathy, or getting out of work. Children are not born with problem behaviors; they learn them. The child with the damaged kidneys in the example above had been carefully (and inadvertently) shaped by poorly informed but well meaning persons to injure himself, eventually ending up with kidney damage and possible death. These problems are described in more detail in later chapters.

Try the least aversive procedure first. For example, you may want to start with a loud "No!" and then use procedures that the child does not like but that appear relatively "innocent," such as 10 or 20 sit-ups, or 5 minutes of jogging around the block, or holding a telephone book for one minute with outstretched arms, contingent on the undesirable behavior. Or, if a child is very afraid of dogs, briefly showing him a picture of a dog when he acts up particularly badly may be enough of an aversive. Another child might hate to throw small bean bags back and forth between himself and the teacher, and a short bean bag session would be sufficiently aversive to help him stop some undesirable behavior. Just as a good teacher can find many ways to reward her child, so she can find many socially acceptable ways to discipline him. If the milder aversives don't work, try a swat on the rear. At the other extreme, painful electric shock has sometimes been used, but we advise against this procedure except in cases where the child's life is in danger. Do not use it without professional supervision.

Use aversives that other parents in the community employ. To facilitate a generalization (transfer) of the learning back into the community, try to find forms of discipline that the community uses and to which community members will not object.

Avoid prolonged use. A child may adapt to aversives and they will lose their effectiveness. Also, prolonged use probably leads to response substitution, such as the emergence of self-stimulatory behaviors (see the next chapter) which the child may use to block the effect of the aversives. If aversives are going to work, they will be effective almost immediately, which means the undesirable behavior should have been essentially stopped after five to 10 applications and should have almost disappeared after the first day of use.

Take one behavior at a time and across environments. If you decide to punish several behaviors, select one behavior and suppress that behavior across all environments (clinic, home, and school) and across all people who interact with the child in order to avoid discrimination. Avoid situation specificity that occurs when the child suppresses a behavior in the presence of those who punish, but maintains a high (or higher) rate with those who do not punish.

Punish early behaviors. If you are going to punish, try to punish early manifestations of the behavior, instead of waiting for a full-blown episode. Early manifestations are weaker than the later ones, and it is easier to stop weak behaviors than strong ones. For example, a tantrum usually builds up over several seconds or minutes. Intervene early.

Keep records. In all of these procedures it is very important to "collect data." That means you should try to get some objective estimate on how often the child engages in the unwanted behavior. For example, count how many times he hits himself in a morning, or how many times he smears per day, or how many times he attacks you in a week. Over a week, a month, or more, does it stay about the same, is he getting better or worse? That's your "baseline," and it will tell you whether or not your intervention works. Your treatment has to produce a change in that baseline; if it doesn't, don't continue. *The effects of aversives have to be documented.* Record keeping is discussed in Chapter 4.

Get some feedback. This includes a "peer review" by other professionals who have experience with aversives. If you can't tolerate the criticism that may be part of honest feedback, don't use aversives. There is always a real possibility that you may be making mistakes when you use aversives, and such mistakes could be costly. Peer review does not eliminate those mistakes, but it reduces them. Persons who are not responsive to their professional colleagues should not use aversives. If you are a teacher, do *not* punish unless the parent is present and agrees to also punish. If you are a parent, never let a teacher punish unless you can see what is going on.

This introduction to aversives may give rise to considerable concern, even distaste in some people. We recommend that you avoid being trapped in some sentimental and popular theory that precludes rational investigation of alternatives. Such may have been the status of punishment with developmentally retarded persons. Probably in the long run, if aversives can be documented to be effective they will become accepted, independent of the public sentiments at the time.

A person may ask whether one can be a useful teacher or parent to developmentally disabled children *without* using physical aversives, like spanking. Without a doubt, the answer is yes. Some children are so responsive to negative feedback that even a minor correction like saying "No" has a major effect. Recent research (Ackerman, 1979) also suggests that developmentally disabled children will learn new tasks in a teaching program that uses contingent positive rewards only. However, in such a program the teacher may not observe a substantial reduction in ritualistic, repetitive (self-stimulatory) behaviors, or behaviors like tantrums and noncompliance, unless contingent aversives are also used. In other words, in order to be a maximally effective teacher or parent, you may have to use physical punishment.

Aversives actually play a very minor role in our programs. We use them to help the child stop or diminish certain behaviors so he can be placed in a teaching situation. The aversives are generally not used after the first week or month. Aversives constitute less than 1% of our interactions. This book is really about teaching and growth; it is about how to free your child and help him stay free. Tomorrow we will know more about how to raise children, and we will not need to rely on aversive control at all.

CHAPTER 3

BEHAVIOR CHARACTERISTICS OF DEVELOPMENTALLY DISABLED CHILDREN

This chapter examines some of the problems developmentally disabled children have in adapting to education, whether it occurs at home or at school. Special behaviors of developmentally disabled children, such as tantrums, excessive ritualistic and stereotyped mannerisms, poor motivation to achieve, and lack of appropriate focus in attention, are closely examined.

When studying the idiosyncrasies of developmentally disabled children, we were reminded that such children are perhaps more different than they are alike. The characteristics discussed in this chapter, particularly in regard to aggression and tantrum-like behavior, may therefore not be true or typical of your child. Many or most disabled children are very vulnerable and nonaggressive; therefore, the section on the management of aggressive and tantrum-like behavior may not apply to your child. However, the sections on motivational deficits or attentional problems may apply.

EXCESSIVE TANTRUMS

Developmentally disabled children often throw tantrums when demands are placed on them. Their tantrums may interfere seriously with their learning of more appropriate behaviors. Your child's tantrums may be minor, such as screaming, or they may be major, such as hitting, scratching, or biting adults or other children, throwing himself on the floor, overturning furniture, breaking glass, or injuring himself by biting himself, banging his head against the wall, etc. Sometimes the tantrum is short-lived and lasts for only a few seconds or minutes. In other cases it can go on for hours on a nearly daily basis for literally years, which sometimes necessitates physical restraints or sedative medication. The tantrums become particularly difficult to control as the child gets older or physically stronger and he can become dangerous to the caregivers. Sometimes a child may be quite unapproachable when he throws a tantrum, only to appear perfectly calm and in total control when the tantrum is over. This has led some people to believe that the tantrum is "manipulative" rather than an expression of a deep-seated emotional problem.

Let us briefly summarize what we know about tantrums.

1. The tantrum is usually the child's response to frustration, such as the loss of a customary reward or a change in routine.

2. The tantrums become stronger if you give in (remove demands) or make a lot of fuss about them. There is compelling evidence that by giving the child attention and concern, contingent on tantrums and self-destructive behaviors, one can shape up and increase such behaviors (place them on acquisition).

3. The tantrums will probably go away if you ignore them. If you can put up with all the screaming and commotion and if the child doesn't hurt himself or you too much, try "working through" the tantrum, acting as if it didn't exist. This is known as *extinction*. Extinction is sometimes hard on the adult and the child because the child will continue to aggress, often showing a peak (an "extinction burst") before the behavior gradually decreases. Time-out (turning away or placing the child in isolation) is sometimes an easy way to handle the tantrums (in that the teacher does not have to put up with all the commotion). Remember, though, that for some children being in time-out is a reward (if the child doesn't like to be in class, he may prefer time-out), so it won't work.

4. Spanking is sometimes a remarkably effective way to stop a tantrum (even though the child may hurt himself much more during the tantrum than you can by spanking him). It is a good idea to catch the tantrum early; once it is full blown, it is harder to control.

5. If the tantrums are initially triggered by frustration, then one may be able to reduce the tantrums by avoiding frustrating situations. On the other hand, by removing frustrating situations altogether, it is unlikely that the child will learn very much. Also, the child eventually has to learn to cope with frustration without engaging in severe tantrums. In any case, keep trying to reduce "unduly" high levels of frustration.

It is extremely important in controlling tantrums, no matter what procedure is employed, that you be on guard so as to not inadvertently reward the child for the undesirable behavior. For example, self-destructive behavior appears to be socially shaped in the first place by persons who did not intend to worsen the behavior, and unless one can now withhold some of those unintended and perhaps subtle rewards, any attempt to stop self-destruction will fail. It is a sad story that the very same persons who intended to help the self-destructive child probably did him more harm than good. Their affection and concern, given contingent on the self-destructive behavior, enslaved him.

It is often the case that, as you start the first lesson (telling him that he has to sit still in order for the lesson to begin) the child will throw a tantrum, perhaps to make you back off and remove your demands. Children are often masters at controlling their parents and other adults through such strong and primitive behavior. In effect *they* decide on how their daily routine should be arranged and what the rules should be. Obviously, you have to reverse those rules.

In the children's defense it must be said that they probably throw tantrums because they have a difficult time understanding what is going on. The tantrums and aggression can be a response to their frustration at not understanding; it is their way of communicating what they want. But that should be no excuse for you to let them continue with their tantrums. We all experience frustration over not understanding. One cannot educate a child who scares his teacher or has to be drugged and restrained to quiet the tantrum-like behavior. Hence the need for *you* to take control of the situation. You have to teach him more appropriate ways to deal with your demands.

Basic Information

Remember, as soon as he has been quiet for 2 or 3 seconds, *reward* him for behaving well ("That's good sitting") and immediately resume the teaching (if you delay presenting him with the demands, that delay may be his reward for the tantrum and will keep the tantrum strong). Gradually increase the time interval required for him to be quiet, that is, not throwing a tantrum.

As far as we can tell, there is nothing "insane," "crazy," or "psychotic" about the tantrums, even though they look very grotesque at times. Some children go so far as to mutilate themselves, biting their hands and banging their heads. Much to our surprise, the data (Lovaas & Simmons, 1969) show that the tantrums and self-abuse are very effective and practical as a means for the child to communicate to you that either he wants affection and attention or that he wants you to stop bothering him, to stop placing demands on him. In fact, our studies on tantrums show how rational such behavior can be.

A main point about handling the tantrums is this: *don't let this behavior frighten you.* Stay cool and rational. The child may look like he is insane, but he is not. He probably is trying to get control over you, and whether or not he is conscious of that intent does not really matter. He is admirably good at it. The more insane he looks, the more he will frighten you, and the worse he will get. In fact, individuals with this behavior have baffled psychiatrists and psychologists for years. Like other people, your child prefers to be in charge and control the situation. Don't let him; *you* take charge.

Many teachers and parents realize how a child's aggressive and tantrum-like behavior will keep him out of his own home and out of good schools where he could learn. All a child has to do is to hit himself on the head or bite himself and he frightens many adults and other children. He is then sent to a more primitive and regressed place and perhaps he is placed on drugs. It is sometimes a very fine balance between his staying at home, or in the community where he can learn, and going some place like a state hospital where he may vegetate the rest of his life. Few people realize that being firm at the right time will settle the child down, keep him "civilized," keep him learning, and keep him out of trouble.

SELF-STIMULATION

Many developmentally disabled children have a variety of repetitive, stereotyped mannerisms such as rocking, spinning, twirling, arm flapping, gazing, tapping, eye rolling, and squinting. We call this kind of behavior *self-stimulation* (short for *self-stimulatory behavior*) because the children seem to use it to "stimulate" themselves. The stimulation can be visual, auditory, or tactile. Usually the behavior is repetitive and monotonous and it may occur daily for years. The following is a summary of what is presently known about self-stimulation:

1. Self-stimulatory behavior is inversely related to the number and frequency of other, more socially acceptable behaviors. When other behaviors are high, self-stimulatory behavior is low. Apparently the child "needs" stimulation, and if he can't get this through behaving appropriately, he will engage in self-stimulation. It appears that there is a need for stimulation, perhaps to keep the nervous system alive. The rocking, gazing, and twirling may be like food to the nervous system; without it, the child's nervous system might deteriorate and atrophy. In this sense, then, self-stimulatory behaviors are necessary for the child. If you do not have a more appropriate behavior to offer him, consider letting him continue to self-stimulate.

2. Self-stimulatory behavior can be used as a reward. We have used self-stimulation as a reward for the child, much like food and water. That is, we may let the child self-stimulate for 3 to 5 seconds as part of his reward for having done something correctly.

3. Self-stimulation decreases or blocks responsiveness to outside stimulation. That is, if the child is self-stimulating during his lesson, it is unlikely that he will pay any attention to his teacher. The rewards derived from self-stimulation are often stronger than the rewards the teacher can offer. Self-stimulation is like drugs: both are difficult to compete with. What we have had to do, then, and what we recommend, is that the teacher actively suppress the child's self-stimulating behavior when she tries to teach. This means that if the child self-stimulates when the teacher is talking to him (when she wants him to pay attention to her), she may physically restrain him, or she may give him a loud "No" and perhaps some other aversive to stop the self-stimulation. (There is a problem in physically restraining the child during self-stimulation, such as holding his hands still, because the contact provided by the teacher may be a reward for the self-stimulation. That is, the child may learn to self-stimulate to get his teacher to touch him.) As soon as he stops the self-stimulation, the teacher rewards him for it ("Good looking" or "Good listening") and gives him his instruction. The teacher may let the child self-stimulate *after* he has behaved correctly, as a reward for being correct.

4. The suppression of one form of self-stimulatory behavior may lead to the increase in another, less dominant form of self-stimulation. For example, if the child rocks a great deal, and such rocking is suppressed, visual gazing may replace rocking. If gazing is suppressed, vocalizing and humming may replace gazing. The task in this case is to help the child develop a form of self-stimulation that interferes minimally with learning and that appears socially more acceptable than some other form of self-stimulation. For example, humming and vocalizing, like gazing, are socially less stigmatizing than jumping up and down while flapping arms and hands. The need for self-stimulatory behaviors may also provide an ideal basis for building play and athletics. This possibility is discussed later in this book.

MOTIVATIONAL PROBLEMS

Developmentally disabled children are often not motivated to learn school-like subjects. It may be that this lack of motivation is caused by the failures and frustrations they already have experienced in such learning, or it may be that their poor motivation is a major reason why they are behind in academic and social skills. In any case, "being correct" is often not rewarding enough. Conversely, "being incorrect" is often not adequately aversive. (However, there are some noticeable exceptions to that inference.) Many of the other nuances and fine points associated with succeeding and not succeeding often pass by the retarded child. Instead of relying on "natural" or "intrinsic" motivation, the teacher needs to construct an explicit reward/punishment system, usually in the form of food and exaggerated social praise, on the one hand, and loud "No"s or physical aversives, on the other. It is a sign of a good teacher that she can find ways to motivate a slow student to learn in as normal a way as possible. The use of rewards and punishment has been discussed in Chapter 1, but let us briefly summarize here:

1. The general rule is this: let the child do whatever he likes to do (eat, self-stimulate, be approved of) *after* he has done what you want him to do. The reward should consume minimal time, say 1 to 5 seconds.

2. Use exaggerated positive rewards in the beginning, while he is learning a task. *After* you know that he has mastered the task, thin the rewards and eventually *expect* him to show you how well he can do, *without* the positive rewards. Thin the rewards slowly for newly learned behaviors, otherwise the behaviors will not be maintained. This is important, because you want to save the positive rewards for *new* learning, rather than just maintain some previously learned behavior.

3. Remember what we said about controlling or minimizing extraneous motivation: don't let him self-stimulate while you teach him. This is so because his self-stimulation and drifting off feel too good for him. Don't expect that you can compete against it, at least not in the beginning. Therefore, suppress the self-stimulation. If he is to self-stimulate, it has to be as a reward for first having done what you wanted him to do.

4. If a child already is anxious about failure, don't punish him for failure. He is punishing himself. You will soon discover that a child who is anxious to start with is an easy child to teach. He has plenty of motivation. All you have to do is to teach him those behaviors that give him a "handle" on his anxiety, the behaviors that help him reduce it.

5. Although you may have to use artificial and exaggerated motivators in the beginning, a good teacher will gradually "fade" out these motivators to make the teaching situation look as normal as soon as possible. "Normalizing" the motivational structure is essential in order to transfer learning across environments and to prevent relapse.

6. *Tokens* have often been used with slow children. Tokens (such as poker chips) are used as "money" for the child to "buy" extras, such as ice cream, special favors, or watching a TV show. The value of tokens is established in the early steps by giving the child something he wants, such as a bite of food, provided he has given you a token first. You may begin by having him give you a token for a bite of food. Once the value of tokens is established, you give him tokens as a reward for some behavior you are trying to teach him. In other words, he may *earn* these tokens, one at a time, by acting appropriately. The tokens can later be cashed in for food, free time, TV viewing, etc. The advantage of the token is that it is an explicit and concrete reward that can sometimes simplify the teaching situation.

    It is, of course, possible to use tokens for discipline as well. The child can *lose* tokens he has previously earned if he misbehaves. Remember, however, that tokens, like food, are "artificial" rewards and should be removed as soon as possible. In this way the child's learning is as natural as possible which helps learning transfer to outside, nontoken environments.

7. Keep in mind that the more unusual (or less "natural") your rewards are, the less your child will transfer what you teach him to outside situations. That is, generalization (transfer) of learned behavior from one situation to another is related to the degree that the two situations have common rewards. For example, if you use food rewards in one situation, then the behavior you build with these rewards may not transfer to another situation where food rewards are not used. Or, the child may behave well when he is hungry (and wants food rewards) and therefore poorly when he is satiated. Again, good teaching transfers the child from artificial rewards to more natural ones, to help generalization of learned behaviors.

ATTENTIONAL PROBLEMS

Another major problem that interferes with the learning of slow children is their difficulty in paying attention. It is possible that this is the main cause of their retarded development. Their attentional problem seems worse when they self-stimulate, when they often seem not to pay attention at all. Poor attention may also be related to poor motivation. If they are not motivated to learn, they probably will not attend to their teacher. The relationship between attention and motivation, however, is difficult to pinpoint. We have sometimes tried to make the children *very* hungry and *very* anxious. Still they show some of the same attentional deficiencies. Perhaps they have several kinds of attentional problems, some related to motivation, some not. Be that as it may, we can now describe some of these problems in more detail than before and suggest ways to work around or reduce them.

The children's attentional problems may lie in an overly narrow attention to external cues. The children often focus on small details and are unable to see the whole picture. They have overfocused or *overselected* their attention. The following examples illustrate overselection. Suppose you show a picture of a man to a normal two- or three-year-old child; that child will label the picture "man." When shown the same picture, a developmentally retarded individual may respond "button," in response to a tiny detail of the person's clothing. We taught developmentally disabled (autistic) children to tell the difference between a girl and a boy. When we took the *shoes* off the figures (or for some children, other pieces of clothing), the children somehow could not tell the figures apart anymore. It seemed that they had learned to tell the boy from the girl by looking at the shoes (or some equally insignificant part) and ignoring the rest of the figure.

Other examples of such overselection relate to the use of prompts. When children are taught to imitate sounds, the teacher may want to use sounds that have distinct visual cues in addition to the auditory ones. In a sense, the visual cues help or guide (prompt) the correct response, as in the mouth movement for producing the sound "ah" or the lip movement in saying "mm." Suppose the children learn to imitate these sounds. Now, when the teacher covers her mouth so the children can't see it, they suddenly go mute; they don't speak any more. They overselected the visual cues and did not attend to the auditory ones. Consider another example illustrating how overselective attention may interfere with transfer (generalization) of learning across situations. A particular teacher taught her children to identify parts of the body, which is a common preschool task. The children learned to point to their ear when the teacher said "ear," point to their foot when the teacher said "foot," and so on. One day a substitute teacher took over the class, and discovered that many of the children were unable to do the task, even though the children seemed cooperative and motivated. When this situation was examined more closely, it turned out that the first teacher, when she asked the children to perform, also made a slight but distinctive gesture with her hand or eyes which the second teacher did not do. Apparently, it was the lack of this gesture that had confused the children. When the second teacher also began to gesture in the same way as the first teacher, all of the children performed well. The children had overselected certain details of the teaching situation and this interfered with their transfer or generalization of that learning to new situations.

We do know that such overselective attention occurs "between the senses," such that if the child *sees* what the teacher is doing, he may not *hear* the teacher's voice. He may focus on *one* channel of input (say the visual cue) while ignoring the other channel (the auditory cue). But he may also overselect *within* a stimulus dimension. For example, with visual cues, which may have shape, size, and color, he may pay attention to only one or two of these dimensions, but not all three. The same problem shows up with auditory cues. For example, in order to learn language the child should pay attention to several cues in your voice, such as the loudness, pitch, and form of a verbal utterance. But again, he may overselect and miss out on what is really being said by just attending to one of these cues, like the loudness. A child will not understand much language unless he can focus on several auditory cues given simultaneously.

Apparently, overselective attention is correlated with the mental age of the child. Children with a very low mental age (the more retarded ones) show more overselective attention than children with higher mental ages.

In summary, then, the perceptual problems associated with stimulus overselectivity center on 1) problems in shifting from prompts to other stimuli, 2) limited generalization (transfer) of learned behavior to new environments, and 3) limited learning or use of environmental cues in general. The question is, what can be done about it? We offer the following suggestions:

1. Try to minimize the extra cues in the teaching situation. For example, if the child is taught to imitate sounds, try to make the visual cues (sight of the teacher's mouth, etc.) unreliable so he does not get "hooked" on such extra cues that fall on the same cue dimension as the teaching cues. For instance, if you are going to teach the child the difference between large and small, start with an extra large object (like a ball, two feet in diameter) compared to a very small ball (one inch in diameter). Later "fade" out this extreme difference to one of more appropriate size. Apparently, it is easier to transfer from prompt cues to training cues when the discrimination is *easy*.

2. Don't reward the child when he gets the right answer with prompts present. Withhold reward for prompted answers. If you don't, the child will learn to pay more and more attention to the prompt, which makes it that much more difficult to fade. For example, suppose you are going to teach the child the difference between a circle and a square (or any other visual cue). Suppose you place two cards, one cue on each card, on the table in front of him. You then say to him, "circle," and prompt the right answer for him by pointing your finger to the card with the circle. He responds to your prompt and he points to the circle. Now, if you do reward him, you may merely be strengthening the bond between your finger-prompt cue and his pointing. *He may not have seen the circle,* and he didn't have to look at it in order to be rewarded. Your finger prompt may have overshadowed (or blocked) his response to the teaching cue (the circle). Incidentally, the more you fade your finger prompt, the more unreliable and minimal you make that prompt, the more he will be forced to attend to the finger prompt, and the less he will see of the teaching cues. Therefore, as soon as possible, *withhold* rewards when he gets the right answer on prompted trials. Only reward him when he gets the right answer *without* prompts. One way to help this along is for you *not* to prompt, to be economical with the prompts, to wait with the prompt, and so on, so as to "force" him to respond without the prompt, hoping he will start searching for the correct cue. Once the child misses out on rewards, which he will if you don't reward him on prompted trials, he will begin to "look around" and to search for other cues. (There is some evidence that unrewarded trials lead the child to overcome some of his overselective responding.)

3. Be on the lookout for accidental prompts. Children are very good at discovering unintended prompts. They will even detect small movements of your eyes when you are visually fixating on the right answer.

4. Start with easy learning first. For example, start by teaching the child the difference between black and white, instead of some color or form cues, like square and circle. There is some evidence that the child will be able to use a prompt, and later drop it (that is, to transfer from a prompt cue to a teaching cue), if you start with an *easy* difference, like black and white.

5. Remember that the children *eventually* learn to use prompts and to "drop" them (that is, to transfer). They can learn to pay attention to more and more cues. They have to learn to do so if they are going to survive. But it takes time.

CHAPTER   **4**

RECORDING BEHAVIOR

Recording behavior may be the only way in which you can learn whether or not a particular treatment works. The different types of behavior usually require different methods of measurement. Two types of behavior (self-destructive and self-stimulatory) and how they should be recorded are discussed in this chapter.

RECORDING SELF-DESTRUCTIVE BEHAVIOR

The most common way to record self-destructive behavior is to record the *frequency* of the behavior because each self-destructive act is usually distinct and succinct, and, therefore, easy to count. Each self-destructive act is called an event and the process is called *event recording;* that is, each time the child hits his head against an object, bites himself, or commits some self-destructive act, one event is counted. Events may occur rapidly, for example, twice every second, or more slowly, like once every minute.

How Long Should You Record?

The length of recording time depends on several factors, including how often the child damages himself, and how much his behavior varies across settings. For example, the child may injure himself frequently in class, but only rarely at the dinner table. In any case, you may want to *sample* his self-destructive behavior. Sampling means that you do not need to record all the time, but only part of the time, perhaps for 10 minutes every hour. Sometimes you may have to record for 10 minutes every hour throughout the day. At other times, it may be sufficient to record for only 10 minutes at a specific hour during the day. How much you need to record depends on a number of conditions, such as how reliable your data are, and how much the clients' behavior fluctuates over time. Sample recordings can provide a reliable estimate of how your treatment procedure is working. When you first start out, or on the first day, you may want to record all instances of self-destruction that occur in 10-minute observation sessions, so that you will have a measure to serve as a basis of comparison for later samplings to assess how the treatment is working.

How to Record

You need a counter that can be reset (like those used to keep golf scores), a good watch, and a data chart to record behavior. Set up a chart (see Table 4-1) that shows 10-minute time periods, and record the frequency of the behavior and make any notes.

How Long to Record before Treatment Begins?

Treatment must start right away if the problem behaviors are so acute that they endanger the child's life. Otherwise, we have usually measured behavior for 14 days before intervening. If the behavior is decreasing, we withhold treatment until the behavior decreases sufficiently to no longer be a problem, or until it stabilizes at a different level. If the behavior stays the same, or rises during the 14 days of recording, we begin treatment. The days that are used to determine a rate against which to measure the effectiveness of the treatment are called a *baseline;* in other words, we often employ a 14-day baseline.

How Soon Can Changes Be Expected?

Change depends on many factors, varying so much across children that no definite rules about when to expect change can be made. In general, physical aversives should work much more quickly than extinction or time-out, and you should see substantial decreases in the behavior within the first hour. If the behavior undergoes extinction, it may increase during the first hour or day and then slowly decrease over the next several days. Sometimes a behavior has all but disappeared after a week; other times it may take an entire month before the behavior is controlled.

RECORDING SELF-STIMULATORY BEHAVIOR

In many cases it is not possible to measure self-stimulatory behavior in terms of its frequency, because self-stimulatory behavior is usually continuous, without discrete onset or offset points. In other words, we can't readily use event recording, as we did with self-destructive behavior, but may instead need to employ a *time sampling procedure.* In time sampling, you divide a certain interval of time (such as a

Table 4-1. Chart for recording self-destructive behavior

Child's Name: _____

Date: _____

Kind of Behavior: _____

Time	Frequency	Notes
9:00– 9:10 a.m.		
10:00–10:10		
11:00–11:10		
12:00–12:10 p.m.		
1:00– 1:10		
2:00– 2:10		
3:00– 3:10		
4:00– 4:10		
5:00– 5:10		

10-minute observation period) into smaller sections (such as 40 15-second intervals). These 15-second intervals are then divided into a period for observation (say, 10 seconds) and a period for recording (say, five seconds). That is, you watch the child for 10 seconds, then you use the next five seconds to record what he did, then watch him again for 10 seconds, record for five, etc. In this way you will have four opportunities every minute to record whether a behavior occurred or 40 opportunities if you observe the child for 10 minutes. A sample data sheet is shown in Table 4-2.

If you put a check mark in the yes column whenever he is self-stimulating, a record of strength of his self-stimulatory behaviors can be obtained by simply summing those check marks for a 10-minute interval. These data can then be averaged over the day, or week, as wanted. You may also want to use a table like the one described earlier in our discussion of the graphing of self-destructive behavior (see Table 4-1).

One easy and inexpensive "aid" in making this kind of observation is to dictate the time intervals into a tape recorder, and to play it back to yourself during the observations through an ear phone. The tape may say, at zero-time, "Line 1 observe," at 10 seconds, "Record," at 15 seconds, "Line 2 observe," at 25 seconds, "Record," etc. This will simplify your recording and you won't have to keep an eye on a stopwatch.

Table 4-2. Chart for recording self-stimulatory behavior

Child's name: _____

Date: _____ Time of recording: _____

Kind of behavior: _____

Line	Minute	Seconds	Yes	No
1.	0	0–10		
2.		15–25		
3.		30–40		
4.		45–55		
5.	1	60–10		
6.		15–25		
7.		30–40		
8.		45–55		
9.	2	60–10		
10.		15–25		
11.		30–40		
12.		45–55		
13.	3	60–10		
14.		15–25		
15.		30–40		
16.		45–55		
17.	4	60–10		
18.		15–25		
19.		30–40		
20.		45–55		

DURATION RECORDING

Some behaviors, like tantrums, are best recorded in terms of their *duration*. The duration of this type of behavior, not the frequency, is the critical factor. A child may only throw a tantrum once or twice a day, but the tantrum may last for hours. What you need to do, then, is to record on any one day whether a tantrum occurred, and how long it lasted. You may want to use a stopwatch to simplify your recordings. A sample data sheet for duration recording is shown in Table 4-3. You need to transfer these data onto a graph so that you can better see what is happening. Record days along the horizontal line (abscissa), and plot the percentage of time (minutes spent in tantrums over the total time he was observed) on the vertical line (ordinate).

RELIABILITY IN RECORDINGS

In any recording procedure, it is important to note whether any two persons agree on the observations, that is, if the recordings are reliable. You can test the reliability of the observer's recording by having a second observer independently record his observation of the same behavior concurrently with the first observer. The data from the first observer are then compared with the data from the second observer. Ideally, a second observer makes "spot checks" on the first observer, to check on agreement or reliability. That is, you don't need to have a second observer present all the time, but to check 10% - 20% of the time. The observations are said to be unreliable if observers disagree so much that two quite different conclusions can be drawn from their data. In general there will be considerable agreement in recording self-destructive behavior and less agreement on recordings of self-stimulatory behavior. If there is strong disagreement, try to define the behavior more concretely, and leave out the more ambiguous kinds. If in doubt, don't score.

Recording procedures have become relatively complex and represent a rather sophisticated area of research. Hall (1972) has written a useful booklet on how to record behavior. You may want to consult an expert on behavioral measurements from the Department of Psychology or School of Education at your local college.

Table 4-3. Duration recording—Sample data sheet

Child's name: _____
Kinds of behavior: _____

Date	Time of onset	Duration	Comment
Jan. 4	9:10 a.m.	15 minutes	
Jan. 4	5:20 p.m.	15 minutes	
Jan. 5	8:00 a.m.	20 minutes	

REFERENCES

Ackerman, A. The role of punishment in the treatment of preschool aged autistic children: Effects and side effects. Unpublished doctoral dissertation, University of California, Los Angeles, 1979.

Axelrod, S., & Apsche, J. (Eds.). *Punishment: It's effects on human behavior.* Lawrence, Kan.: H & H Enterprises, 1980.

Azrin, N. H., & Holz, W. C. In W. K. Honig (Ed.), *Operant behavior: Areas of research and application.* New York: Appleton-Century-Crofts, 1966.

Foxx, R. M., & Azrin, N. H. The elimination of autistic self-stimulatory behavior by overcorrection. *Journal of Applied Behavior Analysis,* 1973, *6,* 1-14.

Hall, R. V. *Behavior management series.* Lawrence, Kan.: H & H Enterprises, 1972.

Harris, S. L., & Ersner-Hershfield, R. Behavioral suppression of seriously disruptive behavior in psychotic and retarded patients: A review of punishment and its alternatives. *Psychological Bulletin,* 1978, *85,* 1352-1375.

Koegel, R. L., Russo, D. C., & Rincover, A. Assessing and training the generalized use of behavior modification with autistic children. *Journal of Applied Behavior Analysis,* 1977, *10,* 197-205.

Lovaas, O. I., & Simmons, J. Q. Manipulation of self-destruction in three retarded children. *Journal of Applied Behavior Analysis,* 1969, *2,* 143-157.

RECOMMENDED READINGS

Basic Learning Theory

Bijou, S. W., & Baer, D. M. *Child Development* (Vol. 1). New York: Appleton-Century-Crofts, 1961.

Navarick, D. J. *Principles of learning: From laboratory to field.* Reading, Mass.: Addison-Wesley, 1979.

Whaley, D. L., & Malott, R. W. *Elementary principles of behavior.* New York: Appleton-Century-Crofts, 1971.

Behavior Modification

Martin, G., & Pear, J. *Behavior modification: What it is and how to do it.* Englewood Cliffs, N.J.: Prentice-Hall, 1978.

Morris, R. J. *Behavior modification with children: A systematic guide.* Cambridge, Mass.: Winthrop Publishers, 1976.

Patterson, G. R. *Living with children* (Rev. ed.). Champaign, Ill.: Research Press, 1976.

Redd, W. H., Porterfield, A. L., & Anderson, B. L. *Behavior modification: Behavioral approaches to human problems.* New York: Random House, 1979.

Sulzer-Azaroff, B., & Mayer, G. R. *Applying behavior analysis procedures with children and youth.* New York: Rinehart & Winston, 1977.

Specialty Books

Baker, B. L., et al. *Steps to independence: A skills training series for children with special needs.* Champaign, Ill.: Research Press, 1977.

Foxx, R. M., & Azrin, N. H. *Toilet training the retarded: A program for day and nighttime independent toileting.* Champaign, Ill.: Research Press, 1977.

Fredericks, H. D. B., Baldwin, V. L., & Grove, D. N. *A data-based classroom for the moderately and severely handicapped.* Monmouth, Ore.: Instructional Development Corporation, 1977.

Henderson, S., & McDonald, M. *Step-by-step dressing.* Bellevue, Wash.: Edmark Associates, 1976.

Huffman, J. *Talk with me.* Bellevue, Wash.: Edmark Associates, 1976.

Kozoloff, M. A. *Educating children with learning and behavior problems.* New York: Wiley, 1974.

Lovaas, O. I. *The autistic child: Language development through behavior modification.* New York: Irvington Publishers, 1977.

Journals

Analysis and Intervention in Developmental Disabilities. Elmsford, N.Y.: Pergamon Press.

Behavior Modification. Beverly Hills, Calif.: Sage Publications.

Child Behavior Therapy. New York: Haworth Press.

Education and Treatment of Children. Pittsburgh: Pressley Ridge School.

Journal of Applied Behavior Analysis. Lawrence: University of Kansas, Department of Human Development.

TASH Review. Seattle: The Association for the Severely Handicapped.

UNIT II

GETTING READY TO LEARN

Unit II outlines a "getting ready to learn" program. Chapters 5 and 6 provide step-by-step procedures for teaching proper sitting and directed attention. Once these preparatory behaviors are taught, interfering behaviors need to be eliminated so that your child is ready to learn. Chapter 7 provides useful information on how to help children overcome their tantrums and reduce other disruptive behavior. (You may find Chapter 7 redundant with Chapters 1 and 2. We recognize this redundancy, but judged it appropriate in an attempt to ensure effective management of disruptive behaviors.)

When you begin the actual teaching it is best to start with something simple, both for your sake and for your child's. We decided to start with the most elementary task, teaching the child to sit in a chair when you give him the instruction "Sit down" (Chapter 5). This simple task is excellent practice because it contains all the elements of a teaching situation: instructions, prompts, identifying correct responses, and rewards and punishment.

We usually start our teaching program with the child and the "teacher" in the middle of the room and the parents and members of the "teaching team" surrounding them to watch the instruction. After a beginning has been made (the "teacher" has taught the child to sit on command), all adults present should be given an opportunity to practice teaching the behavior. Although parents will have a slight edge over team members who have had no experience in teaching developmentally disabled persons, no one should feel embarassed or awkward about learning our teaching methods. When beginning the actual teaching, all adults should teach in the same manner. It is important to keep instructions uniform. Later in the programs you can afford to be more "flexible" and varied, and your child will need that in order to better prepare himself for the outside world. But in the beginning it is best for all adults who teach to use consistent and uniform teaching methods.

You may want to work on two or three instructions ("Sit down," "Hands quiet," "Look at me") during the first session. Don't teach too much in the beginning, however; it is better to establish good control over the basics ("Sit down," "Look at me") before you go on. Some children can perform adequately in response to these commands in less than one hour (or such basic commands may be skipped altogether); others will need a month or more of teaching. Other children will object to your efforts to teach them. In general, your child will "establish" where and how instruction needs to begin.

CHAPTER 5

PROPER SITTING

It may sound surprising, but for certain children, learning to sit correctly in a chair is their first learning experience. It can be a very gratifying step for everyone. Work to get this kind of control before you go on to other programs. Also, remember that since this task is easy to teach, both for the child and the adult who trains him, success is maximized for both. It is extremely important, particularly in the beginning, that both teacher and child be successful. It is gratifying to the child because he has learned something definite, and also because most children like some form of limits. It is gratifying to the adults, and builds their confidence as teachers, because the task is simple enough for them to teach. For some parents, this may be the first time they have had explicit control over their child.

Three commands are extremely useful for helping the child to sit correctly during the teaching sessions: "Sit down"; "Sit up straight"; and "Hands quiet."

"SIT DOWN"

The first command, "Sit down," does not always need to be taught. However, if the child does not know how to sit in a chair, the following procedure is recommended.

Step 1: Choose a chair that is suitable for the child's size. Place the chair directly behind the child.

Step 2: Give the command "Sit down," and then help the child (push him or otherwise prompt him by physically placing him) onto the chair.

Step 3: Reward the child with praise or food as soon as he is seated.

Step 4: Have the child stand up (physically raise him up if necessary) and then repeat Steps 2 and 3.

Step 5: Each time you tell the child to sit down, give him less and less help. That is, gradually fade the physical prompt (assistance) so that he is doing more of the act of sitting down on his own.

Rewards should be given each time the child sits in the chair. Also, in small steps, slowly increase the distance between the child and the chair.

Step 6: If he gets up before you want him to, forcefully (perhaps with aversives) place him back in the seat so that he will become apprehensive about getting out of the chair without your permission to do so.

Step 7: Now introduce the command "Stand up," and prompt him to get up if necessary. Getting up out of the chair may be reward enough. Remember, *you* decide when he shall sit down and when he shall stand up during teaching sessions.

As the child becomes more expert at getting himself into the chair on your command and is able to meet your initial requirement of sitting for approximately 5 seconds, he should soon be required to sit in the chair for increasingly longer periods of time (for some children it may only be 5 minutes at a time, even after a month of training).

While working on other tasks (introduced below) praise the child occasionally for "good sitting" so as to maintain his sitting.

"SIT UP STRAIGHT"

Children can often be seated in a chair but will slump over or slide down in it. When the child does this he is not sitting properly and is generally not attending. The instruction "Sit up straight" helps to get the child's squirming and sliding under good control. The following steps are recommended to teach this command:

Step 1: When the child begins to slouch or slide down in the chair, give the command, "Sit up straight!" Be forceful! Let the child know you mean business.

Step 2: Immediately show the child what you mean by sitting up straight by correcting the way he is sitting. This may require pushing his shoulders back or pulling him up in the chair (prompting).

Step 3: Reward the child for sitting correctly.

Step 4: After several instances of prompting him into the proper sitting position, you should wait for a few seconds after giving the instruction to give him a chance to do it on his own.

Step 5: If the child does not sit up straight within two or three seconds and you sense that he is being lazy or stubborn, force him to sit up. You should make it so the child would rather get himself sitting properly than have you do it for him!

Step 6: Be sure to praise warmly whenever the child sits up correctly on command. Be careful that what you do (by expressing concern and attention) does *not* in fact reward him for slouching. Be mildly aversive as soon as he slouches.

"HANDS QUIET"

The third important command is "Hands quiet." All children fidget, but excessive fidgeting or self-stimulation with the hands is often the cause of a child not paying attention. The child may be sitting perfectly and looking right at you, but if he is fidgeting with his hands or flapping his arms (moving them about) he may not hear a word you say.

"Hands quiet" can mean one of several things: 1) hands are still and arms are hanging at the child's sides, 2) hands are flat, palms down, on the child's legs, or 3) hands are folded in the child's lap. Choose the position that is most natural for the child and *most helpful for you.* Children who fidget with their thumb and forefinger should be taught position 2. With palms down and fingers spread on legs, the temptation to fidget is minimized. For children who don't fidget with their fingers but who flap their hands or arms, position 1 or 3 is appropriate.

Step 1: When the child fidgets, give the command "Hands quiet," and then force the child's hands into the desired position.

Step 2: Be forceful. The child must learn that it is more pleasant for him if he does it himself than if you do it for him.

Step 3: Always reward (with food and approval) the child for following your instruction, even in the initial stages when you are helping him.

Step 4: Gradually decrease the amount of assistance you give the child in getting his hands into proper position on command. Allow the child time to respond to the command and help him only when it is necessary. As the child learns the expected behavior, fewer prompts will be required.

    a.   Say, "Do this," while you perform the desired behavior.

    b.   If necessary, help the child (prompt him) to imitate you.

    c.   Reward him for imitating you.

    d.   Gradually perform less and less of the action yourself after you have given the command.

       (Eventually you will barely have to move your hands at all for him to remember what the entire action is.)

Step 5: As he is catching on to what you want, gradually "thin out" the food as reward, maintaining his correct behavior with social approval only. For example, instead of rewarding every correct response with food, reward the child for every third correct response, then for every tenth response, etc. Finally, "thin out" the social approval, also, so that the child learns that he is expected to sit correctly as a matter of routine.

GENERALIZING PROPER SITTING

After the child is taught to sit correctly in one chair, with one adult in one room, generalize this learning to other places with other people. Have him sit on chairs, on your command, in the living room, kitchen, bedroom, bathroom, etc. Have a variety of adults work as teachers and use a variety of chairs.

       Most likely, tantrums and fussing will take place as you begin to establish control and demand the child's compliance with your requests, however simple and reasonable your requests may be. Chapter 6 deals with techniques for eliminating these interfering behaviors.

CHAPTER 6

DIRECTING AND MAINTAINING THE CHILD'S ATTENTION

This section of the "getting ready to learn" program includes two procedures. The first is teaching the child to visually attend to your face (establishing eye contact). The second is a general procedure for teaching the child basic behaviors such as visually attending to objects in the environment to which you wish to direct his attention.

"LOOK AT ME"

Use the command "Look at me" to establish eye contact. It is generally best to be sure the child has learned to sit properly and to be attentive before you start to teach this procedure.

Step 1: Have the child sit in a chair facing you.

Step 2: Give the command "Look at me" every 5 to 10 seconds.

Step 3: Reward the child with praise and food for correctly looking at your face. In the beginning a correct response occurs when the child looks in your eyes for at least 1 second and looks within 2 seconds after the command is given. That is, it is clear to you that he has looked at you and his response has been sufficiently distinct so that he "knows" what he is being rewarded for. In general, if you have a clear idea of what you are rewarding, he will catch on. Say, "Good looking," and simultaneously feed him.

Step 4: If the child does not visually attend to your face within the 2-second interval, look away for about 5 seconds and then give the command again.

Step 5: Some children will not look at you when you say, "Look at me." Therefore, you have to prompt the response. You can prompt eye contact by holding a piece of food (or something else the child will look at) directly in the line of vision between your eyes and the child's eyes at the same time as you give the command. Therefore, repeat the command ("Look at me") and simultaneously present the prompt (move the piece of food into his line of vision, and level with your eyes).

Step 6: When *eye* contact occurs within the 2-second interval on 10 consecutive commands, gradually and systematically fade the prompt by increasingly hiding it in your hand and by gradually minimizing the movement of your hand over successive commands.

Step 7: To increase the duration of the child's eye contact, gradually delay giving the food while maintaining eye contact with praise. That is, increase the length of time that the child must look before he is given food. Count silently to two before you reward him, then to three, and on to five or more, so that he slowly learns to look at you for increasingly longer periods of time.

Notice something very important in this work: You have established a very clear idea of what is the *correct* response, and you have a clear idea of what is an *incorrect* response. That is critical because you now know when to reward and when *not* to reward. You can be consistent. You know what you want, and you won't hesitate or become obsessed with details that are extraneous to the accomplishment of the final goal. This is very important when you teach slow children. They don't "forgive" your mistakes the way normal children do.

It is best to start teaching eye contact while the child is sitting in the chair because the chair provides a simple teaching situation with little distraction. It is easier for you to get control under these circumstances. However, if the child only learns to look at you while he is sitting in the chair, his new behavior will be of limited value. Therefore, it is necessary to begin to *generalize* this first learning (as you did with his sitting in different chairs). After he has mastered looking at you in the chair, have him look at you when he stands up, when he is in other rooms, etc., and reward him for doing so. Reinforce him for increasingly longer periods of eye-to-face contact, starting with 1-second durations, and slowly increasing the demand for longer looks of 2, then 3 or more seconds before you reward him.

"HUG ME"

The step-by-step procedures for teaching "Sit down" and "Hands quiet" (Chapter 5) and "Look at me" (above) have provided you with a general format for now teaching the child to visually attend to selected objects in the environment as well as for teaching other basic behaviors. You may want to try some of these on your own. For example, one of the early behaviors we teach the child is to give the adult a hug when the adult says, "Hug me." You could arrange the teaching of this behavior along the following steps:

Step 1: Say, "Hug me," and prompt (e.g., physically move) the child so that his cheek makes momentary contact with yours. Reward him with food the moment his cheek makes contact.

Step 2: Gradually fade the prompt while keeping the instruction ("Hug me") loud and clear.

Step 3: Gradually withhold the reward contingent on longer and longer hugs. Move in slow steps from a 1-second hug to one lasting 5 to 10 seconds. At the same time, require a more complete hug such as his placing his arms around your neck, squeezing harder, etc. Prompt these additional behaviors if necessary.

Step 4: Generalize this learning to many environments and many persons. Gradually thin the reward schedule so that you get more and more hugs for less and less rewards.

MAINTAINING ATTENTION

Expect that while you are teaching your child to visually attend he may try to get out of his chair or may start to throw tantrums. Be firm and require proper sitting and no disruptive behavior when you teach. Otherwise, the teaching situation will be pure chaos.

There are many things that can go wrong even in these beginning steps. If the child does not seem to learn or starts to lose what he already has learned, watch for mistakes made by the *teacher*. Generally, it is the teacher who is not performing the teaching sequence properly. Here is where the "staff meeting" comes in handy, to help spot teaching mistakes. One of the most common mistakes occurs when "no" starts sounding like "good." The teacher is momentarily "burned out" and needs to be recharged. The "No" has to sound like hell's fury (sometimes) and the "Good" has to be given with lots of smiles, kisses, and hugs. Ham it up, become an actor, and really exaggerate your expression (as long as the child does not think you are acting and knows you mean business).

A second reason for lack of maintenance is motivational in origin. If you are using food rewards, don't start the teaching session after a meal. As a rule the child won't eat very much if he is full. Don't use big bites (like spoonfuls) or the child will soon become satiated. Instead, during this early learning, be sure the child is hungry (work with him during mealtime, have him skip a meal, give him *small* bites, etc.). This may sound cruel, but it really isn't as long as he is now going to begin learning and the use of food rewards is temporary.

The main problem encountered in "getting ready to learn," however, centers on tantrum control. Eliminating disruptive behaviors is discussed in the next chapter.

ELIMINATING MILDLY DISRUPTIVE BEHAVIORS

CHAPTER 7

This chapter contains procedures that have been designed to eliminate behaviors that the child uses to avoid working or that interfere with teaching. Some children have severe, disruptive behaviors, such as self-mutilation, that are dangerous to their safety. Such behaviors should perhaps be eliminated by procedures other than those described in this chapter, through consultation with professionals, before the child is placed in a teaching situation. If the child's life is *not* in danger through self-injury, it is advisable to proceed with our programs.

Before using any procedure to eliminate disruptive or off-task behaviors, it is important to determine what the child hopes to gain by engaging in the disruptive behavior. There are probably two general causes for the behavior. First, the child may be trying to avoid doing the task. He throws tantrums in order to make you stop and to make you back down. Second, he may simply want more attention from the adult than he is getting at the moment. His fussing, crying, screaming, throwing task materials, upsetting furniture, throwing himself on the floor, arching his back violently, and biting you or himself are all behaviors that can be attempts to escape demands or get attention and make you anxious or uneasy.

PROCEDURES FOR ELIMINATING DISRUPTIVE BEHAVIORS

Straight Extinction

Straight extinction is the most effective and least complicated procedure for eliminating disruptive behaviors. You should act as if nothing has happened. Pay absolutely no attention to the child when he is disruptive and show that his disruptive behavior has no effect on you. That is, don't inadvertently look at him when he is disruptive and don't postpone your instruction because of his disruptions. The child will stop engaging in disruptive behavior when he learns that it brings him nothing in return.

Children seem very clever, sometimes, at knowing when and how to get through to you. Your wincing, hesitating, postponing a trial, or blushing may be all the child needs to keep up with the tantrum.

Straight extinction, however, can usually only be carried out with *mildly* disruptive behaviors. It is impossible to ignore a child when he bites you or breaks furniture. It may be necessary to use punishment and time-out to reduce the magnitude of such severe tantrums, but it is important to remember to return to straight extinction when the tantrums are reduced.

Time-Out from Attention

Time-out is another procedure that can be used to eliminate mildly disruptive behaviors. When the child begins to be disruptive, turn your body away from the child and make sure your face is averted until he stops. Say nothing and remain calm. If this is not enough to stop the disruptive behavior, remove the child from other sources of attention in the room. Face the child toward a blank wall, or position him so that he cannot look at you or others, until he is quiet enough to continue working. Don't scold him while he is quieting down.

Do not attend to your child while he is in time-out. There is no absolute rule on how long he has to be without your attention, but 5 minutes generally seems to be effective. Time-outs exceeding 20 minutes are not recommended because too much teaching time is being lost. Isolating the child until he has been quiet for 5 to 10 seconds can be adequate. Once he is quiet enough to begin working again, praise him for being quiet and calmly reintroduce the task. If the child becomes disruptive immediately after you reintroduce the task, repeat the procedure. Let the child know that he receives no attention from you for behaving badly and that he must continue going back to task.

Time-out should not be used if your child self-stimulates frequently. In this case, your child may find time-out as enjoyable (reinforcing) as your attention because he can self-stimulate freely while you ignore him. Time-out will also fail for those children who want to escape or avoid your demands. In fact, in such cases the use of time-out worsens the child's behavior.

Corner Behavior

This procedure is a form of time-out from attention with the added feature of physical restraint. Some children are very vicious when being disruptive. They kick, scratch, bite, or hit to gain attention and to avoid working. Corner behavior should be used only if your child is aggressive when disruptive or if he will not stay still when the time-out procedure is used.

When the child begins to be disruptive, immediately force him to a nearby corner of the room. Make him face the corner with his arms extended behind him and away from his body. Press his arms flat against the two walls forming the corner. If he kicks, his legs should also be spread with as much surface of the leg touching the two adjoining walls as possible. Hold the child in this position until he quiets down. This is an *extremely* uncomfortable position and the child will not want to be held that way for very long.

As soon as the child has quieted down and is no longer struggling to kick, scratch, or hit, release him, praise him, and return to working on the task. The child may begin to strike out as soon as he is released, or shortly afterward. Restrain him in the corner immediately. Repeat this procedure as often as necessary. Let him know that trying to injure others is definitely *not* allowed and that your endurance is greater than his on this issue! As always, return to the task and continue working until you feel it is completed to *your* satisfaction, not his.

Working Through the Task While Using "No!"

If extinction is impossible to carry out, and if time-out doesn't work or seems inappropriate to use, try working through the task while simultaneously forcefully telling the child, "No!".

When the child begins to engage in disruptive behavior, he should be told "No!" immediately and *very* forcefully. Try not to stop the task because that may be rewarding to him and counteract the effects of "No." Sometimes it is helpful to pair the "No!" with a loud noise such as slapping the table hard or clapping your hands loudly in front of the child's face. In general, the command should specify the particular behavior, such as "No screaming!" or "No laughing!" In this way the child hears exactly what it is you want him to stop doing. Keep the command short, however. In certain cases, such as throwing task materials off the table, where a complete verbal description of the unwanted behavior would be cumbersome and perhaps confusing to the child, it is best to leave the command short and just use "No!"

The child may respond to your "No" in one of three ways:

1. The child may stop his disruptive behavior. If this happens, praise him for stopping ("Good quiet," or "Good sitting") and proceed with the task.
2. The child may become *more* disruptive. He may fuss to such an extent that the task cannot be continued (e.g., he may throw materials involved in the task on the floor). In this case, you may want to escalate the aversiveness of "No!" (e.g., becoming louder, slapping him once, etc.). Make your command so aversive and persistent that he would prefer to have you stop giving your command than to continue being disruptive.
3. The child may become less disruptive, at a level low enough to allow the task to continue. For example, the child may stop a loud tantrum but continue to whine. In this type of situation, proceed with the task as though the child were not disruptive at all. That is, try straight extinction. When the child responds correctly, praise him especially warmly. You will thus be praising (reinforcing) the behavior you desire and ignoring (extinguishing) the unwanted, disruptive behavior.

The child may often start being disruptive as soon as, or shortly after, the task is reintroduced. Repeat the procedure. Let the child know he must complete the task and that his being disruptive will not get him out of completing his assignment. With most small children, a loud "No!" is sufficiently aversive to stop the disruption. In some cases a sharp slap to the thigh is recommended while saying "No!" A strong slap on the rear will usually stop a tantrum if other procedures have failed. The aversives are sure to stop the tantrum quickly (so you can proceed with teaching).

Sometimes, however, it will not work that easily. This will be the case when the child is extremely negativistic and is actually rewarded by your being angry and punishing him. The more you punish him, the more he will become disruptive. Usually, in such cases, if you get really angry and hard, you can stop him. But it may take weeks or months, a time that will be very taxing on your mental and physical health. You may have to fall back on extinction, working through the tantrums. Or you may try some form of overcorrection, as discussed in Chapter 1.

Finally, should your commands and the child's disruption escalate into long shouting matches and if you have too many reservations about spanking, then you should probably use plain extinction or combine the "No!" with the time-out procedure. Shouting matches may be an indication that your child finds some enjoyment in seeing you raise your voice and become angry so that the procedure is not effective. Also, keep in mind two important possibilities when you use aversives. First, the child may adapt to them if you use them for any length of time. If aversives are to work, you should see their effects after 10 or 20 applications. Second, the child may learn to use a form of self-stimulatory behavior to block out his external environment to shield him from surrounding stimuli. This is more likely to occur with the prolonged use of aversives.

MASTERING UNIT II

How long does it take to accomplish Unit II? For example, how long does it take for a child to stop his tantrums, or to learn to sit in a chair, with hands on his lap, looking at you? Some children have mastered Unit II in one hour; others have needed a whole month. Even after a month, some children throw tantrums, but the tantrums may be so weak that one can move forward to Unit III. In any case, children vary enormously in their rate of learning, even within a group that has scored within the same range on IQ tests. Of course, it will also depend on how good you are as a teacher, how much control you have of effective positive reinforcers to shape alternative behaviors, how forceful you are, how much help you have, and so on. In any case, you need to complete this unit on preparation for teaching and get some control over the child. It will make teaching other programs much easier.

Once you have mastered Unit II, the confidence that it gives you will go a long way. Probably more things have happened to your child than just his sitting still. Some of these things are hard to measure. Having a more specific role than before, he may start to feel more trust and affection toward you as you become capable of doing more things for him. You take on more stature in his eyes.

RECOMMENDED READINGS

Carr, E. G., Newsom, C. D., & Binkoff, J. A. Stimulus control of self-destructive behavior in a psychotic child. *Journal of Abnormal Child Psychology*, 1976, *4*, 139-153.

Carr, E. G., Newsom, C. D., & Binkoff, J. A. Escape as a factor in the aggressive behavior of two retarded children. *Journal of Applied Behavior Analysis*, 1978, *13*, 101-117.

Koegel, R. L., & Couvert, A. The relationship of self-stimulation to learning in autistic children. *Journal of Applied Behavior Analysis*, 1972, *5*, 381-387.

Plummer, S., Baer, D. M., & LeBlanc, J. M. Functional considerations in the use of procedural time-out and an effective alternative. *Journal of Applied Behavior Analysis*, 1977, *10*, 689-705.

Rincover, A., Newsom, C. D., Lovaas, O. I., & Koegel, R. L. Some motivational properties of sensory stimulation in psychotic children. *Journal of Experimental Child Psychology*, 1977, *24*, 312-323.

UNIT III

IMITATION, MATCHING, AND EARLY LANGUAGE

The programs in Unit III should make the job of teaching your child much more interesting. Chapter 8 describes ways of teaching your child to imitate your movements. You teach him to raise his arms, to touch his nose, to clap his hands, to stand up, to smile, and so on in imitation of your actions. Once he can imitate your actions, you can help him in many tasks, such as showing him how to play with toys, how to dress, and how to use facial expressions. Imitation is an extremely powerful teaching device, and is probably the primary way that normal children learn from adult society. You must remember that children learn at different rates. Teaching children who have little or no imitation skills will probably go slowly, whereas other children will readily imitate some of your actions at times. With such children it is more a question of expanding what they already know and, very importantly, to get control over their imitations so they can use them at the right time. Chapter 8 contains an important section that should be read with care. It pertains to "random rotation" and to "discrimination learning problems." The learning processes discussed in this section are basic to all the programs in this book.

The program in Chapter 9 teaches the child to match one object or a simple visual form (along the dimensions of size, shape, or color) to an identical or similar object or visual form. For example, the teacher places a variety of different objects on a table in front of the child, he is given one object (a replica), and is taught to identify ("match") that object with the corresponding object on the table. The program on matching objects or forms is very similar to the program on imitating ("matching") movements. There is no magic in the sequence of teaching matching of movements before teaching matching of objects; you could just as easily reverse the order. We run the two programs just about concurrently.

Chapter 10 describes a program on following verbal instructions (early receptive speech). Essentially, the program in Chapter 10 enables the teacher to obtain *verbal control* over the behaviors that were taught in Chapter 8. For example, instead of the child merely raising his arms (or clapping or smiling) in imitation of the teacher, the teacher now begins to verbally instruct the child with commands, such as "Raise your arms," "Clap your hands," or "Smile," gradually fading out the prompts of manual

59

movement until the child can respond to the verbal instruction alone. At this point you clearly can see how adult society is beginning to exercise more and more appropriate control over the child.

Chapter 11 is the most difficult program in the book. It describes how to teach a mute or largely nonverbal child to imitate sounds and words so that he can learn to speak. Whereas the programs in Chapters 8 and 9 deal with imitation or matching of *visual* cues, verbal imitation obviously deals with matching of *auditory* cues. It may be that developmentally delayed children have special problems with perceiving and processing auditory cues (as compared to visual cues). Or, it may be that auditory matching as in speech is much more complex than is visual matching. In any case, Chapter 11 will test your teaching skills for sure. If you can teach verbal imitation then you are an unusually competent shaper, for it is a very difficult teaching task.

Once you have taught the child some imitative behavior, you have the basis for programs pertaining to play skills, which is the subject of Chapter 12.

Finally, Chapter 13 discusses optimizing learning, as in maximizing generalization of new learning to new environments and helping ensure that the new learning lasts.

Unit III is a comprehensive package. By this time you are deeply involved in the teaching programs; an ideal teaching situation may involve 6 to 8 hours of one-to-one instruction daily. Not all settings can provide for that much teaching, but keep in mind that the more your child is taught, the better off he will be.

At this point your child will be learning several programs concurrently because there is no meaningful ending point for any of the programs introduced in Unit III. This allows you to introduce variability in his schedule, and to make both your and his day more interesting.

IMITATION OF SIMPLE ACTIONS

CHAPTER 8

Children normally acquire complex behavior, including play and sports, by observing the behavior of others, and in the case of language, by hearing others speak. Thus, children seem to learn the majority of their social, recreational, and language skills through imitation. After working with developmentally disabled children, you can observe how these children fail to imitate your behavior, or that they imitate you at the wrong time. Perhaps their failure to learn important behaviors from people in their everyday lives can be attributed to their inability to imitate appropriately.

Our research has demonstrated rather conclusively that the child must first learn to imitate the less complex behaviors of his peers and of adults before he is able to imitate the more complex skills. The programs in this chapter teach the child the rudiments of generalized imitation (what some may refer to as the establishment of imitative tendencies or capacities). Specifically, your child is taught to copy, or imitate, gross motor behaviors (e.g., raising the arms, tapping the knees, touching the nose) when you say, "Do this," and perform the activity. This newly established imitative behavior can then be used to teach self-help skills, appropriate play, sports, and other acceptable social interactions. Imitation of the behavior of others can do much to enhance the overall social and intellectual development of the child. Bear in mind also that the basic purposes of imitation training are to teach the child to pay more attention to the people around him and to become more interested and excited about what others are doing, and, in general, to enable the child to behave more appropriately in his environment.

Once the child has learned to sit quietly in a chair for a reasonable length of time (about 2-5 minutes) without engaging in any disruptive behavior and can visually attend to the teacher's face, non-verbal imitation training can begin. It is important to note that eye contact may develop further after the child learns several imitative behaviors. However, if the child frequently engages in disruptive behaviors, such as self-stimulation or excessive tantrums, eye-to-eye contact should be established before teaching begins. If the child is not looking at you, he probably will not see your instruction, which means that you may have to continue suppressing tantrums and self-stimulation and continue to reward eye contact as you are beginning to teach imitation. You may find yourself working hard while the child is just sitting there, rolling his eyes, smiling, flapping his hands, drifting off, or whatever. You should stop those behaviors. Let the child know that you mean business and that you will not put up with the whining, crying, fussing, tantrums, self-stimulation, or any other distracting actions that interfere with his learning. You will no doubt find that your child will come to respect you as you acquire more control over him.

A record of the child's progress should be kept during the training. You, or an attentive observer, should record the child's progress by indicating the trial number, the behavior you are trying to teach the child to imitate, and whether the child responded correctly or incorrectly or required a prompt. Another method of recording would be having an "impartial" observer watch you and the child and then give you feedback on your teaching methods, such as your use of prompts. The child should be imitating behavior in some way after 1 hour. By that time you should know whether the child is improving or standing still. If he is standing still, you probably need to improve your teaching skills. You then have to go back and examine aspects of your teaching method, such as your use of rewards and prompts, and the level of the child's self-stimulation; you may have to become more strict, or change your method of teaching in some other way.

We start the imitation training by teaching the easiest behaviors first, such as Arm raising.

GROSS MOTOR IMITATION

Arm Raising

Step 1: The child is seated opposite you with hands in lap and is attending to your face.

Step 2: *The stimulus.* Loudly present the verbal command, "Do this," while simultaneously raising your arms straight up over your head. If the child does not respond by imitating your actions, you must prompt him so that he responds correctly.

Step 3: *The prompt.* Repeat the verbal command, "Do this," while raising your arms as in Step 2. After raising your arms, hold the child's forearms and raise his arms over his head and hold them there for a second. Or, you may have an assistant stand behind the child and prompt him (raise his arms for him). Also, verbal commands, such as "Raise arms," can be used as prompts for some children. When the child responds correctly, reward him with praise for good arm raising, or give him a bite of food. Try to reward the child while he still has his arms raised.

Step 4: *Fading the prompt.* If the child does not respond on the next trial by raising his arms directly over his head without the prompt described in Step 3, you should prompt him for several trials and then lessen, or fade, the prompt slightly over the next several (say 10) trials. For example, say, "Do this," and then lift the child's arms up so that they are parallel and directly over his head and then let go of them, after which you immediately position your arms over your head. If the child keeps his arms up on his own for even a second, immediately reward him. If he does not keep them up, go back to using the prompt described in Step 3.

Step 5: If the child responds appropriately on several consecutive trials with the prompt described in Step 4, you must fade the prompt even further in order to arrive at your goal. Give the verbal command, "Do this," and then take hold of the child's forearms and gently pull his arms upward (don't hold on very long) as you raise your arms over your head. If the child keeps his arms up over his head in imitation of you for even a brief period, reward his actions. If he doesn't respond appropriately, go back to the prompt described in Step 4.

Step 6: Even though the prompt described in Step 5 may enable the child to respond correctly, you must fade this prompt even further. Instead of actually taking hold of the child's hands and pulling them up as in Step 5, simply push his arms up in the right direction with your fingertips as you are raising your arms over your head. If the child raises his arms in imitation of you, reward him immediately and try using no prompt at all on the next trial.

Assuming the child responds correctly on each successive trial, you should gradually fade the prompt until the child eventually imitates you without any prompting whatsoever. Remember to fade the prompt slowly. The child should be successful on several consecutive trials at a given level of prompting before the prompt is faded or reduced. If the child does not respond by imitating you when you use a reduced or more faded prompt, go back a step to a more effective or "obvious" prompt; that is, use a prompt that you know will enable the child to respond correctly. However, be sure that a reduced or weaker prompt would not do just as well. Many times the child will not need such overt or extensive prompts as you might think. He simply may not be paying attention to the situation at hand. One common characteristic of many children is that they will do as little as possible of what you want them to do, if they feel they can get away with it. Therefore, be stern and matter-of-fact with your child as you go through these steps. You should move to the next step when the child can respond correctly *without any prompting* on several consecutive trials. The child *responds to criterion* when he responds correctly on 9 out of 10, or 18 out of 20, consecutive trials.

The next behavior you want to teach should be different from the first behavior so that your child can easily tell them apart. We teach "Touching nose" next because it is quite different from "Raising arms."

Touching Nose

Step 1: The child is seated opposite you and is visually attending to your face.

Step 2: *The stimulus.* Say, "Do this," while simultaneously raising one of your hands and touching your nose with one forefinger.

Step 3: *The prompt.* If the child does not respond by touching his nose, or if he makes the mistake of "raising arms" (which is likely), you must begin a series of prompting procedures, depending on how the child responds. For example, if he makes no response at all, you must give the verbal command, "Do this," and simultaneously take one of the child's hands, touch his nose with a finger, and hold it there, while also touching your nose with a finger on your other hand. Immediately praise the child for "good touching."

If the child responds by raising his arms, you must say "No" loudly and distinctly, since it is clear that child is not yet able to pay close attention to what is going on. After saying "No" do not look at the child for 5 seconds, and then begin the next trial. Say, "Do this" and prompt him as indicated in this step.

Step 4: *Fading the prompt.* You should slowly fade all prompts so that the child will be able to imitate your touching your nose without any prompting at all. For example, after using the prompt described in Step 2 for several trials, fade this prompt so that you merely guide the child's hand to his nose and then let go before he touches it. If he keeps his hand on his nose for even a second, praise him profusely for his "good touching." If he does not keep it there, use the prompt described in Step 2. Once the child has responded correctly with this faded prompt try fading it even further for a few consecutive trials. After a few successes at this level of prompting, try fading further. For example, you may just pull the child's hand out of his lap and in the general direction of his head. If he touches his nose, praise him accordingly and fade the prompt even further, or try no prompt at all. If he then fails to touch his nose, you must go back a step and use a "more obvious" and less faded prompt.

Introducing Random Rotation

When the child can respond to criterion (responds correctly on 9 out of 10 consecutive trials or on 18 out of 20 consecutive trials) with the two responses learned thus far—arm raising and nose touching— begin mixing trials. It is extremely important that you intermix trials of these two responses *randomly* because the child may become used to a given sequence (e.g., arm raising, then nose touching, then arm raising, then nose touching, etc.) and may not really be learning to imitate behavior.

The teaching process that underlies these programs is called "discrimination learning" in the technical literature. It is a basic process and a very powerful one. Essentially, it says that if a response (A) is rewarded in one situation (X) and *not* rewarded in another situation (Y), then situation X will cause response A to occur (situation X will "cue" or "set" the occasion for response A to occur). The importance of random rotation procedures in helping the student to discriminate the correct or desired cue can be best illustrated by presenting some common teaching problems.

Problem 1. Suppose the teacher asks the child to "Raise arms," and the child behaves correctly and is rewarded. If the teacher repeats this instruction several times and the child continues to respond correctly, all the child may be learning in that situation is to perseverate, that is, to repeat the response that was rewarded earlier. In other words, he is learning that a particular response, when rewarded, is a cue for him to repeat that response. He may *not* learn to raise his arms to the teacher's cue, "Raise arms." This can be tested by saying "San Francisco," or make any other verbalizations, or by just readying yourself to give the instructions. If the child raises his arms under these conditions, he has obviously not learned what you intended—to respond to the cue, "Raise arms."

Problem 2. If the teacher alternates between two instructions, so that every second instruction is identical (e.g., "Raise arms," "Touch nose," "Raise arms," "Touch nose," and so on), the child may simply be learning to systematically alternate between two responses. That is, he is learning that, if one response (raise arms) was rewarded on one trial, then that is the cue for him to try the other response (touch nose) on the next trial. He may be learning a particular *order* or *sequence;* he is *not* learning to imitate your action. You could test this by giving him one instruction, such as "Touch nose." If you then stay with the fixed alternating order of instructions, he should get the first, and then all remaining commands, correctly. If you place your instructions in random rotation, he would fall back to chance responding, that is, he would achieve 50% correct.

Problem 3. Suppose the teacher gives one instruction ("Raise arms") and the child responds incorrectly (touches his nose, for example) and is not rewarded. If the teacher now repeats her instructions ("Raise arms") and the child responds correctly and now is *rewarded,* what the child may be learning is to switch responses if a particular response is not rewarded. Withholding of the reward by the teacher becomes a cue for him to change behavior. The student tries to solve the problem not by attending to the instructions, but based on whether or not he gets a reward. One way to reduce such a problem is to (gradually) withhold rewards unless the child gets the right answer on the first try, without first self-correcting.

Problem 4. Suppose the teacher "guides" the child by looking to the place of the correct response, for example, by looking above the child's head when she says, "Raise arms," and looking at his nose when she says, "Touch nose," The teacher may or may not know that she is providing such extra assistance. What may well happen in this situation is that the teacher's visual gaze becomes the main cue for the child's responding, whereas her verbal instructions remain nonfunctional. Many disabled children have problems processing more than one cue simultaneously, and may learn visual cues more quickly than auditory cues.

The purpose of introducing these sample problems (many more could be added) of how one may inadvertently misdirect a child's learning is to remind the teacher to carefully monitor her steps. It is to everyone's advantage when the teacher suspects that it is *her* teaching that underlies the child's learning problems, not the child's. The more you know about discrimination learning, the more you realize how easy it is to teach mistakes. Developmentally disabled persons learn, perhaps as quickly as anyone else. They do not necessarily learn what the teacher "intends" that they learn, but they may learn what she is reinforcing them for.

This is the reason for the emphasis on random ("chancy") presentations of the first two actions (sometimes arm raising, sometimes nose touching). It may help you to write out a random order before you give the commands, such as 1 (arm raise), 2 (touch nose), 2, 1, 2, 1, 1, 2, 2, 1, 2, 2, 1, 2, 1. If the child can respond to criterion when trials of the two responses are randomly mixed, go on to teach the next behavior. If the child cannot respond correctly when the two actions are randomly mixed, use the random rotation procedure described below.

Step 1: Present the first action trained (raise arms) to the child while saying, "Do this." If the child does not imitate you correctly, prompt the response. The first prompt should be the weakest one used in training the response (e.g., perhaps tapping the child's hands). If this prompt fails to produce a correct response, the strength of the prompt should be increased on successive trials until a correct response is produced. Once the child is responding correctly, fade the prompt in the same manner as in the initial training. Present trials until the child responds correctly, with no prompt, for five consecutive trials.

Step 2: Reintroduce the second action trained (touch nose). Present trials until the child responds correctly with no prompt, for five consecutive trials.

Step 3: Alternate Steps 1 and 2 randomly until little or no prompting is needed the first time that an action is performed.

The two actions now are presented in a randomized rotation. Slight prompting may be necessary on the first few trials. If slight prompting does not result in correct responding, repeat the procedure until the child responds to criterion.

Clapping Hands

Step 1: The child is seated facing you and attending to your face.

Step 2: *The stimulus.* Give the verbal command, "Do this," while simultaneously clapping your hands together several times.

Step 3: *The prompts.* If the child does not respond appropriately (that is, makes no response at all, responds with a behavior already learned, or makes an otherwise incorrect response), you must begin to use a series of prompts that will ensure correct responding. In the case of hand clapping, it is easy when two persons are present to help the child with prompts. Seat yourself face-to-face with the child as you have been doing, and have an assistant kneel or sit behind the child. As you say, "Do this," while simultaneously clapping your hands, have the assistant grasp the child's forearms from behind and begin clapping the child's hands in imitation of you. Immediately praise the child for "good clapping" and give him a bite of food, if you are using food as a reward for correct responding.

Step 3: *Fading the prompt.* Have your assistant fade the prompt slowly. For instance, after you present the verbal command and clap your hands, have your assistant clap the child's hands together once or twice, and if the child claps even once more on his own, praise him profusely. On successive trials the prompt may be faded to only lifting the child's hands into a clapping position. On each trial, provide a prompt that will ensure correct responding. If the child fails to respond appropriately on any given trial, go back to using a stronger prompt that will enable the child to respond correctly. Remember to be sure that a weaker prompt would not do just as well. Be firm with your child and insist that he attend to you and the action you perform or model for him.

Variation for Clapping Hands

Here's an alternative prompting method if you have no other person around to help in teaching your child to imitate you in hand clapping:

Step 1: See Step 1 of "Clapping Hands," above.

Step 2: As you say, "Do this," take the outside of the child's hands in your own hands and actually clap his hands for him. In this way both of you will be clapping at the same time. After several hand claps, immediately praise him for "good clapping."

Step 3: *Fading the prompt.* Give the verbal command and take the child's hands and clap them together once or twice and then clap your own hands several times while saying, "Do this." Immediately reward the child for "good clapping."

You must continue to fade the prompts you have been giving. Instead of actually clapping the child's hands for him, give the verbal command and take the child's hands and just place them together in a hand-clapping position. Immediately clap your hands several times. If the child responds by clapping his hands even once, reward him immediately and, on the next trial, use an even lesser prompt. If the child fails to clap his hands, go back to Step 2.

Step 4: Give the verbal command and begin clapping your hands. If the child does not imitate you, use a prompt such as lifting his hands off his lap. Then continue clapping your own hands and saying, "Do this," once or twice. If the child fails to respond appropriately, you must go back a step and use a more obvious prompt. In this way, you should be able to effectively teach the child to clap his hands in imitation of you without your assistance.

When the child can respond to criterion by correctly imitating you, start mixing trials with the three behaviors learned thus far—arm raising, nose touching, and hand clapping—using the random rotation procedure. Remember that the child *must* correctly imitate the *random* presentations of the behaviors. Otherwise, he may start responding to the particular order, or sequence, that you have inadvertently developed in choosing the responses you want imitated. Therefore, your task is twofold if the child has problems imitating these three responses. First, you must require the child to pay strict attention to you. Second, you must monitor your order of presentation of these responses.

After the child can reliably imitate all three responses, choose at least 10 new responses from the list below and teach them to your child. If one of the first three responses seems particularly difficult to teach your child and the task is becoming too time-consuming, choose another response from the list below as a substitute. Use your own ingenuity in developing and then fading prompts.

Additional Manual Imitation Responses To Be Taught

Tap nearby table	Touch knees
Stand up	Touch head
Touch tummy	Touch teeth
Touch elbow	Pick up an object from table
Stamp feet	Touch tongue
Throw kisses	Touch ears
Wave "bye-bye"	Touch shoulders
Put arms out to side	Touch eyelid
Raise one arm	Turn around (standing up)

Notice that we did *not* group all the "head" responses (touch head, mouth, eye, tongue) because they would look too similar and would confuse the child. Spreading them out makes it easier for the child to tell them apart. Eventually, the child has to learn to distinguish behaviors that look very similar (such as the various "head" responses), but that training comes later.

IMITATION OF FACIAL EXPRESSIONS AND GESTURES

Some psychologists and psychiatrists have theorized that an important problem with developmentally disabled children is that they lack a "body sense" or a "sense of self." Whether or not this is the case remains an open question and one that probably never will be answered to everyone's satisfaction. The purpose of teaching the child to imitate facial expressions and gestures is to make him aware of and attentive to his own facial expressions, body postures, and gestures. The drills and exercises described in this section can help the child become more aware of you and his own physical self and behavior as he moves about in his environment. Facial expressions and gestures in particular are more subtle and complex than the behaviors taught in the previous section. Therefore we do not begin training these until the child has mastered a number of gross motor imitations.

It is probably best to start working in front of a mirror. Use one that is big enough for both you and the child to see each other.

"Opening Mouth"

Step 1: Sit together in front of the mirror and have the child attend to your reflection. Say, "Do this," and then open your mouth wide.

Step 2: If the child does not imitate you, prompt him. Say, "Do this," and manually open his mouth. Praise him, and on successive trials fade your prompt so that he can reliably imitate you opening your mouth.

Step 3: After the child can imitate you opening your mouth in front of the mirror, begin teaching him in a face-to-face position. Say, "Do this," and then open your mouth wide. If he does not readily imitate you, again use a prompt such as the one described in Step 2. Fade this prompt so that the child can reliably imitate you.

After you have taught the child to imitate you opening your mouth, try teaching any or all of the behaviors listed below by first having the child imitate you in front of the mirror and then in the usual face-to-face situation. Teach the behaviors the same way that you taught the imitation of the gross motor behaviors. By this point, you should be able to develop and fade prompts that will enable the child to eventually imitate you without prompting. Remember to present the trials randomly in order to avoid ordering or perseveration of the child's responses.

Additional Imitative Responses to be Taught
in Front of the Mirror and then in the Usual Face-to-Face Position

Smile	Frown
Smack lips	Pout (lower lip out)
Shake head no	Nod head yes
Puff up mouth with air	Bite lip
Pucker up lips	Roll head in circles
Brush teeth	Wink (close one eye)
Stick out tongue	

Remember that the child should be able to imitate each newly learned response when it is intermixed with previously learned responses before you begin to teach new responses.

MAKING PROGRESS IN IMITATION TRAINING

By recording the child's progress, you should find that each new response is learned more easily than the previous ones. In fact, when the child can respond correctly by imitating you without any prompting the *first* time a novel response is presented, you will have taught your child an *imitative set* or tendency, which is exactly what we have been working toward! The amount of time that is required to teach this imitative set, or what is also called *generalized motor imitation,* varies enormously from one child to another. Thus, some children need more prompting and slower fading of the prompts, whereas others require little or no prompting at all. Some children have mastered 60 imitative behaviors within 1 week of 1-hour sessions per day, and others have required 3 or 4 months of more intensive training. We are uncertain about the reasons underlying these large individual differences in mastering behaviors.

We recommend at least 3 to 4 hours of training a day when the child is only receiving manual imitation training. Later, when additional programs are introduced, you should probably have a minimum of 1 hour of imitation training per day. It would be easier for you and your child if *several* assistants now helped you with the teaching. You have to shape the basic steps for the child to imitate, but then others could take over from there, at first merely *maintaining* what you have taught. Later, as these assistants begin to understand the basic teaching procedures, they will be able to teach the child new imitations. It is important that the imitation program be run by as many persons, in as many surroundings (e.g., house, car, park), as possible in order to keep the child alert all day, to keep him learning.

CONCLUSION

Imitation is one of the most important behaviors your child can learn and you should now extend it to several parts of his life. For example, you should now be moving him out of the chair as much as possible and teaching him to imitate you in different locations, such as in different parts of the house, in the car, or on a walk. If possible, have several other persons teach him too. That is, generalize the training.

Use your imagination and expand teaching into other areas. If he has begun to imitate your movement and gestures, you may want to model dancing steps for him and teach him to dance. Imitation should be used as much as possible when teaching the child tasks such as brushing his hair (you shape him to imitate you when you brush your hair), brushing his teeth, and making his bed. You should expect some problems with teaching new tasks, but the problems should be reduced each time because each new task requires that the child pay attention to something he has not seen before.

The play program in Chapter 12 is a direct outgrowth of the manual imitation program we just described. You may want to go on to that chapter at this point so you can begin to teach your child some free-time fun activities.

CHAPTER 9

MATCHING VISUAL STIMULI

Identifying the similarities and differences between objects is one of the fundamental skills of learning that a child must acquire before he can move to more advanced skills. For example, the child learns that some objects go together because they look the same (e.g., same color or same size) or that objects go together because they have the same use (e.g., utensils). A child must learn to utilize his past experiences in detecting similarities between present objects or events in order to benefit his present learning situation and to transfer learning from one situation to another. Being able to detect similarities among diverse situations can help provide regularity and "smoothness" in a child's behavior.

One way to help children learn to detect similarities between events is called *matching-to-sample*, or *learning to match*. Quite simply, the child is handed an object and is taught to place that object next to the identical (or similar) object in a group of objects on a table in front of him. For example, he may be taught to place a shoe next to another shoe, and not next to the cup or the book that are also on the table. He learns to put "like with like," or to match. This chapter presents a program on matching that is relatively easy to teach, flexible, and extremely useful. Most children enjoy this program a great deal.

You will be teaching your child to match elements in their concrete form (as three-dimensional objects) and in their abstract form (as pictures). The child will also learn to match concrete objects to their corresponding abstract representations (matching an object to a picture). As you learn how to teach these matching procedures, you will be in a position to create new programs to fill a particular child's needs. For example, a program for early reading would involve teaching a child to match an object to a written word denoting that object.

NECESSARY MATERIALS

Select some objects and pictures that are readily available simply by hunting through your house. It is suggested that you make use of items with which the child has regular contact so that what he is learning will be immediately meaningful to him. For example, food items (such as cookies, pieces of fruit, vegetables), toothbrushes, hair brushes, silverware, and small articles of clothing (such as shoes and socks) are ideal to use in the early matching tasks.

Objects that exist in identical pairs, such as two brown shoes, two white glasses, or two metal spoons, are necessary for the early matching programs. Later programs require similar versions of these various objects. Other programs require that the child match an object with a picture of that same object (which can be taken from a magazine) and then later match the object with a picture of a similar object. Magazine pictures should be mounted on index cards or thin pieces of cardboard so that they are easy for your child to handle.

Additional materials are needed for teaching the child to match colors and shapes. Two squares of each different color to be matched are needed. Pieces of construction paper, at least 3 inches by 3 inches in size, can be used for this task. Three-dimensional and two-dimensional representations of various shapes, in different colors and sizes, are needed for the shape-matching tasks. It is suggested that a set of wooden blocks be used for the three-dimensional forms, and that the two-dimensional forms be made from construction paper.

MATCHING IDENTICAL THREE-DIMENSIONAL OBJECTS

Begin by teaching your child to match *identical three-dimensional objects*. In the following explanation the letters A, B, and C represent those items that are on the table; the letters A', B', and C' represent the corresponding items that you will hand to your child for him to match.

One problem that is likely to occur in any step of the matching tasks is that of the child not looking at the items on the table before him. As a result, he tends to place the item to be matched on the table without looking at the other items. Such a problem may be partly avoided if you direct your child's attention to the items on the table before you start each trial. For example, you can direct your child's attention to the objects on the table by telling him "Look here," while pointing to each item individually, making sure, of course, that he follows your finger prompt with his eyes. Or you can help him follow your finger as you draw a continuous imaginary line behind the objects.

The task of directing and building the child's attention is one of the most difficult problems any adult faces in teaching developmentally retarded children. Even though the child is looking directly at the objects you want him to evaluate, there is absolutely no guarantee that he is "seeing" them. "Seeing" is not the same as "looking." Teaching a child to pay meaningful attention to the task (to "see" or to "hear") is a slow process. As we understand this problem right now, such attention is built through "discrimination training." That is, after the child has responded to the *wrong* object (and has lost out on the reward, or otherwise was admonished) but at the same time was rewarded for responding to the *right* object, then slowly his attention should be built. He will have to *attend* to the right object in order to be rewarded and not admonished. Once you have this attention, the teaching of the behavior *per se* seems easy.

If your child makes an incorrect response after he demonstrates that he has acquired knowledge of the step you are presently teaching him, you may want to become louder and more firm in the way that you let him know that he is wrong. If your child has no consequences to suffer once he knows what he is supposed to do, it would seem pointless for him to even care about the task; he may just as well be playing games with you. So don't be afraid to let him know that you are upset when he responds incorrectly out of carelessness. At the same time, should your child respond correctly, and particularly if he responds correctly without your prompting him, reinforce him heavily. Remember that the contrast between "Good" and "No" should be substantial.

Your child probably should not be attending to this task for more than 15 minutes at a time. If he makes several incorrect responses within a session, be sure to end the session after he has made a correct response. If necessary, you should help your child make a correct response by prompting him so that the session can be terminated after he is correct. This has a twofold purpose: your child will have ended the session feeling successful and he will also learn that he cannot be allowed to leave a session without having met your expectations in some way.

One final note to get you started. As in all other programs, make sure you have your child's attention. Make sure he is looking and listening to you before you begin the trial. Do not allow him to drift during any trial. If you do, it is very likely that he will respond incorrectly and you will have been wasting your time and his time.

Step 1: Matching Simple Objects — First Pair

Choose the first pair of objects that you wish your child to match (hereafter referred to as objects A and A . This need not be any particular object, but it should not be too complex in its features or shape. For example, begin with a pair of yellow cups. Place one yellow cup (object A) on the table directly in front of your child and clearly visible to *him*. Take an identical yellow cup (object A') and hold it out in front of your child, making sure that he looks at it. (You may need to point to the item while telling him, "Look here.") While handing A' (the cup) to your child, instruct him, "Put same with same." Your child should take cup A' and place it on top of or near cup A on the table.

Some children will have difficulty knowing where to place the object on the table. One way to help such a child is to place A on a sheet of 3 inch by 10 inch paper, or in a pie tin, and to reinforce the child for placing A within that same area. The piece of paper (or the pie tin) helps him define the correct response; it also helps him to look at *where* to place the object (particularly if the adult moves the paper to different positions on the table from one trial to the next). You want to avoid having him passively (without looking) placing the object on the table.

Once he places A correctly near A, heavily reinforce him. If you feel that your child needs more experience with this step, continue for 20 or 30 trials. You must remember, however, that there is only one object present, so your child may become bored. You are likely to have lost his attention by the time you are ready to begin the next step.

Since you are just beginning to teach your child to match, it is highly unlikely that the task will go this smoothly. It is possible that your child will have no idea of what you want him to do. If this is the case, you have to prompt his placement of A as you tell him, "Put same with same." As soon as he has learned to pick up A , you may fade the prompt by merely pointing to the area of the table beside object A, that is, directing him where to place A'. Reinforce him after he has placed A' on the table. Work on the placement of A' until he can place A' adequately on the table without prompts.

Step 2: Matching Simple Objects — Second Pair

Select the second object (B) you wish to teach your child to match. It should be as different from the first object as possible. For example, do not choose a fork if the first object was a spoon, or do not choose a glass if you have trained him on a cup. If your first object (A) was a cup, choose a spoon, or a sock, for the second object (B). Place A and B (the cup and the spoon) on the table in front of the child, so that the objects are equidistant from him. Next, hand the child B' (a spoon identical to the one on the table), and tell him, "Put same with same."

If his placement is incorrect (he places B' near A), do not let him self-correct (that is, switch to the right response after he has made the wrong one). Merely say, "No," retrieve B', and start the trial over again, using a prompt if necessary to help the child respond correctly. The main problem with self-correction during early training is that the child may merely learn to switch from one response to another, without really looking at anything. We find it helpful not to let the child self-correct in the early trials. On the other hand, self-correction in later learning may be essential. Self-correction affects each child in a different way. The best approach is to be flexible and to try different procedures to see which approach benefits your child the most.

If your child has responded correctly (placed B' on the table near B and not near A), reward him. Continue to present B' while keeping the positions of objects A and B constant until your child has met criterion. The reason for leaving A and B on the table in the same position is to allow your child to use the position of the objects as a prompt. All children may not need such a position prompt (you may be able to rotate the position of A and B on the table from the onset), but many do.

If this position prompt does not prove effective in guiding the child's response, you may do some additional prompting, such as isolating item B on the table and then fading item A into place beside it. To do this, place B closer to your child than to you. Present your child with item B', and with each new trial, gradually move item A forward on the table until it assumes a position beside item B. Repeat the positioning process above until your child has met your chosen criterion.

Step 3: Matching Simple Objects — Random Presentation

Objects A and B should be placed on the table equidistant from the child's midline. Keep the position of A and B on the table constant throughout this step and randomize your presentation of objects A' and B'. For example, present A' for two trials, then B' once, A' once, B' for three trials, etc. Since your child will not have matched object A' with A since Step 1, it is suggested that in the first few trials you present this item alone. (At the start of a new session you may want to refresh your child's memory by running a few trials from the step just completed before proceeding with the next.) Hand objects A' and B' to your child and reinforce his correct responses as you have in the earlier steps; repeat this step until he has met criterion. You may need to do some prompting (by pointing to the correct object on the table) in the early stages of Step 3. You must remember that in the two previous steps your child was matching only one object at a time. Although your child may know which objects to match, he may now be confused by the fact that he has to deal with two objects at once in two different positions.

There are several ways in which you may inadvertently mislead your child in these early stages. First of all, if object A is closer to your child than object B, it is very likely that he will match object A' or B' with the closest object regardless of whether or not it is a correct match. Therefore, try to make both items on the table equidistant from your child's midline, and see to it that they are equally close to his side of the table.

If you have a tendency with each new trial to change hands when you are giving the objects to your child, or if you hold the arm you use somewhat off-center toward one side or another of your body, you might unintentionally direct your child to the object on one side of the table. For example, if you give the object to your child with your left hand, you could inadvertently be directing your child toward the object on your left. Since your tendency is to change hands as well as items with each new trial, it would seem logical for your child to follow such a lead. To avoid this, it is suggested that you be consistent with the hand you use in giving your child the objects in every trial; in addition, when you hand your child the objects, hold your arm out as close to the midline as possible.

Make sure you avoid making many body cues or facial gestures during the trials. It is very easy to inadvertently guide developmentally disabled children with such body cues. After you have handed your child an object, make sure that you do not lean your body to one side or the other. Do not place either elbow on the table during the trial. Do not look at the correct object before you hand your child the object, and don't look while he is in the process of matching. Do not smile or frown as your child approaches the correct or incorrect item in the processing of matching. If your child is unsure of the task, it is very likely that he may look at you for cues such as these to provide him with additional information. Withhold any feedback until he has committed himself.

Step 3 is perhaps the most difficult one in the program. Because he has so many choices, the child has to learn some rules in order to succeed. He may learn the basic step in matching at this point, and if he does he is over the worst. Or, he may simply have learned that A' goes on one side of the table and B' goes on the other. To help him do a "real" match (and to avoid position cues), the following procedure may be used.

Step 4: Matching Simple Objects – Random Positions

Place objects A and B on the table so that they are about equidistant from your child's midline. With each new trial randomize (interchange) the objects (A' and B') you present to your child, as in the previous step. In addition, randomize the *position* of the objects (A and B) on the table. That is, sometimes A is on the right side, sometimes on the left. Continue with the trials until the child meets criterion.

Step 5: Matching Simple Objects – Three Pairs

Remove either object A or object B from the table and replace it with a new object (C). Make C different from A and B. For example, it you have used a cup and a spoon, let C be a sock. Repeat Steps 2 through 4 using C and the other object you have left on the table. (In Step 2, object C will replace object B.) When you complete Step 4, reintroduce object B, and repeat Steps 3 and 4 using all three items by keeping the positions of all three objects on the table (A, B, and C) constant while randomizing the order of presentation of the objects you hand to your child (A', B', or C'), and by randomizing the positions of the objects on the table as well as the objects that you hand to your child.

Step 6: Matching Simple Objects – Four or More Pairs

Introduce a fourth object (D), in the same way that you did object C, that is, by repeating Steps 2 through 4 with object D and one of the other objects with which your child has already met criterion. When criterion is achieved for Step 4, reintroduce one of the other two objects and repeat Steps 3 and 4 with three objects. Finally, reintroduce the remaining object and repeat Steps 3 and 4 with four objects. When this is completed, you can continue to introduce new objects into the task. Simply repeat Steps 2 through 4 with the object you are introducing and one of the objects with which your child has already met criterion; then repeat Steps 3 and 4 until all of the old objects have been reintroduced.

You may find that your child becomes confused with too many objects, or that after a while you run out of space on the table. If this happens you may continue to teach new objects to your child and reduce the number of items in the task simply by not reintroducing as many of the old items when you repeat Steps 3 and 4. Perhaps four or five objects are optimal on the table at any one time.

Table 9-1 represents the first 5 steps of the training sequence in outline form to help facilitate their progression.

Once the child has learned to match a dozen objects, the difficult part of your task is completed, and it's going to be relatively enjoyable for you to design new matching programs. Many children enjoy the matching programs and their motivation often improves. The basic matching procedure can be used for a number of new tasks.

MATCHING IDENTICAL TWO-DIMENSIONAL ITEMS (PICTURES)

You may find it easier to teach your child to match two-dimensional objects if they correspond to the three-dimensional items he has just learned.. For example, if you taught your child to match identical cups or spoons, you may want to teach him to match identical pictures of those cups and spoons.

Teaching your child to match pictures can proceed in the same manner as we have outlined above on teaching matching with three-dimensional objects. When matching pictures, have your child place the picture he is holding on top of the one on the table to be matched.

You should mount pictures from magazines on index cards or thin pieces of cardboard so that they are sturdier for your child to handle. There are several factors inherent in the pictures that may cause problems, particularly if you have found the pictures in magazines. You may want to cover, or remove, the border on the picture. In many cases, borders may hinder the child in matching because he may attend to the border instead of the picture itself. Similarly, you should try to cut out the pictures as uniformly as possible because your child may attend to the shape of the picture (e.g., circle or square) and not to the picture itself.

You may find that some pictures are oriented vertically and that others are oriented horizontally. Pictures of different orientations should not be used until the child is more proficient in matching. At that time you may want to reintroduce other distracting features as well (borders, different sizes or shapes), since the child very likely has learned to attend to the relevant features by this time.

Table 9-1. Outline of matching steps

| | Object | |
	Given to child	On table
1: First pair	A′	A
2: Second pair	B′	A and B position fixed
3: Random presentation	A′ and B′	A and B position fixed
4: Random position	A′ and B′ intermixed	A and B position intermixed
5: Three pairs	A′, B′, and C′ intermixed	A, B, and C position intermixed

Imitation, Matching, and Early Language

MATCHING THREE-DIMENSIONAL OBJECTS
WITH IDENTICAL TWO-DIMENSIONAL REPRESENTATIONS

Pairs of objects and pictures are needed for this task. Place the two-dimensional picture on the table and hand your child one of the corresponding three-dimensional objects so that he can place the three-dimensional object on top of its two-dimensional counterpart. In addition, the command for this task is "Put *(object)* with *(object),*" e.g., "Put shoe with shoe."

At the onset of this task, your child should be able to visually discriminate between the three-dimensional item and its two-dimensional counterpart; otherwise he would never have been able to complete the two previous tasks. Granted, making the connection between a three-dimensional item and its two-dimensional counterpart may be confusing to your child; it is confusing to very young normal children as well. However, matching objects to their symbolic representations is basic in the educational process and is an important task for the child to learn. Proceed with the training in the same way as in earlier matching-to-sample training.

MATCHING OBJECTS IN CLASSES

In this task you will teach your child the basic concepts of learning to match similar, but not identical, objects. For example, you may want to teach him the relatively simple concept that different kinds of shoes go together, even though they are not identical in their appearance. Later you may want to teach matching of more complex objects, that is, objects that are more varied in size and shape, such as clothes, foods, and animals.

Essentially you need to introduce groups of objects whose members differ only slightly among each other. For example, if your child learned to match identical brown shoes, you will need to teach him to match the brown shoe with a black shoe, a red shoe, or a striped shoe. Place the object your child originally learned to match on the table along with objects of different classes, and proceed as in earlier matching-to-sample training. With each new trial involving that object, hand him a different version of the object. Gradually "stretch" the concepts you teach to include many heterogeneous members forming one homogeneous set.

MATCHING GENERALIZED TWO-DIMENSIONAL OBJECTS

Pictures of the objects you used in matching objects in classes are needed for this task. Place two different pictures (of two different concepts) on the table, and then give the child a picture to be matched with one of them; prompt and reinforce as before. For example, you may place pictures of a spoon and a brown shoe on the table; then give him a picture of a similar object from one or the other class, such as of a fork, or a red shoe and tell him to match.

MATCHING GENERALIZED THREE-DIMENSIONAL
OBJECTS TO GENERALIZED TWO-DIMENSIONAL REPRESENTATIONS

All of the objects and pictures of the objects used in the two previous tasks are needed for this task. Select one item from one class and one item from a different class of two-dimensional objects and place these two items on the table. Hand your child a three-dimensional object belonging to one of the classes represented by one of the items on the table and ask him to match. With each new trial, hand your child a different three-dimensional object belonging to a class represented by one of the items on the table, and have him match it to the appropriate picture. In practice, this may work as follows: place a picture of a shoe (e.g., a lady's shoe) and a picture of a spoon on the table in front of the child. Now hand him a brown shoe, and ask him for the appropriate placement. Reward as before. Then rotate the pictures, and give the child a knife, then a fork, then another shoe, and so on. He is learning to identify classes of different objects and to match these against symbolic (two-dimensional) representations of those objects.

Be aware that learning to match members into sets that are defined by a common function is difficult and may require some prior conceptual (language) skill. Therefore, very advanced matching may have to await prior language learning, which we will introduce in Units V and VI.

MATCHING COLORS

Since color itself is not an object, you will only be able to teach your child to match colors presented in a two-dimensional form. As discussed earlier, you will need two or more identical colored squares for each color you introduce. Follow the same steps used for teaching matching of objects. Since it is less difficult to visually discriminate among colors than pictures or objects, and since your child will already have a good idea of what matching is all about by the time this task is introduced, he should learn these tasks reasonably quickly. You should use the instruction: "Put (color) with (color)." The best procedure is to keep a program in operation for about three to four weeks (1 hour a day or more); if the child makes no progress, set the program aside for a month or so, and then start over again. If he still does not improve, you may begin to suspect some underlying problem, such as color blindness, but this happens rarely.

MATCHING SHAPES

The same sequence of steps described for object and picture matching is used for teaching your child to match shapes. Since the child has just completed color matching, there may be some confusion if the color of the item you hand to your child is the same as the color of another item on the table. For example, if a yellow square and a green circle are on the table and you hand your child a yellow circle, he may attend to the color, and not to the shape, of the item he matches. Therefore, it is suggested that you eliminate any confusion on tasks until your child has grasped the idea of both tasks. One way to avoid matching shapes on the basis of color is to use all black forms. Later, when you introduce differently colored shapes, make sure that every shape presented is a different color, or that all shapes on the table are the same color. In either case, we recommend that the item you hand to your child be a different color from the corresponding item on the table, and that you hand your child a differently colored version of that item with each new trial. In this way you teach your child to attend to the shape, and not to the color, of the items.

The materials for this task may be obtained by simply cutting different shapes from differently colored cardboard, construction paper, or plastic.

Later you may want to teach your child to match generalized shapes by introducing shapes that differ in size. For example, place a large (12-inch) card with various shapes (a triangle, a square, and a circle) on the table in front of the child. Now hand him a card with a small (2-inch across) shape of a triangle and ask him to match. This procedure can then be carried out for other shapes, such as squares or circles.

OTHER PROGRAMS

There is virtually no end to the kinds of concepts one can begin to teach by using the matching procedures outlined in this chapter. Matching is an extremely powerful teaching device. For example, you can use it to teach the child to identify groups of behaviors, and to match pictures expressing different feelings (happy versus sad faces) or activities (like eating, sleeping, or driving). Similarly, you can teach early reading, by teaching the child to match a card containing a printed name (like Mom) with a picture of his Mom (versus pictures of Dad or sibling). Or, you can teach numbers, by teaching the child to match a card displaying a particular numeral with a card containing a group of dots (later use objects) equal to the numerical quantity. The various matchings can be made very subtle, thus requiring considerable intellectual behaviors on the part of the child. Our experience with matching has been very favorable, and it is a program that can be kept going through almost all of the other programs.

Surprisingly, perhaps, many children learn to enjoy matching. The matching task acquires its own reward value since the detection of *similarity* between events is rewarding for the children. You may observe that the same things happens with the verbal imitation drills (Chapter 10), where some children become echolalic, apparently matching your voice for the sheer fun of it, or with teaching non-verbal imitation (Chapter 5). The child begins to enjoy acting like the adults who teach him.

CHAPTER 10

FOLLOWING VERBAL INSTRUCTIONS

This program is designed to teach your child to understand some of what is said to him. Specifically, this program will teach your child to respond correctly to simple instructions or requests, such as "Stand up," "Give me a hug," or "Raise your arms." This is known as training in "receptive language" because the child is taught to "receive" your verbal message and to act appropriately in response to that message.

This program on early receptive language should be taught after the child has acquired the imitation responses taught in Chapter 7. Remember, your child has made a start in receptive speech by responding to such commands as "Sit down," "Hands quiet," and "Look at me." The program is easy to teach. It will help both you and your child and he will be easier to manage. This is particularly true when you begin to teach him the meaning of statements such as, "Wait, we'll do it later," or "Don't touch the stove, it will burn you."

Some parents and teachers will say, "Well, he already knows and understands these early commands, so I can skip this step and go on to more advanced work." What they mean is that *sometimes* the child will do what they want, *sometimes* he says amazing things, or *sometimes* he looks as if he knows what is being said. That's good: the child shows potential. However, it isn't very helpful for either of you for your child to be so unpredictable. Therefore, our advice to you is to teach the early steps in this program carefully and to *establish control,* which means that *you* control these early behaviors so that he does what *you* want him to do, when you ask him to. Obtaining good and reliable control in the early stages of the program builds a solid basis for later learning. You do not want your child to exhibit tantrums or self-stimulation, but rather good sitting on chair, good *eye-to-face* contact with hands down, and *reliable* (predictable) responses (obedience) to early instructions ("Stand up," "Sit down," "Raise arms"). If you cannot control your child now, you probably will not be able to later because the programs will soon become more difficult to teach. On the other hand, you will be pleased and surprised how much more relaxed and content the child will seem once he knows you are in the driver's seat, once he knows what is expected and understands that he can't get away with all the nonsense and crazy behavior, and once he is in a learning situation where he can be a successful student for a change. Do not be impatient and jump ahead; it is important to build the basics first. It is as necessary here as it is in any other life venture. A child can't do the advanced work if he doesn't have the fundamentals down.

EARLY RECEPTIVE LANGUAGE

For all of these sessions, have yourself and your child seated in chairs facing each other, about 2 feet apart.

"Raise Arms"

Step 1: *The stimulus.* Begin teaching your child by presenting the instruction, "Raise arms." Say it loudly, slowly, and clearly. Make sure that the child is not self-stimulating, that he is sitting up straight in the chair, and that he is looking at you. Do not give him a complicated command, such as, "John, listen to me, now I want you to raise your arms." Such a statement contains too many unnecessary words (noise), and will prevent your child from attending to (discriminating) the critical or *relevant* part of your instruction, which is simply "Raise arms." Make sure there is a distinct pause (three to five seconds) between your instructions. If your child responds to criterion (responds correctly to 9 out of 10, or 18 out of 20, trials), go on to the next behavior. If your child does not respond correctly, go on to Steps 2 and 3.

Step 2: *The visual prompt.* Since the child has already learned to imitate the action of raising arms, you should raise your arms immediately following the instruction as a prompt for the child to do likewise. If the child fails to imitate this action, you can either reestablish the imitation, or you can physically prompt the child. Have the child exaggerate the response; make him keep his arms raised for 2 or 3 seconds before you reward him. This should help him know (discriminate) why he is being reinforced.

Step 3: *Fading the visual prompt.* Gradually and systematically fade your prompt by performing less and less of the visual prompt following presentation of the instruction "Raise arms." For example, after the child responds correctly for five consecutive trials, raise your arms so that your hands are only as high as your head. The child must still raise his arms straight up in the air to receive the reward. With each trial gradually reduce the prompt, that is, raise your arms so that your hands are at shoulder level, then at chest level, and then at waist level, until you provide no visual prompt at all.

Sometimes it can be very expedient and helpful to see if the child can respond to the instruction without your having to go through all the fading. This can be determined by withholding the prompt for a trial or two. These are called *probe trials.* They "probe" to see if the child has already learned the response. Some children learn very quickly, so you can skip all or some of the fading. If the child cannot perform the instruction, go back to using the prompt and then fade it. In all cases, the child must raise his arms straight up in the air and should be required to hold them there for 2 or 3 seconds before receiving a reward.

It is important that the child learns to raise his arms *when you tell him to.* If you let him raise his arms "at will" during this early learning he will probably not learn to listen to you. Therefore, if he raises his arms at other times, say "No!" loudly and stop him.

When the child can raise his arms on command to criterion, begin teaching the next behavior.

Imitation, Matching, and Early Language

"Touch Nose"

Step 1: *The stimulus.* Present the instruction, "Touch nose." "Touch nose" is an appropriate second stimulus because it sounds and looks different than "Raise arms." You should not pick a stimulus that is similar to the others during the early learning because you want to maximize the child's success. For example, "Arms out," may be too much like, "Raise arms," and may confuse the child during the early stages. It becomes critical in later learning that the commands be similar in order to build the child's attention to detail as much as possible, but it is just too difficult in the beginning. If the child responds to criterion to "Touch nose" teach the next behavior. If he cannot respond correctly go on to Steps 2 and 3.

Step 2: *The visual prompt.* Since the child has already learned to imitate this action, you should prompt his behavior by touching your nose immediately following the instruction so that the child will do likewise. Physically prompt the child if he fails to imitate your action. The child should be rewarded when he imitates you by touching his nose. Make sure that the child keeps his finger(s) on his nose for 2 or 3 seconds before providing the reward.

Step 3: *Fading the visual prompt.* Once the child is readily imitating you, gradually and systematically fade the prompt. For example, after the child correctly imitates the nose-touching response for five consecutive trials, bring your finger toward your face but hold it about 1 inch from your nose, then 2 inches, then 3. Next, gradually raise your hand with finger pointed only to the level of your chin, then your chest, until you are providing no visual prompt at all. In all cases, the child must place his finger(s) directly on his nose and should be required to hold it there for 2 or 3 seconds before receiving his reward. When the child can touch his nose on command to criterion, go on to random rotation.

Random Rotation

If you have just finished teaching "Touch nose" and you now say "Raise arms," the child will probably touch his nose instead. The child really does not understand yet what the different instructions mean; he hears what you say as "noise." Your job now is to teach him that the two instructions are *different;* you will be teaching him to discriminate. Random rotation is part of this process.

Step 1: Present the first instruction ("Raise arms") again. If your child does nothing or performs an incorrect response, say "No!" loudly; repeat the instruction and prompt the correct response. The first prompt should be the weakest one used in training the response. If this prompt fails to produce a correct response, a stronger prompt should be used on the next trial. Continue to increase the strength of the prompt on succeeding trials until the child responds correctly. Once the child is responding correctly, fade out the prompt again, as you did in the initial training of the response. Continue training until the child has responded correctly with no prompt for five trials. (Be sure your child's failure to respond is not due to a failure to attend to the task. Remember how he has handled problems in the past. If he is wrong he will become frustrated. Some of the old aggression may reappear or he may start to self-stimulate again. Don't let him act like that now.)

Step 2: Present the second instruction ("Touch nose"). Prompt the child so he gives the correct response to that instruction. When he responds correctly with no prompt for three trials, present the first instruction ("Raise arms") again. Prompt and repeat as before. After two correct trials, switch back to the second instruction, and repeat as before. Once the child masters these two commands easily on the first try, go on to Step 3.

Step 3: It is important to make certain that the child knows the difference between these first two instructions before teaching the next one. Therefore give the child a series of trials presenting the two instructions in a random order. For example, ask him to touch his nose two times, then raise his arms once, then touch his nose once, then raise his arms three times, and so on. It is important to keep changing the sequence and the frequency of the instructions so that the child cannot figure out a pattern and use this pattern rather than your instructions as a basis for responding. For example, if you go regularly from one instruction to the other he will learn to alternate those responses and won't really listen to your instructions. Don't repeat the same command too many times in a row, because you may teach him to perseverate, that is, to repeat the same thing over and over. You want to be sure he is using your *words* as a cue for his response. Continue to present trials until the child responds to criterion.

Multiple Requests

Now you may introduce additional requests, such as "Clap hands," "Sit down," "Stand up," and "Pat tummy"; other instructions can be found in the list of nonverbal imitations in Chapter 7. First teach the correct response to the instruction, and then intermix it with the first two instructions. Do this for about 10 instructions, so that the child gets a thorough drill.

As you continue to present new requests, always test to be sure that the child can still respond to previously learned instructions and to the new instruction when it is interspersed with the others. Use random presentations of the various instructions to test the child's comprehension.

If you find that the child is having difficulty with one of the instructions, go back and work on that instruction to get a correct response. Present only that instruction and prompt the correct response if necessary. Continue this retraining until the child responds to criterion. Then return to randomly presenting all learned instructions, initially giving more trials of the problem instruction to be sure it has been learned.

Once the child can correctly master 5 to 10 instructions, you should keep him very busy by having him respond to the various commands. Give him a command every 5 seconds or so (that's 12 commands a minute), and take a 1-minute break every 10 minutes. Work with him in this way for at least 1 hour a day, ideally, 3 or 4 hours spaced apart during the day. "Surprise" him occasionally, throughout the day, with various commands. The point is to keep him busy doing useful things (in order to reduce his self-stimulation and other bizarre mannerisms), to "tune his head" to listen to you, and to teach him to pay attention. Remember to give your child lots of kisses, hugs, and other goodies for doing the right things (he could be kissed a dozen times a minute this way, if he can take all that loving); and don't forget the sometimes necessary sharp smack on the behind if he starts to self-stimulate or doesn't follow your commands.

Notice that this kind of exercise is quite simple and can be carried out by relatively naive and untrained assistants, such as older siblings or high school students. Remember to generalize the training so that the child responds while he is standing up, when he is in other parts of the house, and when he is outdoors. The child can be kept quite busy now, wherever he is.

PRE-TRAINING SOPHISTICATED BEHAVIORS

The next group of instructions requires slightly more sophisticated behavior on the child's part than that needed for the early instructions. For example, the child must be able to deal with objects not within his immediate reach. This "pre-training" is for teaching the child to label his own actions and to begin labeling objects in his environment. The procedures used for teaching these tasks are similar to those used in the previous section.

"Get (Object)"

Step 1: *The stimulus.* Place an object (a book, a glass, or a brush) on the table within easy reach of the child. Choose an object that is easy for the child to retrieve. Begin by presenting an instruction, such as "Get book." If the child responds to criterion, try another instruction, which may be "Get brush" or "Get glass" (see below). If not, prompt the correct response (Step 2).

Step 2: *The prompt and fading the prompt.* Present the instruction "Get book" while manually guiding the child's hand to the book, having him hold it, and moving it toward you. Take the book and reinforce the child. Place the book back on the table, repeat the instruction and start fading the prompt; that is, give only as much physical guidance as is necessary to have him complete the response. Once the child responds to criterion, gradually move the book farther and farther away from him on the table, and eventually ask him to retrieve the book from a different part of the room or from a different room.

Step 3: *Labeling objects.* The next instruction after "Get book" is mastered may well be "Get brush" or "Get glass." You must be sure that the child is discriminating between objects and not just choosing the object because it is on the table. The correct response requires correct labeling. We have suggestions to help your child respond correctly to your instructions. First, it seems easier for a child to identify an object by associating it with a familiar functional behavior rather than just pointing to it. For example, it is easier for a child to identify a hair brush when he hears the instruction, "Brush your hair" rather than the instruction "Point to brush." Second, it is easier for the child to reach for a glass of milk when you say "Drink glass milk," than when you say "Point to glass." Therefore, use instructions containing the action (e.g., "Drink glass milk") to get the child to retrieve the object, and then slowly fade the action ("drink"), ending up with just the name of the object (glass), which he then hands to you.

Step 4: *Introducing new instructions.* As the child's learning progresses, gradually add new instructions for him to handle new objects, such as "Get toast" or "Get doll." Later you can give two instructions for two objects at the same time. Begin this part of the task with one object on the child's left and one on his right. Gradually move the objects away from him (6 feet, 12 feet, and eventually in another room) so that he has to move around and search to get them for you. The more instructions the child has mastered, the busier you can keep him.

Now let's turn to a different kind of instruction, requiring slightly different training steps.

"Turn on Light" (Manipulating Objects)

Step 1: *The stimulus.* Begin by presenting the instruction, "Turn on light." If your child responds to criterion, teach another behavior. If the child does not respond correctly, prompt the correct response (Step 2).

Step 2: *The prompt.* Present the instruction while you and the child are standing at the light switch. After stating the instruction (avoid more than 1-second delays), take the child's hand, bring it to the switch, and assist the child in the motion of turning on the switch. Reinforce the child for this prompted response. Then turn off the light, wait several seconds, and present the instruction again. Prompt the child only as much as necessary. For example, following the instruction, wait for a second or two to see if the child will reach for the switch before prompting this action. Once his hand is on the switch, whether he put it there or you prompted this action, wait a second to see if he will operate the switch unassisted before prompting this action.

Step 3: *Fading the prompt.* Fade the prompt by touching or holding the child's hand more lightly and by removing your hand from the child's hand before he presses the switch, then before he reaches the switch, then when his hand is half-way to the switch, and so on until he is carrying out the motion unassisted. Remember to allow the child to succeed at each level of prompting a few times before reducing the prompt further. Remember, do not let him turn on the light without your having instructed him first. You want him to learn to listen to you.

Step 4: This step teaches the child to respond to this instruction when he is not standing within reach of the light switch. Once he is responding to criterion on the original task, move a few feet from the light switch and present the instruction. If the child fails to respond, prompt him by giving him a gentle push toward the switch. If he still fails to respond, move closer to the switch. When the child can cross the room and turn off the light to criterion, begin teaching a new behavior.

You will find that some behaviors may be rewarding in themselves. For example, children who like to turn lights on and off may not need to receive an additional reward for completing the task. However, you must be sure that the child is responding to your instruction, and not rewarding himself, when he turns on the lights. If he does so without being asked, you must show your disapproval so the child learns that he must attend to your instruction and not do as he pleases.

Teaching Affectionate Behavior

You can use the methods discussed in this chapter to teach the child affectionate behaviors, such as hugging, kissing, patting you on the head, or stroking your cheek. There are many questions one can entertain about this way of training affection: "Can affection be trained in the first place?" "Won't it be 'shallow'?" "Is it right when affection has to be taught?" "Shouldn't it be spontaneous?" There is no really good answer to these questions, except that the training works. (In fact, it is possible that normal children learn affectionate behavior in the same manner.) Children who have been taught to show affection are easier to work with, and if they are not taught affectionate behavior, they will never know whether or not they like it. Also, it is important to consider your needs and what *you* want, not just what the child wants. Children who show affection are part of the reinforcement adults need when working with children. So, for the sake of the child and your own "survival," the child ought to be taught how to show affection toward others.

MORE COMPLEX BEHAVIORS

Your child can be taught to respond to many other instructions of a similar nature. Try to teach the child behaviors that will be useful to other members of the family as well, such as "Close the door," "Turn off the TV" and "Pick up the toys." As you teach new behaviors, remember to review the previously learned behaviors, retraining any that may have been forgotten. Also remember to present these instructions off and on throughout the day, so that the child is kept busy listening to you, and acting appropriately. He has to learn to be alert for your instructions, so that you gradually break through the indifference and self-stimulation. Keep him busy.

As you finish the training outlined in this chapter your child should know how to follow several instructions, imitate many actions, sit still for reasonable (5-minute) periods of time, and reduce his self-stimulation. The length of time required to achieve these results depends on the individual child. For some children it may take only a week; others may require several months. It is impossible to tell who is going to move fast and who is going to move slowly before you start the training. We do know that if the child moves rapidly in this learning program he will move rapidly in subsequent programs.

Certain unexpected benefits will begin accruing at this point. Your child will start to look more grown up, his eyes will look more alert. At the same time, he will begin to sleep better at night, because he is tired from all the hard work of training. There are many other desirable side effects. The child probably will become more attached to you emotionally (all our children did), and he will be better able to handle everyday frustration. He should start to show more varied affect, so that he will look more joyful (at successes), or more anxious and sad (at failures). In short, he will start to look more and more like an average child.

DIFFICULTIES

As you will soon find out, many things can go wrong even in the early steps of this program. Some children are very lazy. For example, they will barely respond to the command "Raise arms," acting as if their hands were made of lead. Don't accept that kind of behavior. If the child performs inadequately, his behavior may begin to look like some other action (like "Touch head"), and he will end up confused. Let him know you are displeased (yell at him and perhaps spank him if you have to) when he performs poorly.

Also, it is true in these programs that the child may now begin to tantrum. You should expect tantrums and anger when you introduce new programs because the child has been handling new demands and novelty in this way for several years. You cannot get him to stop that kind of behavior immediately. You have no choice but to try to eliminate the behavior when it appears; otherwise it will take over completely.

The child may be slow in learning these programs because you are letting him self-stimulate too much, and he is paying little attention to you. Self-stimulation may come back because you just get tired and depressed from using aversives and being so hard on the child. That's very human. But remember, it becomes increasingly easy to keep the self-stimulation in check, and eventually it will require very little effort on your part.

If your child seems to have a hard time learning early commands, which are very easy for most children, check and see if *you* are doing something wrong. Your rewards and punishments (your "Good"s and "No"s) may be sounding alike to him. We mentioned this possibility before. It is one of the most common mistakes one makes in working with these developmentally disabled children. You should try to *act* angry, or try to *act* very sweet. Ham it up. The more dramatic you are, the better. "Good" should be full of soft sweetness and goodness and make him smile. "No" should be full of loud anger and threat and should make him mildly apprehensive.

Other problems may arise that are specific to the program you are teaching. If you fade the visual prompt by raising your arms less and less, the child may continue to imitate you and will thus raise his arms only as high as you do. If this happens, *physically* prompt or guide the correct response by gently pulling the child's arms up by his hands until his elbows are straight. Then let go of his hands and reward him when he has continued to hold his arms up unassisted for several seconds. If he lowers his arms when you let go, pull them up again and reinforce only after several seconds of unassisted arm raising. Gradually and systematically fade this prompt by pulling more lightly on the child's hands and by letting go of his hands earlier and earlier, for example, when his hands are at head level, then at shoulder level. Continue to reward only for correct responses: raising the arms straight above the head.

You should also be on the lookout for the child's tendency to "hook on the prompt." Children with developmental disabilities are often distracted, rather than helped, by extra stimuli such as prompts. For example, if you are inadvertently moving your eyes in the direction of the desired response when asking the child to get a particular object, the child will very likely begin attending to your eye movements (rather than to what you say), and learn the wrong cues. Try to make sure you do not give him such extra cues.

The task of teaching your child should be enjoyable and rewarding for you; a lack of enthusiasm or discontent on your part does not make for the best learning environment. You must take breaks from the task of teaching. Breaks are as necessary for you as they are for the child; take care not to burn out. You could arrange your teaching schedule so that family and friends are able to watch the child respond to your teaching. Also, because you work so closely with the child, you may not notice his achievements as clearly as those who observe. Feedback from observers is your reinforcement to continue.

CHAPTER 11

VERBAL IMITATION Imitation of Sounds and Words

The program in this chapter is the most difficult one in the book. It outlines the first steps in teaching your child how to talk, that is, it teaches him how to imitate speech, beginning with sounds and words. Most slow children find it very difficult to learn to imitate speech. It is easier for them to learn to imitate actions and gestures (Chapter 8). It is wise to start teaching this program early and to devote a part of each day to verbal imitation training. The amount of time you put into verbal imitation training depends on how important you feel it is for the child to talk, relative to the other skills he needs to acquire. We spend about half of the teaching time on the language programs, which in the beginning means that we spend a great deal of time, upward of 4 hours a day, teaching the child to imitate speech. You probably will not make much progress on speech unless you spend at least 1 hour a day on the training, preferably one-half hour in the morning, and one-half hour in the afternoon, when the child is in his best form. Ideally you should also try some imitation training at different times throughout the day.

It is wise to mix the training a bit so that the verbal imitation training is mixed in with nonverbal imitation, receptive commands, and so on. Perhaps every 3 to 5 minutes of verbal imitation training you should present some trials of already mastered material from other areas. This helps reduce the monotony of the training.

Teaching language is a complex job and we shall only present the beginning steps in this book. Those who experience considerable success in this introductory program may want to consult a book we wrote specifically on language training, *The Autistic Child, Language Development through Behavior Modification* (Lovaas, 1977), that includes more complex training for language programs.

Before you begin to teach verbal imitation, you must be warned that not all children can learn to talk using the program we have outlined in this book. It is difficult to say beforehand which child will learn, and which will not. If the child is less than 6 years old, and particularly if he already uses complicated consonant-vowel combinations, then he probably will learn quickly. On the other hand, if your child is over 6 years old, and if he is not making some sounds or words involving "difficult" consonants (such as k, g, p), but merely gives an occasional vowel ("ooh," "ah"), then it has been our experience that he will progress very slowly. Perhaps all children can learn some speech, but this may require such a tremendous expenditure of effort that the verbal imitation program becomes rather impractical, considering all the other skills a slow child must learn. If you work for 2 or 3 months on verbal imitation training and your child is not making much progress (cannot imitate five or more succinct sounds), then you should consider minimizing or dropping the program. You may want to come back to it later. A child can learn to communicate effectively without actually using his vocal cords; he can learn to "talk" with his hands. Chapter 24, on manual signing, is for those children who fail to learn verbal imitation. If you find that your child is not learning to talk, spend time strengthening his abilities in other areas.

The child who becomes proficient in verbal imitation does not simultaneously learn the meaning of the sounds. He is merely learning to imitate words. Unit V, "Intermediate Language," contains programs for teaching meaning. If your child already has acquired *some* echolalic speech, it is still important to have him undergo verbal imitation training so that *you* get good control over his imitations. Finally, at the same time that you begin work on the language programs (which probably will never be completely mastered by the slow child), start teaching your child other skills. Because it will take some time to finish this program on verbal imitation, we usually introduce the child to our play program (Chapter 12) at this point. Also, we introduce some more practical programs before we teach more language. Therefore, Unit IV deals with basic skills the child needs to take better care of himself, such as eating and dressing. Programs for teaching more advanced language are found in Unit V. However, you should keep practicing the verbal imitation program for part of each day, mixing this program with earlier programs and with the play program. Verbal imitation is a hard skill for your child to learn, and he will need lots of practice.

The program in this chapter is composed of five phases: 1) increasing vocalizations, 2) bringing vocalizations under temporal control, 3) imitation of sounds, 4) imitation of syllables and words, and 5) imitation of volume, pitch, and speed of vocalizations.

PHASE I: INCREASING VOCALIZATIONS

A vocalization is any sound made with the vocal cords, including grunts, laughter, babbling, "ah's," and "ee's." The goal of this phase of the program is to increase the frequency of these vocalizations. You want your child to learn that verbalizing will be rewarded with food and praise, and that he can control the supply of food, praise, and other rewards by making sounds, so that he will not use his ability to vocalize just for self-stimulation.

Step 1: You and your child should be seated face to face and about 1 to 2 feet apart. Since children typically "clam up" (stop vocalizing) when they are anxious, it is important that the situation now be as friendly and happy as possible. Try to avoid using too many aversives for tantrums and self-stimulation because that will quiet him down too much. Any tantrums and self-stimulation should be at manageable levels by now.

Step 2: Say, "Talk," and immediately reward each vocal response with praise and food. You may repeat the instruction every 5 to 10 seconds. Try to establish a nice "flow" or "natural pace" to your requests of "Talk." If you are doing it right, then your pleasant, happy manner, your timing of "Talk," and the nature of your rewards should help prompt vocalizations, which you can then reward.

Step 3: If your child does not make any sounds, you may physically prompt him with tickling, caressing, or bodily activity (like jumping), which may induce him to vocalize. Immediately reinforce any sounds that your child makes. If this type of prompting fails to produce any vocal response, you may want to backtrack to the program on "Imitation of Facial Expressions" (Chapter 8) and intermix that training with the prompts for vocalizations.

Remember that even this early step will be hard to learn for almost all the children. Even if a child is used to vocalizing a lot, it will take him a long time to "catch on" to the notion that vocalizing produces effects on you. It seems obvious to you that he should catch on to that quickly, but it will not be obvious to him. Technically, there may be two problems involved: 1) his early speech may be controlled by eliciting stimuli (that is, it may be *respondent*) and therefore difficult to bring under *operant control* (that is, under the control of rewards given contingent on his behavior), or 2) the early speech has been a form of self-stimulation, that is, the child has been getting his reward through the sensory feedback involved in the act of vocalizing itself. Bringing the behavior under the control of your external rewards, then, takes time.

You can consider Phase I mastered when the child makes roughly 10 or more vocalizations per minute, over 2- or 3-minute time spans. In other words, the phase is mastered when it looks like he is getting the idea that he can control the supply of food and other reinforcers from you by vocalizing.

PHASE II: BRINGING VOCALIZATIONS UNDER TEMPORAL CONTROL

The goal of Phase II is to teach the child to make a vocalization within 3 seconds after you say, "Talk." In Phase I you taught him that he could control the supply of rewards by vocalizing. Now you will teach him something a little more complicated. He will get these rewards by vocalizing, but only if he first *listens* to you vocalize. It is a beginning step in teaching him how to listen, and, in a sense (within less than 3 seconds), he will be rewarded.

Step 1: You and your child should be seated face to face and about 1 to 2 feet apart.
Step 2: Say, "Talk," and reinforce each vocal response that occurs within about 3 seconds after your demand with praise and food. These trials should continue until the child makes a vocal response to your instruction within about 3 seconds for 10 consecutive trials.
Step 3: The interval between your instruction and his response should now be decreased to about 2 seconds. That is, your child must now make a vocal response within 2 seconds after you say, "Talk."
Step 4: When the child has succeeded at a 2-second interval for about 10 consecutive trials, the interval is further decreased to 1 second. When the child has made vocal responses within 1 second after the demand is stated (and the sooner the better) for 10 consecutive trials, go on to Phase III.

"Spontaneous" vocalizations (that is, vocalizations that occur outside the time interval following your request to "Talk") should be rewarded less profusely, by nodding and saying, "Good talk." You should reserve the big reinforcers (food, kisses) for vocalizations that occur within the time interval. Some people may prefer not to reinforce "spontaneous" vocalizations at all during the early training, because it probably makes the child's task harder—he cannot discriminate which behavior is being reinforced. That is, if he is being rewarded for being spontaneous, he may not learn that he is being rewarded for vocalizing at a specific time.

The training is now becoming more complicated—you have more options, and it is not always obvious which course of action is best. You are not the only person who does not know exactly what to do. No one has worked out all the details yet; perhaps that is why some children catch on to the imitation program, and others do not. Since you don't always know which program is best, try different ones. Try one approach consistently for a few days and see how it works (collect data on how well the child is doing); then switch to another approach, and see if the child improves. If you have a team working with you, have one or two persons teach one program, let the others try a different one, and then compare how the child is doing on the two programs. This method should not confuse the child unless each person tries something different from trial to trial. Experiment. Be prepared to make mistakes. There is no way to find out what method works best for your child if you are unwilling to make mistakes. As far as the child is concerned, he has to get used to inconsistency and mistakes, since the world is full of them. It is better if your child gets his first lessons in inconsistency and mistakes from you because you can best help him handle his reactions to that. *You* have to be consistent in collecting data so that you can decide what works best. Once you find the right program, you should be consistent with your training.

PHASE III: IMITATION OF SOUNDS

The goal of Phase III is to teach your child to imitate specific sounds that he will later use in saying words. Your child should initially learn to imitate about 10 sounds, including at least three consonants. A sample group of sounds is:

| a | ("ah") | b | ("buh") | f | ("ef") | d | ("duh") | k | ("kuh") |
| m | ("mm") | o | ("oh") | e | ("ee") | u | ("uh") | t | ("tuh") |

The first sounds to be brought under imitative control may be sounds that the child frequently emitted while you were increasing the amount of his vocalizations, or they may be sounds that he made when you were establishing temporal control, or they may be "easy" sounds, like "ah," "mm," "oh." (Wait with s, k, g, l, and so on because they are more difficult sounds.)

The First Sound
The following procedure can be used in teaching your child to make his first sound in imitation of your sound.

Step 1:   You and your child should sit face to face about 1 to 2 feet apart.

Step 2:   On each trial, say one sound, such as "ah."

Step 3:   On the first five trials, any sound that the child makes within 3 seconds of your sound and that is even just a rough approximation of the sound you made, is rewarded. For example, in early training, if you are saying "ah," and he is giving you "eh," that is acceptable.

Step 4:   For certain sounds, the child may fail to match, even roughly, the sound you make. In these cases, visual and/or manual prompting should be used to produce a rough approximation of your vocalization.

In the *visual prompting procedure* exaggerate the shape of your mouth when you say the sound. For instance, when saying "ah" you should open your mouth very wide. Reinforce your child for imitating the shape of your mouth whether or not he vocalizes. If necessary, open his mouth for him. When the child has successfully imitated the shape of your mouth, then demand that the child imitate the shape of your mouth *and* make a sound. The resulting vocalization should be at least a rough approximation of the sound you made. The visual prompting procedure is continued until the child has roughly approximated the sound you made for five consecutive trials.

In the *manual prompting procedure,* you hold the child's mouth in the appropriate shape while the child vocalizes. Thus, you can manually prompt the sound "mm" by holding the child's lips together when he vocalizes. The prompt forces the child to produce at least a rough approximation of your sound. A speech therapist can give you many suggestions on how to prompt difficult sounds, such as trying a mild gag to produce consonants g or k, or depressing the child's tongue with a tongue depressor to get a good "ah." The full prompt is used until the child has roughly matched your sound for five consecutive trials. The prompt is then gradually *faded* until the child has roughly approximated your vocalization without any manual prompting for five consecutive trials.

Step 5: After the child has roughly approximated your vocalization on five consecutive trials (using the procedure in Step 3 or Step 4), the child's response is *shaped* to more closely match your vocalization. That is, on successive trials, you should reinforce responses that more closely match your vocalizations. Specifically, on a given trial you should reinforce a response only if it approximates your vocalization as closely as, or more closely than, the last reinforced response. However, if your child fails to match your sound closely enough to be reinforced for a number of trials, backtrack and reinforce a less accurate approximation to keep his vocalization "alive." If your child receives too little praise he will lose interest in the imitation task.

Step 6: The *shaping* of the child's response is continued until the child can accurately imitate the sound you make. When the child has correctly imitated the first sound for 10 consecutive trials, imitation training of the second sound can begin.

The Second Sound

The second sound chosen for imitation training should be quite *different* from the first sound. For example, if "ah" was the first sound taught, "mm" would be an appropriate second sound.

Step 1: Steps 1 through 6, used in teaching the first sound, are the same steps used for teaching the child to imitate the second sound "mm."

Step 2: After the child has correctly imitated the second sound, "mm," for 10 consecutive trials, reintroduce the first sound, "ah." Continue to present trials until your child has responded correctly for five consecutive trials.

Step 3: Repeat Steps 1 and 2 until the child makes, at most, one error the first time you say each sound.

Step 4: You should now begin random rotation with the two sounds, for example: "ah," "mm," "ah," "mm," "mm," "ah," "ah," "ah," "mm," "ah." If the child loses one of the sounds during this step, go back and rebuild it, then place the two sounds back into random rotation. Continue to present trials in random rotation until the child has imitated you correctly to criterion. Your child is now ready to learn to imitate a third sound.

Sounds 3 Through 10

Step 1: The procedure for teaching the remaining sounds is the same as that for teaching the first two sounds.

Step 2: After each new sound is acquired by the child, you should mix presentations of the new sound randomly with presentations of the sounds learned earlier (so as to keep the old learning intact) until the child has responded correctly to criterion.

Step 3: When your child can imitate six to ten sounds, you should begin the next phase, building syllables and words. However, you should continue to teach your child to imitate the remaining sounds in the list.

Again be aware, as you are working on verbal imitations, which is a hard job both for you and the child, that the child may "regress," that is, start to tantrum and self-stimulate. If that is the case, you have to go back and settle him down. There is no sense in trying to work with a child who is squirming and paying no attention, at least not when you are demanding difficult learning, as in verbal imitation. Yet, as we said, you have to go easy on the aversives in this kind of training.

Also, since the work is very tedious, consider "sprinkling in" various instructions that the child can follow successfully in order to break up the monotony and to help him retain a sense of success. For example, once in a while (every 2 minutes or so) give the child a nonverbal imitation to imitate (such as, "Arms up," "Touch stomach," or "Touch nose") or some simple instruction (such as, "Stand up" or "Pat the table").

PHASE IV: IMITATION OF WORDS

Word List

mama	up	open	tummy
papa	eat	pee pee	eye
bye bye	cookie	go	milk
down	water	baby	out

The words you choose to teach should be composed of sounds that the child can readily imitate. For instance "banana" should be chosen only if the child can imitate the sounds "ba" and "na." "Tickle" should be chosen only if the child can imitate the sounds "t" and "k." It's easier to start with words that have "like" sounds (homogeneous chains) like "mama" or "papa," or nearly like sounds, like "cookie" or "baby." Words composed of very dissimilar sounds (heterogeneous chains) like "table" and "clock" should be presented later.

The First Word

Step 1: For the first few (20-50) trials, say a word, such as "mama," and reinforce any approximations that include the main sounds in the word. Thus "ma," "mam," "ma-a," or "muck" are adequate initial approximations of "mama"; "daga" is an adequate initial approximation of "doggie."

Step 2: If the child makes an adequate initial approximation to the word on the first few trials, you should use *shaping* on the later trials to make the child more closely approximate your verbalization. That is, in a given trial, reinforce your child's response only if it approximates your word as closely as, or more closely than, the last reinforced response. Continue the shaping procedure until the child's approximation of the word is consistently clear enough to be readily understood by most people. The child's response need not exactly match your pronunciation; an adequate imitation of "tickle" would be "tihka" or "tihko."

Step 3: For some words, your child may fail to approximate even roughly your word on the first trials. For example, the child may fail to imitate one or more of the sounds that make up the word (component sounds). An inadequate approximation of "mama" is "ah," "milk" is inadequately expressed as "mah," and an inadequate approximation of "doggie" is "dah" or "gah." In these cases, you must build the word using a shaping procedure. Divide the word into its component sounds and present each sound as a separate trial. Thus, "mama" breaks down as "mm"—"ah"—"mah"—"mah mah"—"mama." The child imitates each component when it is presented, and is reinforced for repeating each component. In the following sample sequence the "good" said by the adult represents the reward you use during the exercise, such as food or social reinforcement.

Adult: "ah"
Child: "ah"
Adult: "Good!...mah"
Child: "ah"
Adult: "mm"
Child: "mm"
Adult: "Good!...ah"
Child: "ah"
Adult: "mm"
Child: "mm"
Adult: (May wait for the child to say, "ah.")
Child: "ah"
Adult: "Good!" (Repeat sequence.)

The point of the training here is that you want the child to "chain," or "hook up," two different sounds so that, once he has said one sound, that is *his* cue for the second sound. For example, "mm" becomes *his* cue for saying "ah" without your giving him the "ah" first. You do this by gradually fading your cue ("ah"), eventually waiting him out.

Building the first word is a difficult procedure to write out in detail, and you may have to improvise to help a particular child along. For example, if you are working on "mah," the child may give you "ah" when you say "mah" because the last sound in your "mah" is "ah," which is the strongest sound for him, since he heard it more recently than "mm." He may give you "mah" if you say "mm." Therefore, stay with saying "mm" for a while, then fade in the "ah" in your "mah" *slowly,* retaining his "mah" with rewards.

After the child has performed the sequence correctly on five consecutive presentations, you should gradually, in the succeeding sequences, speed up the rate at which the sounds are presented. As the rate of presentation speeds up, the reinforcements presented between the component sounds gradually are dropped. At this point the sequence may be:

Adult: "mah"
Child: "mah"
Adult: "mah-mah"
Child: "mah"
Adult: (Waits for the child's second "mah" or minimally prompts.)
Child: "mah"
Adult: "Very good!"

It is important to intermix presentations of one-syllable and two-syllable units, for example, "mah," "mah-mah," "mah-mah," "mah," in order to help him discriminate between those two kinds of sounds.

The child may persist in making slight pauses between the sounds of the word for quite some time ("mah...mah"). However, these pauses gradually can be eliminated by selectively reinforcing only those instances in which the child says the word with less pause.

The Second Word

The second word chosen for imitation training should be quite different from the first word. For instance, if "mama" is the first word taught, "baby" is an appropriate second word. You may accept "baba" or "bebe" as adequate approximations. The second word, like the first, should be composed of sounds that the child can imitate separately.

The second word should be taught in the same way the first word was taught. After the child has correctly imitated the second word for 10 consecutive trials, you should begin random rotation of the two words. Use random rotation in the same way as we have described earlier. Present the first word to the child. Continue to present this word until the child has correctly imitated it for five consecutive trials. You may need to prompt the word on the first few trials by separating the word into its component sounds as you did in the initial training. Now reintroduce the second word. Continue to present trials until your child has responded correctly for five consecutive trials. Then present both words until the child makes, at most, one error the first time you present each word. Randomly rotate the order in which the two words are presented.

Words 3 Through 10

The procedure for teaching the remaining eight initial words is the same as that for teaching the first two words. After your child learns to imitate each new word, you should mix presentations of the new word with presentations of the words learned earlier using random rotation until the child has responded to criterion.

When the child can imitate 10 words consistently, you should begin the next phase: imitation of volume, pitch, and speed. Concurrently, however, the child should be taught to imitate the remaining words on the list, the names of people with whom he interacts regularly and any other labels that would be functional and useful for him in his environment, such as "Up," "Down," and "Open."

Introducing Additional Words

When you shape words that contain different sounding units, start with the last unit of the word and work backward. This is called "backward chaining." For example, if you work on "mommy," first train "mee," then put "mah-mee" together. If you train "cookie," then "kie" is initially enough for him to get his reinforcer (cookie); later demand that he say "coo-kie." Usually what will happen when you take apart a word like that is that it will sound "mechanical" or awkward at first, almost as if it were two separate words. Don't worry about that—you will be reinforcing him for better approximations over time, so that eventually it will sound natural.

Remember to teach words that can be made functional for the child, that is, words that he can use to fill his needs and desires. For example, "Up" is good, because he can be taught that he has to say that in order to get up out of the chair. "Cookie" is good, because saying that gets him a cookie. "Open" is good because he can be taught that saying "open" means he will be let out of doors.

Imitation, Matching, and Early Language

Many children can be overheard to say some words before you begin training, but they do not say the word when you ask them to, and they rarely use the word appropriately. Our advice is to try to get reliable hold of these words, and, if that does not succeed, go back, simplify things, and gain control. Demand simple sounds and/or words to start with, get reliable imitation first, then become more elaborate later.

Finally, present many informal rehearsals of words and sounds the child can imitate. Do it everywhere, and present it as an enjoyable game, hoping he will learn to like his imitations. If he does, he will become "echolalic," which is good, because he will "play" with speech, imitate you a lot, even if he doesn't know the meaning of what he says (you can teach him meaning later). If he does not begin to spontaneously imitate your speech, and if each word is very difficult for him to learn to express, even after several months of training, then you have a child who will probably not talk a lot later on. You will have to supplement his vocal speech with manual (hand) signing, which is described in Chapter 24. Don't get too upset about this, however; some people do quite well without speaking a lot.

PHASE V: IMITATION OF VOLUME, PITCH, AND SPEED

As your child learns to imitate his first words, he may show problems in the areas of volume, pitch, and overall speed with which he says his words. These problems can be remedied using shaping.

Volume Imitation

Step 1: Begin by saying in a very loud voice one of the sounds that your child can imitate. Reinforce the child simply for imitating the sound on the first trial. In succeeding trials, shape the child to match your volume. That is, on each succeeding trial you reinforce the child only if he imitates the sound correctly *and* if the volume of the response is as loud as, or louder than, the volume of the last reinforced response. You may try to prompt a loud volume by getting the child excited and moving around, or by actively gesturing for "loudness" as would a school cheerleader or symphony conductor. The drill is continued until the child is matching your volume.

Step 2: Make the second sound in a near whisper. Prompt softness by being very quiet and gentle, settling yourself and the child down. Put your finger on his lips. The child is reinforced only if he imitates the sound correctly and if the volume of the response is as soft as, or softer than, the volume of the last reinforced response. Training is continued until the child is matching your near whisper.

Step 3: You should now randomly rotate the loud sound and the soft sound. Present the loud sound with its prompt (the "loud" gestures) and the soft sound with quiet movement. Gradually fade these prompts. Randomly vary and rotate the two sounds. The drill is continued until the child can shift from loud to soft easily.

Step 4: Next introduce and train new sounds one at a time at either a loud or a soft volume. Continue to drill the child until he can imitate each new sound at the appropriate volume.

Step 5: When the child can appropriately match the volume of a sound the first time that the sound is presented, you should begin to present words that the child can imitate in order to generalize the imitation of volume to words. The drill is continued until the child can imitate the volume of a word the first time that that word is presented in a session.

Step 6: If you want to be extra fancy at this point you can begin teaching him the meaning of the words "loud" and "soft." Say, "loud," very loudly, and reinforce him for imitating it. Say, "soft," in a whisper; reinforce as above. Consider now that your loudness (decibel level) is a prompt for his loudness, which you may now want to fade so that you end up saying "loud" and "soft" at equal (conversational) volume, while you maintain, with reinforcement, his two different volumes. That is, he gives the appropriate decibel level when you say "loud" or "soft" even though your decibel level stays the same.

Pitch Imitation

The procedure for teaching your child to imitate pitch is very similar to the procedure used in teaching volume imitation.

Step 1: Begin by saying a sound that the child can imitate at a *high* pitch. Over a sequence of trials shape the child's response to match your pitch (e.g., by reinforcing closer and closer approximations of your pitch).

Step 2: Present a second sound that the child can imitate, this time at a *low* pitch. Again, shape the child's response to match your pitch.

Step 3: The two sounds are now presented in random rotation. The drill is continued until the child is shifting pitch easily.

Step 4: Introduce new sounds next. Continue the drill until the child can imitate the pitch of a sound the first time that that sound is presented in a session.

Step 5: After the child can imitate the pitch of sounds the first time that they are presented, begin to present a three-sound cue, such as "da-dee-da," saying the sounds at different pitches (low-high-low). Shape the child's response until he can imitate the pattern of pitches that you make. When the child has mastered one three-sound cue, a second one is introduced with a different pattern of pitches, and the child's pattern of pitches is again shaped to match your own. New three-part cues are introduced and the child's responses are shaped until the child can imitate the pattern of pitches the first time a given pattern is presented.

Imitation of Speed

Step 1: Begin by repeating a sound that the child can say three to four times at a rapid speed. A typical cue is "da-da-da" or "mee-mee-mee." As in teaching the child to imitate pitch or volume, first require the child to imitate only the sounds of the cue, and then gradually shape the child, over trials, to imitate the speed at which the cue is spoken.

Step 2: Now present a second cue at a slow rate. Then present these two cues in random rotation until the child can shift the speed of imitation easily.

Step 3: Present new cues at either a fast or a slow rate, and shape the child's response on each cue until it matches the speed of your presentation. Introduce new cues until the child can imitate the speed at which a cue is spoken the first time that it is presented.

Step 4: Words that the child can imitate should be presented next, and the child should be required to imitate the speed at which the word is said as well as imitating the word itself.

CHAPTER 12

APPROPRIATE PLAY SKILLS

This chapter outlines the program for using the nonverbal imitation skills your child has acquired as a basis for teaching him to play with toys, to participate in recreational activities, and to do art work. Brief pointers on the selection of toys that seem to facilitate the learning of play skills for developmentally disabled persons are also given.

In our treatment programs, we discovered early that by using imitation it became possible to teach the developmentally disabled child a number of complex behaviors, which would seem virtually impossible to teach otherwise. This seems particularly true in teaching language. If the child were not first taught to imitate sounds (Chapter 11), it is unlikely that he would have been taught to talk, to use words and sentences, or to use meaningful language. For the same reason, the learning of the complex skills involved in playing with toys, in drawing, and later in self-help skills is always preceded by intensive training in imitation of more simple behaviors described in Chapter 8. If your child cannot correctly imitate the simple behaviors, he probably will not be able to reach most of the goals that are outlined in this chapter. Remember, also, that the earlier programs on imitation are only a partial solution to the kind of training that the child needs for mastering play skills, sports, and art. Although the child will imitate an adult in many ways, there are always some behaviors that are too novel for him to imitate, and that have to be trained separately. Examples of such behaviors are presented throughout this chapter.

You should have by now a fairly good understanding of the basic steps involved in shaping so the programs underlying play skills, sports, and art are not discussed in as much detail as the earlier programs. Rather, we will take special notice of the specific difficulties that may arise as those particular programs are taught.

Before you start teaching any activities, you may want to keep in mind that some children develop an interest in a certain activity. In other words, the behavior becomes self-reinforcing, which means that the child is in good shape for beginning to learn; however, some children could not care less about the learning activity. You will not know that until after the child has had the exposure to and has acquired some proficiency at the task. Should your child remain disinterested in the task, even after you have worked with him for a while, then there is really no sense in continuing with that activity at that time; perhaps you may want to return to it later. After teaching several of the activities described in this chapter, it is probable that your child will take a liking to one or more of them. Your goal should be to teach some constructive activity that looks "appropriate," that will acquire its own reinforcing properties, and that will then replace the stereotyped, ritualistic, and inappropriate behavior called self-stimulation. In all likelihood, play, art, and sports are basically self-stimulatory in nature. That is, completing jig-saw puzzles, shooting baskets, and dancing do not really solve any of the world's problems, but it feels good (to some people) to do these tasks. The task itself generates the kind of sensory feedback rewards that serve to maintain the child's interest in the task. The trick is to teach a child appropriate forms of self-stimulatory behavior, which will replace socially undesirable, inappropriate forms of that same class of behavior.

PLAYING WITH BLOCKS

One very useful activity for any child to learn, and one of the easiest tasks to teach, is building with blocks. Because of the nature of this activity, make sure that you have duplicate sets of blocks. As you play with a particular kind of block, the child gets to play with the same kind of block. You want to teach the child how to build a particular structure with blocks; you then let the child build his own, using yours as a model. Eventually, it is hoped that the child can be instructed to "Go play with blocks," or that he may do so on his own initiative and build the structures you have taught him through modeling. In this fashion he can be taught independent play (discussed later in this chapter); that is, he can be taught to play constructively with materials in his environment without your constant supervision and direction.

In preparing to teach this activity, you and the child should sit facing each other across a table wide enough to provide good separation between two working areas (each 1 foot square), but small enough to provide easy access to a supply of blocks, which you place between you and your child on the side of the table. In the beginning you may want to have just a few blocks in this pile, but as training progresses, you should add blocks so that there are more from which to choose. If the table cannot accommodate two separate working areas, move onto the floor, which should be cleared of unnecessary objects. The floor will do just as well, provided that the child has a clear view of his working area as well as yours.

Step 1: Take one block from the pile and place it in front of you and place a similar block in front of the child. In teaching this behavior, as well as in teaching other behaviors, you should start with the simplest form. This may be to simply touch your block, and to teach your child that he can touch his block in imitation of your touching. You can start with the instruction "Do this," and then touch the block, prompt the child to touch his block, reinforce, and gradually fade the prompt. In the beginning, he may touch your block, but you should prompt and reinforce him for touching *his* block. Eventually you should be able to touch your block, and he should touch his block in imitation of your action. Then go on to teach more complicated behaviors, such as lifting your block and putting it back down. Prompt and reinforce him as before for imitating your behavior. Perhaps the next step would be for you to pick up your block and tap it a couple of times on the table or the floor; then prompt your child to do likewise, and fade the prompt, until the child masters the task.

Step 2: Now teach the child to handle two blocks. You may begin this task by placing two blocks in front of you and two similar blocks in front of the child. Now touch one block and then the other. Prompt your child to do likewise; fade the prompt and reinforce in such a fashion that, once you have touched the first block and then the second block, the child will act similarly. A simple extension of this kind of activity will occur when you pick up one block and put it on top of the second block, directly in front of you, and then prompt and reinforce the child to do the same with his blocks. Once a child can imitate you stacking two blocks on top of each other, go on to using three or four blocks, so he is involved in imitating you building a "tower."

Step 3: Once the child has begun to move blocks around and arrange them in a tower, it is a relatively easy step for you to arrange your blocks to construct more imaginative structures, such as a "bridge." This particular task requires you to demonstrate building the bridge. In separate and distinct moves, place two blocks side by side and place one block on top, touching both the blocks underneath. Prompt and reinforce the child for matching your moves. It may be helpful for you to instruct the child by saying "Do this" or "Do as I do" because this may serve initially as a "ready signal," which tells him to pay attention to what you are doing. Once he has learned to match your separate moves, "condense" the imitation by completing your structure before he is allowed to start. Now you are teaching him to match "final products," not just separate moves. Once he has built a bridge in this way, then he could build a bridge with a tower next to it. Later he may learn to imitate your building a house (eight or more blocks in a rectangular shape) then a house next to a bridge next to a tower, and so on. If you build several structures like that, you can introduce new objects, such as taking a doll and placing it inside the "house," or placing a toy cow inside the "corral."

Step 4: This step may have to wait until *after* the child has completed Unit V (Intermediate Language). Once the child has learned the necessary components of building in imitation of you, you may want to remove your structure and then ask your child to build that structure. Then gradually, once he has built the structure—a tower, for example—teach the child to call it a tower. While you are fading your structure as a prompt, teach him to follow the instruction, "Build a tower." The purpose of this step is to bring his toy play under your verbal control, so that you can just tell him what you want him to do with the blocks. You don't have to do all the work.

The kinds of combinations and creations that you can make with blocks and objects (toy animals, toy figures, clay) can be quite complex and imaginative. You have made a beginning in teaching your child how to play appropriately.

PLAYING WITH TOYS

One of the early tasks in teaching appropriate play skills is to teach your child to play with simple toys, such as dolls and trucks. Again, as is the case with teaching block play, buy two of each toy. If you want to teach your child to play with dolls, the first steps, then, would be very simple. Pick up your doll and prompt the child to do likewise; fade and reinforce until the child picks up his doll in response to your request "Do this," or "Let's play dolls." In subsequent steps you would not only pick up your doll, but put the doll in your arms, and then prompt and reinforce the child for doing likewise with his doll. Other steps would include rocking the doll back and forth, patting the doll on the back, laying the doll down, covering the doll with a blanket, and feeding it. Remember to prompt when necessary and to reinforce.

Later you may want to teach the child to wash the doll, to dress it, to put it on the potty, and so on. Remember that each of these are reasonable complex behaviors. It is ideal if you can teach the child to engage in these behaviors through imitation because the more the child can imitate you, the more he will learn from you.

It is hoped that you may now be able to see how you could teach the child to play in a similar manner, using a truck or any other toy. A truck does lots of things: it stops and goes, it can be driven through a city (made of blocks), it can be filled with gas, it can be loaded and unloaded. You may want to verbalize your actions, teaching the child (if you can) to describe his own behaviors as he plays. The more programs you can run concurrently, the better off everyone is. Remember to start with a simple task, such as just moving the truck back and forth.

The advantage of having duplicate sets of toys or objects is that the child does not have to "remember" what it is you want him to do; a toy is immediately available for him to use in imitating you. After he becomes increasingly proficient in matching and imitating you, then you may want to delay, in gradual steps, the completion of his task, so that the time interval between your behavior and his is gradually lengthened. This is done with the goal in mind that eventually you will need just one set of objects for imitative play. You would perform the task first, then hand the toy to the child, and ask him to do as you did. This kind of delay between your behavior and his requires that he remember what you did. Memory, the storing of such information, is probably learned, and there is every evidence that your child could also learn to store such information.

PARTICIPATING IN RECREATIONAL ACTIVITIES

Once you get the feel for how to teach imitative play, as when you use blocks, trucks, and dolls, it is a relatively easy task to extend this kind of behavior to activities such as sports and dancing. Suppose you want to teach your child to play with a basketball. Get two balls, and pick up your ball while telling your child "Do this"; prompt and reinforce as before. Drop your ball and catch it and instruct your child to do likewise. In some activities you will use a lot of direct imitation, but it also will become apparent as you get going that for some of the more difficult tasks you have to do a lot of *hand shaping* (that means physically guiding your child through the sequence of acts comprising the behavior you want him to perform and then reinforcing him for doing it). Suppose you are going to teach a child to catch a ball after it bounces on the floor. Almost invariably you will have to teach him to catch a ball as a separate act. This act is taught by having the child hold his arms outstretched and then merely placing the ball in his arms, reinforcing him, and then very slowly and in gradual steps, tossing the ball to him from increasing distances, such as from 2 inches, 6 inches, and then 1 or 2 feet. That is, you may have to *hand shape* some of the components in the kind of imitative act you are trying to teach. If you are concerned with teaching him how to shoot baskets, teach him first to bounce the ball off a wall, and then, with a basket at eye level, teach him to drop the ball through the hoop, gradually raising the basket in small steps (6 inches at a time) to the point where he actually has to throw the ball into the air to make it fall through the hoop.

This may seem like a terribly arduous task, and an extremely impractical way to teach a child to play basketball. It is. For some children, it just is not going to work, but it is surprising that for some children shooting baskets becomes a reinforcing activity and some become quite expert at it. You just won't know until you have tried.

If your child is no star at shooting baskets, perhaps he will be a great dancer. Many developmentally disabled children are very fond of music, and many have a great sense of rhythm. For such a child it is relatively easy to teach dancing in response to music. Turn on his favorite record, stand facing the child, tell him "Do this," and start with some very simple behavior, such as rocking from one foot to the other. Prompt the child if necessary. In gradual steps, then, introduce more elaborate behavior, such as moving your foot forward and backward, bending your knees, turning your body to the left and then nodding your head to the right, and turning completely around. Again, if the child doesn't do this through imitations, prompt him to get the behavior underway, physically move him through the actions.

As will become obvious to you when you begin to teach dancing, some children love to dance and become very good at it, while others never quite get the knack. Children are different—some are good at some things, some are good at others. Your child is just like everybody else in this respect.

There are many behaviors that are useful and fun that you can teach a child by modeling the behavior first, and then prompting and reinforcing him for matching your models. Sometimes you have to be a "ham" to act out the kinds of behaviors that serve to break up the kind of plastic, rigid appearance of many children who are developmentally disabled. They often behave without much expression, and you must teach them how.

The programs for block building and playing with dolls and trucks, as well as the beginning of athletics and dance, are examples of teaching your child to participate in recreational activities. It is virtually impossible to write a training manual that would include all the kinds of play and recreational activities the child could be taught; nor is this necessary. It is necessary for the adults around the child to construct individual programs so that the needs and goals of the particular child are met.

DRAWING AND WRITING

Drawing and writing are elaborate behaviors that can be taught as an extension of the child's training in nonverbal imitation. The program for drawing pictures is discussed in detail; the program on writing is very similar, and follows naturally from drawing. The final goal of the program on drawing is to teach the child enough skills so that he can draw recognizable figures and objects in response to your request, "Draw a picture," or so that he will pick up a crayon and draw when he sees crayons and paper. He may draw figures that he has learned through imitation, and he may draw original, creative ones. As with normal children, developmentally disabled children differ widely in their interest in drawing. Some children are extremely creative in drawing, producing intriguing figures and some interesting work; you won't know if your child will do this unless you get him started.

Drawing

Step 1: *Tracing.* With a pencil, draw a single horizontal line on a piece of paper. Give the child a crayon and prompt him to trace directly over your pencil line. Say "Do this," and actually guide the child's hand with a crayon over the pencil line. After you have completed this tracing, praise the child for "good working," or "good drawing." Repeat this procedure while you gradually reduce your prompts. You may find that the child is not watching the drawing, but rather is attending to something other than the task at hand. Clearly, he must watch what is going on, and you will have to bring his attention to the paper, pencil line, and crayon. As in all the other tasks you have taught, help the child attend to the task at hand by positively reinforcing him for being correct and giving some reprimand (or withholding the positives at least), for being incorrect. When the child can reliably trace your *single* horizontal line without any prompting, draw another horizontal line and ask the child to trace over both pencil lines.

After mastering this, require correct tracing over a single vertical line. Although the child may be able to trace horizontal lines, vertical lines are a new experience, and may require prompts. Once the child can discriminate and reliably copy horizontal versus vertical lines, have him trace double vertical lines, and then lines that intersect. The child can be taught to trace shapes such as triangles, squares, and circles and eventually he will be able to trace box figures.

Remember to praise the child when he correctly traces your pencil marks and to reproach him for incorrect responses or for not paying attention to the materials in front of him. Also, before advancing to a more complex task (i.e., going from tracing a single vertical line to tracing double vertical lines), be sure the child has mastered the previous task and can trace your line(s) without any prompting. The time it takes to learn the skills described in this step varies considerably for individual children. Some may pick it up in a few minutes, whereas others may require a month of patient teaching.

Step 2: *Copying.* Begin to teach the child to copy or imitate your pencil lines instead of requiring him to trace over them. That is, the child must draw his lines next to, below, or above your lines. As in Step 1, grade the material in very small steps, starting with single horizontal lines, go on to double horizontal lines, then use single vertical lines, double vertical lines, lines that intersect, triangles, squares, and eventually box figures.

You may find at this point that it will be easier to facilitate drawing by using a chalkboard built into a desk with an attached chair. This will provide the child with all the necessary drawing materials in one place. Of course, such a tool is optional.

Step 3: *Advanced copying.* Using the skills learned in the above two steps, the child can be taught to imitate your drawings of various geometric shapes, and then he can move on to copying small animals and plants, such as dogs, cats, and flowers, and eventually larger and more complex objects, such as human figures, houses, and trains.

At this point you may begin requiring the child to imitate your use of color. For example, you draw a flower using red, yellow, green, and orange crayons and require the child to correctly imitate your use of these colors.

Step 4: *Original drawing.* Original drawing is quite complex and may have to be postponed until after Unit V. Once the child has learned the necessary components involved in imitative drawing, the behavior can be shifted from imitation of your drawing to a verbal request, such as "Draw a picture." This may at first require you to prompt the child by taking his hand and guiding it through the beginning phases of a drawing. Fade your manual prompt slowly so that the child can make a drawing on his own, when he is asked.

This newly acquired behavior can be gradually brought under the control of more appropriate stimulus contexts (other than "Draw a picture"), such as the child's sight of objects in his environment, either in concrete form or in a representation, as in magazine pictures. At this point, it may become apparent that the child has taken a great interest in a particular area. For example, he may show an affinity for drawing animals, or he may show an interest in sequences of objects, such as numbers or the letters of the alphabet. A strong enough interest can provide the child with an "internal source of motivation" that will greatly enhance the effectiveness of your attention and praise. To be consistent, we would probably call it an advanced form of self-stimulation. Also, the drawing skills learned thus far may prove so pleasurable to the child that you can begin to train him to occupy his free time engaged in this appropriate form of play rather than other, inappropriate forms of self-stimulatory behaviors.

Writing

The program for teaching your child to write can be structured in much the same way as that for drawing. First, teach your child to trace simple horizontal and vertical lines and curves as in Step 1 above. Then move on to tracing, and finally copying, letters. When your child has mastered these skills, teach him to copy, and then write on his own, simple words or phrases.

INDEPENDENT PLAY

All the procedures described thus far have been employed in the presence of an attending adult. You have probably observed your child when he is alone and unattended; too often the child reverts to drifting inattention or to inappropriate self-stimulation when left alone. Therefore, you can begin teaching the child to continue activities such as the ones described in this chapter when no adult is present.

The teaching of appropriate independent play can be approached in the following manner. First, you should teach the child to play with toys in your presence, without your active participation. You should teach him to play with two toys and then gradually add more until all available toys have been introduced. Or you may want to instruct the child to complete some simple tasks, such as "Build a bridge," or "Draw a flower." As the child begins to play, gradually fade yourself from the child by sitting farther and farther away from him, eventually leaving the room, so that the child is left alone for a minute. If the task(s) are completed or if he is working on the task upon your return, praise the child profusely. If the child does *not* finish the task, reprimand him, ask him to do it again, and prompt his play by standing at the door (or nearby) for a shorter period than before. In gradual steps, the number and complexity of tasks required and the time allowed to complete them can be increased. During this time, you can occasionally leave the child alone with play materials (coloring book, crayons, paper, magazine pictures, and puzzles), with *no instructions,* so that the mere presence of toys begins to cue his playing. On such occasions, the child should be observed as unobtrusively as possible and should be allowed to remain unattended only as long as he uses these play materials appropriately. If he remains unoccupied for a total of 5 minutes or if he engages in any inappropriate behaviors, such as self-stimulation, for a total of 15 seconds, remove the child from the room, terminate play with the materials and perhaps have him do something he does not like all that well, such as household chores, or difficult language drills. You should be able to gradually increase the amount of time the child stays in the room engaged in appropriate independent play. Although it will take some effort on your part to teach the child the rules of this kind of play, it should become apparent that, once he has learned what you expect, he may be capable of gaining enjoyment from it, just as any other child would.

TOY SELECTION

Not a great deal of factual information is available on toy selection, that is, on whether one can help children play more by selecting a particular set of toys over some other set. However, we feel that it is worthwhile to give more attention to toy selection. We have suggested that many developmentally retarded children spend a great deal of their time in primitive, repetitive, and monotonous behavior in an apparent attempt to provide their bodies with needed auditory, visual, vestibular, proprioceptive, and tactile stimulation. We have already argued that one goal of a good toy-play program may be to substitute appropriate toy play for the more bizarre-looking behaviors. That is, you can probably select toys to "channel" or "substitute" a more appropriate form of self-stimulatory behavior for a less appropriate form of self-stimulation (e.g., rocking). In other words, you may be able to provide the child with the needed reinforcers (visual, auditory, vestibular stimulation) by teaching him to play with toys, instead of acting bizarre.

Hill and McMackin of the Lynne Developmental Center in Dallas, Texas, recommended that the child be observed and his various kinds of self-stimulatory behaviors be noted in order to classify the kinds of sensory stimulation a particular child is seeking. The following categorization, including examples of the inappropriate behaviors, has been developed:

Visual Stimulation   The child gazes at lights, fixates at rotating objects, regards his hands, flaps his fingers in front of his eyes.
Auditory Stimulation   The child vocalizes, hums tunes, clicks his tongue, taps furniture.
Tactile Stimulation   The child strokes his own body parts, pinches himself, places his fingers in his mouth.
Vestibular Stimulation   The child rocks his body, bounces, spins his body.
Proprioceptive Stimulation   The child's body assumes strange positions in space; he postures, toe walks, holds his head to one side.

Hill and McMackin suggest that an initial toy selection to reduce *visual* self-stimulation should include toys such as flashlights, whirling lights, wheels, an hourglass, magnetic swinging balls, Light Brite pegs, a Flash Gordon gun, pinwheels, an Etch-a-Sketch, a Pachinco machine, a pinball game, a kaleidoscope, View Master, Slinky, tops, and wind-up toys. For those children who twirl string, try fishing-rod games or string puppets.

For replacement of *auditory* stimulations select toys that make noise. For example, use clackers, bells, whistles, talking toys, buzzers, a toy piano, music boxes, a radio, noisemaking push-pull toys, hair dryers, stethoscopes, or music of any type.

For replacement of *tactile* stimulations, select items that touch the body. Examples are an autoharp, Silly Putty, vibrators, facial scrubbers, soft furry toys, puppets, gum, body paints, and blankets.

For replacement of *vestibular* and *proprioceptive* stimulations, try selecting items that recreate the motion or position. Examples are a rocking horse, a rocking chair, large physical therapy balls to roll on, barrels to roll on and in, wagons, a spinning office chair, a hammock, many forms of playground equipment such as swings, trampolines, and teeter-totters.

Many of these toys or items will be "favored objects" the moment they are introduced. On the other hand, the child may have to be extrinsically reinforced (e.g., with food or praise) so that he will handle certain toys. It is difficult to determine how long to maintain the child on extrinsic reinforcement for "good playing" before the reinforcing value of the toy itself "takes over." The rule may be to try different toys during this training and "exposure" period, for upward of a week per toy.

If a child becomes quite attached to some toy or activity (like music), then access to that toy or activity can be his reward for engaging in some behavior that he does not like that much. For example, playing with a toy (even for a few seconds) could become his reward for sitting attentively in a chair and learning some task necessary for more adequate social functioning.

Hill and McMackin also suggest a useful shaping procedure within a particular play activity. For example, a child who is a *body rocker* can be placed in a rocking chair and reinforced for rocking in that position. Then, in gradual steps, teach him to stand next to a chair while rocking a doll in the chair, to rock the doll in a crib, then to swing another child on a swing. In that fashion there may be a progression and elaboration in the child's play.

Keep in mind that no child would take interest in a toy if he were not exposed to that toy. Remember also that *some* developmentally retarded children show elaborate play, as when they assemble complex puzzles, play intricate musical selections, or manipulate numbers at an advanced level. These are examples of the "splinter skills," or isolated areas of superior functioning so often found in developmentally retarded children. You will never know whether your child has these explicit skills unless he gets the opportunity to discover and develop them himself.

CHAPTER   **13**

GENERALIZATION AND MAINTENANCE

Generalization, roughly analogous to transfer, is one of the most important concepts or processes in teaching. Generalization is concerned with the efficiency of teaching, that is, determining the change in the child's behavior specifically as a result of what he has been taught. This chapter draws heavily on a paper by Carr (Note 1).

Generalization is usually divided into two aspects: stimulus generalization and response generalization.

STIMULUS GENERALIZATION

If you are a teacher, and you have taught your student well in class, you may wonder whether he will manifest what you have taught him in class in other environments as well. If you are a parent and you have taught your child some important things at home, you may wonder whether he will behave accordingly in school or elsewhere in public. These are questions of *stimulus generalization*. Stimulus generalization is the extent to which a behavior that is taught in one situation is subsequently performed in another situation, even though that other situation was not involved in the original teaching. Whether or not a particular behavior will generalize across environments cannot be determined beforehand. Sometimes behavior generalizes, sometimes it does not. You should help the behavior generalize, if it does not initially generalize. There are certain procedures that help ensure stimulus generalization.

1. *Work in several environments.* If your child is only being taught in one environment (such as in school or in a clinic) and not in other environments (such as at home), then over time he will discriminate between the different environments, and little, if any, stimulus generalization will be observed. To remedy this, the child should be taught in more than one environment. Whatever he is taught at school should be taught at home, and vice versa.
2. *Have several "teachers."* It is critical, particularly with developmentally disabled children, and especially the older ones, that many "significant adults" teach the child. Too often, a child who is behaving very nicely and learning well with a teacher behaves poorly and does not learn any con-

structive behaviors from the parents. The rule should be that all adults teach. After a certain number of adults teach the child, his discrimination between adults breaks down and the new appropriate behaviors generalize across all adults.

3. *Program common stimuli.* It may help, at least in the beginning, to make home and school similar in appearance. Have some of the same toys at home that the child has at school. Try to create the home mealtime environment at school (e.g., sitting at a table covered with a tablecloth). If he plays well with some children at school, try to have the children visit and play with him at home. Before the child begins school, play school with him at home using school-like equipment; it will then be easier to transfer the new behaviors to school later.

4. *Common reward schedules.* If a behavior is on a very "thick" (continuous or nearly so) reward schedule at home, and it is suddenly shifted to a thinner (intermittent) schedule at school, the behavior will probably not generalize, at least not after the first few days. Such abrupt changes in reward schedules are likely to take place when the child goes to school, if for no other reason than because the ratio of children to adults is different in the two places. To avoid such changes in reward schedules, try to thin the child's reward schedule at home before he goes to school. Also, have extra teacher aides present at school during the first few weeks to provide for an initially thicker reward schedule.

There are a large number of other dissimilarities between environments that may have to be attended to in order to maximize generalization. Remember the basic rule about stimulus generalization: if you don't get it, build it.

RESPONSE GENERALIZATION

Response generalization refers to the extent that you can produce a change in a larger number of behaviors by only working on one behavior. For example, by teaching the child to sit and look at you on command, does he become generally more compliant or attentive? If you teach him to hug and kiss you, does he start to like you more? It is clear that, as with stimulus generalization, we are in part dealing with practical teaching efficiency: how much behavior change do you get for free when you teach one or a limited set of behaviors? Some degree of generalization, be it stimulus or response, is critical for successful teaching. You have to get some changes "for free" because you cannot build all behaviors in all situations.

Procedures for obtaining response generalization are less clear than in working with stimulus generalization. The following suggestions are offered for maximizing response generalization:

1. *Build communicative responses.* Build and strengthen those aspects of language that are functional in getting the child what he wants. For example, it may be more helpful to build verbal requests for things your child wants (e.g., "cookie," "juice," "open," "stop," "swim") than descriptive labels (e.g., "nose," "ear," "green") because in many instances functional speech will replace more chaotic behavior, like self-stimulation and tantrums, which may in part be based on the fact that the child cannot express his wants appropriately.

2. *Build "practical" self-help skills.* For the same reasons, a child will probably greatly benefit from learning any behaviors that will increase his self-sufficiency and facilitate his getting what he wants. Being able to open a door, to take off wet pants or a hot sweater, or to ride a bike places him in more immediate contact with the rewards he seeks.

Imitation, Matching, and Early Language

3. *Build appropriate play.* Certain kinds of play are appropriate substitutes for less appropriate forms of self-stimulation. For example, a child who spins everything he sees (ash trays, cups, dishes) can be taught to use a spinning top, thereby reducing the amount of inappropriate self-stimulation. Similarly, dancing may well replace rocking, and so on.

4. *Build compliance.* Once adults acquire control over two or more behaviors which the child has already mastered (such as "Sit down," "Stand up," or "Close the door"), a number of other (already mastered) compliance behaviors will increase simultaneously.

    It is important to note again that there is a great deal of individual difference across children in regard to this and similar response generalization. For example, a child will evidence "generalized compliance" insofar as there exists a set of already acquired compliance behaviors. In effect, you are achieving control where some control already existed. For some children, generalized compliance may not emerge.

5. *Teach observational learning.* Ideally you should teach the child, at some point, a *process* whereby he can learn. In the chapters on nonverbal and verbal imitation (and in Chapter 34 on observational learning), programs are presented whereby the child learns "on his own," by merely observing behaviors of other people, and without direct shaping.

6. *Building new social rewards.* As you interact constructively with the child, when you as a person come to mediate important gratifications and aversives, your person will acquire meaningful reward and punishment properties. In other words, adults will acquire a larger range of controlling properties, and the child's behavior will become increasingly shaped without the adults explicitly doing the shaping. New behavior will be built through more informal interactions.

7. *Building intrinsic rewards.* Perhaps the child's largest gains will take place when he learns to discriminate (attend to) rewards inherent in the task or the behavior. Methods for building such intrinsic rewards are not known, but a minimal requirement is to extensively expose the child to the behavior several times. Although relatively little is known about this process, there are examples that it operates. If you teach a group of mute children to imitate your sounds and/or words, a certain portion of the children will become imitative on their own; they will become echolalic. That is, they will continue to imitate the adult even though there is no explicit or socially controlled reward for doing so. Their mere "matching" of verbal outputs appears rewarding to them. The task of imitating has become its own reward.

MAINTENANCE: GENERALIZATION ACROSS TIME

There is obviously little merit in teaching a set of behaviors only to see them disappear some months or years after your efforts have stopped. We learned some very bitter lessons in that regard. After painstakingly teaching language and other complex behaviors to several developmentally disabled children, we discharged the children, and 2 years after we had terminated teaching we observed a comprehensive loss. We reinstated the teaching programs for a short time and recovered many of the earlier gains, only to observe a second loss some 3 years later. These follow-up data have been extensively discussed elsewhere (Lovaas, Koegel, Simmons, & Long, 1973).

    There are certain steps you can take to protect the gains that your children will make in your program. Build that protection into your initial teaching program. The following points should help you make use of generalization in your teaching programs.

1. Make the transition between school and other environments imperceptibly small. In other words, create the school environment everywhere so that the child cannot discriminate when he is out of

school. The best way to do this is to train the parents and other significant adults to be teachers. In this way, there is no "discharge," no "vacation," for the child. His posttreatment environment is no different from his treatment environment.

2. Use an intermittent ("thin") reward schedule. While you may initially reward a child for every correct response, once the behavior is learned, start "missing" some rewards; for example, arbitrarily skip rewards to perhaps a third of his correct responses (select the ones to skip at random). The child will "tell" you how quickly you can thin. If his behavior starts to weaken, then "thicken" the reinforcement schedule. Eventually, you may end up with one reward for every 10 or 20 correct responses, or perhaps less.

3. Use rewards that the child will receive in his natural environment. Artificial, exaggerated, or school-type rewards, such as grades or tokens, are not likely to be found outside the teaching situation. Try to "normalize" the rewards as soon as possible.

4. Teach functional behaviors. Teach the child behaviors (that part of language, play, self-help) that get him important reinforcers in his everyday life. Teaching some erudite task that does not get him anything on the outside will not be maintained on the outside either.

Maintenance of behavior change can be attributed to generalization. Behaviors will be maintained to the extent that the child cannot discriminate between school and no school (or clinic, no clinic) settings. There are other, less well-known variables that effect maintenance of gains. Some variables pertain to the memory storage capacity of the organism. Perhaps a retarded child also is one who has a poor capacity for long-term storage of learning. The relationship is difficult to determine; relatively little is known about long-term memory storage in mentally retarded persons.

RECORDING LEARNING PROGRESS

You may want to consider recording the child's progress on the various programs described in this Unit. In general, we advise against such recordings because they are so time-consuming and one can generally judge progress on the concrete and specific tasks in this manual by whether or not several observers agree that there has, or has not been, any noticeable learning. If you do wish to record, you should begin when the child has come to a stand still; that is, when he seems not to be making any progress on a task. How long do you work on a task before you decide no progress has been made? That depends on the task, how intensively you work with the child, and so on. If you have worked for a week, a couple of hours a day, and he appears to make no progress, then you have a problem and you should start recording. Recording will allow you to determine a "baseline" against which to decide what alternatives may be effective. You may want to consider a trial-by-trial format for recording learning data. Remember that a trial was defined as beginning with the teacher's instruction; it includes the child's response or failure to respond, and it may include prompts and consequences such as rewards and punishment. The most simple recording scheme for trial-by-trial data would simply indicate if instructions were given, and whether the child was correct or not. A sample recording sheet is shown in Table 13-1. To record data, simply circle the trial number as each instruction is given, and give a check mark in the corresponding column if the child is correct.

You may want to group the data by averaging the number of correct responses to all the trials given in one day (sum of correct responses divided by total number of trials given). This information may then be graphed as shown in Figure 13-1. Grouping the data into "blocks" of a day will allow you to

Table 13-1. Simple recording form for step-by-step trial data

Child's name:
Date:
Instructor:
Behavior:

Trials	Correct response	Trials	Correct response	Trials	Correct response
1		11		21	
2		12		22	
3		13		23	
4		14		24	
5		15		25	
6		16		26	
7		17		27	
8		18		28	
9		19		29	
10		20		30	

determine whether, for example, your child has stopped responding to a particular type of instruction (Days 3 and 4, Figure 13-1), and to check on the success or failure of different teaching methods you may try (Days 5 through 9, Figure 13-1).

By using this kind of graphing, you will be in a better position to ascertain whether your child is improving, staying the same, or getting worse. It is a baseline against which to evaluate new ways of teaching. These new ways may include: 1) dropping the prompt and "waiting him out," 2) simplifying or otherwise changing the instructions, 3) giving stronger negative consequences for incorrect responding, and 4) interspersing different kinds of learning.

Suppose you have tried to teach the child a task for 1 to 2 hours a day, for a week and he has made no progress. You try different kinds of procedures in an attempt to improve his performances, but he still shows no improvement over the next 2 or 3 weeks. At that point you may want to drop that task and return to it in a month or so. Sometimes the child will change enough in that time interval (or you will) so that when you return to it, he may be able to learn it.

Figure 13-1. Sample recording form for grouped average correct responses. Days 3 and 4 show low averages, indicating that the child is no longer learning the task being presented. On Day 5, an attempt is made to improve the situation by giving stronger negative consequences for incorrect responses. However, this does not seem to work well; Days 5 and 6 show continued poor performance. On Day 7, the instructions are simplified, and great improvement is shown. A high average of correct responses is again obtained on Days 8 and 9, indicating that the child is improving with the new teaching method.

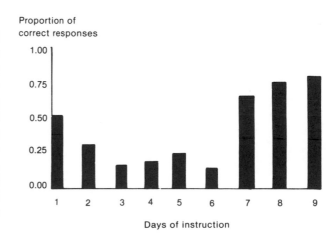

REFERENCES

Lovaas, O. I., Koegel, R. L., Simmons, J. Q., & Long, J. S. Some generalization and follow-up measures on autistic children in behavior therapy. *Journal of Applied Behavior Analysis*, 1973, *6*, 131-165.

RECOMMENDED READINGS

Lovaas, O. I., Berberich, J. P., Perloff, B. F., & Schaeffer, B. Acquisition of imitative speech by schizophrenic children. *Science*, 1966, *151*, 705-707.

Metz, J. R. Conditioning generalized imitation in autistic children. *Journal of Experimental Child Psychology*, 1965, *2*, 389-399.

Rincover, A., & Koegel, R. L. Setting generality and stimulus control in autistic children. *Journal of Applied Behavior Analysis*, 1975, *8*, 235-246.

Sidman, M., & Stoddard, L. T. Programming perception and learning for retarded children. In Ellis, N. R. (Ed.), *International Review of Research and Mental Retardation* (Volume II). New York: Academic Press, 1966.

Stokes, T. F., & Baer, D. M. An implicit technology of generalization. *Journal of Applied Behavior Analysis*, 1977, *10*, 349-367.

Reference Note

1. Carr, E. Generalization of treatment effects following educational intervention with autistic children and youth. In Wilcox, B., and Thompson, A. (Eds.), *Critical Issues in Educating Autistic Children and Youth*. To be published, 1980.

UNIT IV

BASIC SELF-HELP SKILLS

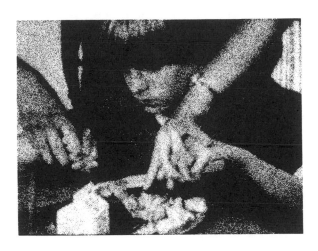

Many developmentally disabled children have difficulty learning basic self-help skills. They often require an enormous amount of help and effort from the attending adult in order to be "socially appropriate" in skills such as dressing and toileting. However, with careful teaching and patience, most of these children can learn quite complex self-care skills. Your child is no exception; once he becomes more self-sufficient, he will become less of a burden on his family or caregivers.

This Unit contains programs for teaching your child to feed, toilet, dress, and undress himself, and programs for teaching him to brush his hair and brush his teeth. Obviously, your child needs more self-help skills than the few we have outlined in this Unit, but enough pointers are given in these programs so that you are able to construct your own.

The feeding and toileting programs *may* be started after your child has progressed through Unit II, the "Getting Ready to Learn" unit of the manual. Dressing, hair brushing, and tooth brushing are more complex programs and should be started after your child has learned generalized motor imitation and can follow several verbal instructions. Do not try to teach too much at once. Choose one skill at a time and work with your child regularly until he masters it.

The programs on self-help skills, discussed in Unit IV, were written to enable the teacher to proceed without the student having completed the programs on imitation of simple actions, which were described in Chapter 8. Therefore, the programs in Unit IV rely on breaking the various complex behaviors down into smaller elements and using physical prompts, such as manually guiding the student through the behaviors. It was the intent of the program on imitation in Chapter 8 to facilitate the student's progress with the acquisition of complex behaviors, such as self-help behaviors. To the extent that the student can imitate (or learn to imitate) the adult, the *prompt* that the teacher uses to elicit the correct student behavior should be her own (modeled) behavior, rather than physical guidance. Early and continuous training in imitation of gestures should facilitate the student's mastery of Unit IV.

The programs for teaching self-help skills in this book are introductory, and many may find them inadequate for their purposes. We have made extensive use of the programs developed by Baker, Brightman, Heifetz & Murphy (1977) and the programs developed by Watson (1972). Watson's programs may be particularly helpful for the severely retarded.

115

CHAPTER **14**

EATING

Children are generally taught to spoon-feed themselves first because the spoon is the easiest utensil to manipulate. As in teaching any complex behavior, eating should be broken down into small steps and a verbal cue given for each step. It is recommended that complex eating skills, like dressing skills, be taught using the backward chaining process. In this process, the child learns to perform on his own the last step in the sequence first, then the next to the last step, and so on, until he can perform all the steps on his own.

For teaching this behavior, choose a spoon that your child can manipulate easily. You may want to invest in a small child's spoon if his hands are very small. Your child should learn to feed himself independently a little faster if he is not struggling with a spoon that is too large and clumsy for him. Putting the food in a bowl instead of on a plate should also help the child obtain better control of his food. When teaching the child to eat with a spoon, you should use soft foods, such as applesauce, pudding, or yogurt, because they are easier to put on a spoon than chunks of meat or vegetables.

You may want to break down the use of a spoon into four steps. Note that in a true backward chaining paradigm, you should start with Step 3, (that is, the adult places a full spoon in the child's hand), but since there are so few steps involved, we have usually been successful starting with Step 1.

Step 1: Say "Pick up spoon," and then place your hand over your child's hand and arrange his hand so that it grasps the spoon. With your hand still over his, lift up his hand, spoon and all. Praise him for picking up the spoon. You should teach your child to master this response before you go on to the next step.

Step 2: Say "Get food," and guide his hand so that the spoon dips into the bowl. The act of getting food on the spoon will be difficult; make sure that you show him how to turn his wrist to make the spoon dip downward. Praise him. Once he has placed food appropriately on the spoon, go on to Step 3, his reinforcement for completing Step 2.

Step 3: Say "Eat," and gently apply pressure under his clenched hand so that he lifts the spoon containing food upward toward his mouth. Praise him. Continue to guide his hand with the spoon in it to his mouth. Your child will probably open his mouth to accept the spoon naturally. Praise him as you help him put the spoon in his mouth. If he's hungry, he'll get the idea soon enough. Be sure to praise him for each step.

Step 4: Once the spoon is in his mouth, you may need to remind him to take it out. Some children do not naturally reject the spoon from their mouth but continue to "mouth" it. Say, "Spoon down," and guide his hand, still grasping the spoon, away from his mouth and onto the table. Praise him.

If your child self-stimulates a lot with his hands or with the spoon, or if he frequently tries to put his hands in the bowl, tell him, "Hands quiet," and insist that both hands stay flat on the table until he is ready to take the next bite with his spoon. Be sure to praise for quiet hands.

When your child has swallowed the food in his mouth, begin the sequence again with, "Pick up spoon." You should discourage your child from "shoveling" his food. Make sure that your child has finished the first bite before starting to take another.

When your child has been through the entire sequence enough times that you can feel he is learning the task, begin to fade out your assistance. Start by letting him perform the last step in the sequence first on his own. For example, let your child put the spoon on the table by himself. Praise him generously. When your child has released the spoon on his own a couple of times, let him perform on his own the whole sequence of taking the spoon from his mouth and putting it on the table. Always give the verbal cue "Spoon down" at this stage and be sure to praise enthusiastically.

Continue to give less and less assistance; that is, let your child perform more and more steps on his own. Fade out your assistance *slowly,* making sure your child has had several successes at each stage before requiring him to do more by himself. Eventually, you will also want to fade out all your verbal cues. Wait a few moments before giving the cue to see if your child even needs a reminder. If he does, you may be able to indicate what the next step is by some visual cue, such as pointing at the spoon and then at the table for "Spoon down."

This sequence of behaviors was taught without the adult *modeling* appropriate use of the spoon for the child. Instead, the child was prompted through manual assistance and reinforced for each step. In the long run, it is better to teach a behavior by using a combination of modeling and physical assistance. It is a good rule to try to demonstrate (model) the action yourself before you physically prompt it. If he imitates you, you save a lot of effort. If he does not imitate you, then your demonstrating the actions (as you physically prompt him) will teach him more about imitation. The more he is taught to do in imitation of you, the easier it will be for him to learn later.

Once your child can readily feed himself with a spoon using soft foods, graduate to a bowl of bite-size portions of solid foods. You should only have to prompt getting the food on the spoon and perhaps making sure the spoon is held steady before it goes into the mouth so that food does not fall off. Your child should be able to perform the rest of the steps on his own.

You can teach the child to use a fork and a knife in the same manner. Break the task down into small steps, use verbal cues for each step, fading out your assistance slowly, beginning with the last step first.

Basic Self-help Skills

DAYTIME TOILET TRAINING

CHAPTER 15

Toilet training your child requires an initial time investment on your part. Be prepared to spend about 6 hours working on the task with your child. Using the procedure described in this chapter, adapted from the methods developed by Azrin and Foxx (1971), we have usually been successful in toilet training the child in one day. It takes a lot of work in the beginning, but after your child is trained, you both will be happier persons.

PREPARING FOR THE PROGRAM

The following suggestions should aid you in toilet training your child:

1. Your child should not be wearing diapers during training. You should have about 12 pairs of training pants on hand. You will need enough so that you can change the child into dry pants each time he soils them.
2. Your child should be able to easily manipulate his clothing. Have your child wear simple clothing, such as slacks with an elastic waistband or a short skirt.
3. Your child should be comfortable sitting on the toilet. It is important that the child need not have to struggle to keep from falling in. To avoid this problem you can use a potty chair or put a child-size toilet seat on the regular toilet. If you use a regular toilet for training, provide a low stool or block on which the child can place his feet while sitting on the toilet.
4. You should keep plenty of your child's preferred beverages on hand. You want to increase the child's fluid intake so he will eliminate more frequently.
5. You should also keep small food treats (e.g., nuts, dried fruit, candy, chips) ready in the bathroom to use as rewards. You should choose treats that will increase the child's thirst so that his fluid intake is increased.

The next section contains the major steps for the overall procedure of toilet training. Additional toilet skills are discussed in the last section.

INTENSIVE TRAINING

Step 1. *Sitting on the Toilet.* The goal of this step is to make it clear to your child that he is expected to eliminate in the toilet. This is accomplished by placing your child on the toilet and giving him many liquids to drink. Reward him profusely every time he eliminates. This step usually takes about 2 hours. During this time the child should be completely undressed in order to avoid the possible confusion of having to remove clothes. (Later, some clothing may be left on.)

If your child eliminates, praise him enthusiastically and give him hugs, liquids, and food. Remember, the more he drinks, the more often he will eliminate, and the more often he can be rewarded. After you have rewarded him for his performance, allow him to leave the bathroom for about 10 minutes to play, before returning to the toilet.

If your child does not eliminate, praise and reward him every 3 minutes or so for "Good sitting."

Step 2: *Building Independent Toileting Skills.* The goal of this step is for the child to learn to go to the toilet in order to eliminate there. Your child should be seated on a chair next to the toilet. He should still be undressed during this step.

If your child goes to the toilet and eliminates, reward him immediately, while he is still on the toilet, with liquids, hugs, and other rewards, and give him a short break. When he returns to the bathroom, place his chair a little farther away from the toilet and put training pants or underwear on him.

If your child does not eliminate after 5 minutes, reward him for "Good sitting." Remember to give him plenty of liquids.

If your child eliminates while sitting on the chair, have him go through an overcorrection procedure:

1. Reprimand him strongly for eliminating in his pants.
2. Have him clean his clothes and the chair.
3. Give him a shower. Optimally, a cold shower should be given; at least, it should not be a pleasant shower.
4. The child should not receive any rewards for a 5-minute period.
5. Place your child back on the toilet until he eliminates there.

Step 3: *Increase Toileting Skills.* The goal of this step is for your child to gradually learn to go to the toilet when it is some distance away, that is, walk to the bathroom, remove his clothing, and eliminate in the toilet. Place the chair farther away from the toilet each time your child is successful. Also, with each success, add more pieces of clothing.

If your child eliminates in the toilet, praise him enthusiastically, while he is still on the toilet. Give him a short break, and, when he returns, move his chair farther away from the toilet, and add an article of clothing.

If your child does not eliminate after 5 minutes, reward him for continuing to sit in the chair.

If your child eliminates in his pants, have him go through the overcorrection procedure outlined in Step 2. Move the chair closer to the toilet and remove an article of clothing.

You should continue with Step 3 until your child can successfully get up from the chair, go to the bathroom, remove his clothing, and go to the toilet. When your child has mastered Step 3, go on to Step 4, Maintenance.

Step 4: *Maintenance.* This step involves checking your child's pants every 15-30 minutes. Ask your child, "Are you dry?" You may have to prompt him to answer this question by helping him place his hand on the crotch area of his pants so that he can feel for wetness.

If your child is dry, praise, cuddle, and kiss him. Reward him also with some treat that he likes.

If your child is wet, reprimand him ("Bad! Wet pants!") and have him go through the overcorrection procedure. Then return to Step 3. Continue with Step 3 until your child can get up from the chair and eliminate in the toilet.

If your child independently toilets, reward him profusely.

With continued success, lengthen the time between "dry pants checks," until it is no longer necessary to check.

Fading Out Prompts and Returning to Normal Schedule

Once your child understands what is required of him, you will want to gradually fade out your physical assistance, the amount and frequency of the reinforcers, and, finally, your verbal cues. After you have followed through with this intensive training for 2 to 3 days, you will want to return to a more normal schedule:

1. Give "dry pants checks" before or after meals or snacks, and at naptime and bedtime. You may also want to have these checks at times when your child is most likely to eliminate.
2. When accidents occur, reprimand as usual, and have him go through overcorrection.
3. Avoid putting diapers on your child again. If necessary, instruct babysitters and teachers in your procedure so that they will not continue to use diapers.

ADDITIONAL TOILETING SKILLS

The following toileting skills should be taught after your child has learned successful toileting.

Wiping If your child eliminated, and it is necessary to wipe:
1. Instruct your child to "Get some paper," while helping him get enough toilet paper from the roll.
2. Praise him for getting the paper.
3. Help your child grasp the paper correctly, then say, "Wipe yourself," while helping him through the entire motion of wiping.
4. Praise him for wiping.
5. When your child has wiped himself, instruct him to "Drop the paper," while helping your child release the paper and drop it into the toilet.

Getting Off the Toilet
1. Tell your child "Stand up," or "Get down," while prompting him to do so, if necessary.
2. Praise him for getting down.

Dressing .
1. Say, "Pants up," and prompt your child by helping him take hold of the waistband of his pants and using his hands to pull the pants up to his waist.
2. Praise him for pulling up his pants.

Flushing the Toilet

1. Tell your child to flush, and prompt him by guiding his hand to the handle and pushing firmly to flush the toilet.
2. Praise him for flushing.

CHAPTER 16

DRESSING

The skills involved in learning to *undress* are not only closely related to those involved in learning to dress, but also are more easily taught. Therefore, undressing is usually taught first to ensure the success of the child.

It is recommended that "backward chaining" be used in teaching undressing and dressing. This essentially means that the child be taught the last action in a sequence of actions first, then the next to the last, and so on, until the first action in that sequence is taught last. However, you will want to prompt your child through the entire sequence a few times before insisting that he learn the individual actions himself.

UNDRESSING

Children usually learn first to take off their shoes and socks, then their pants, and then their shirts. It is recommended that you teach the items in this order and that you work with one item until the child is able to remove it by himself.

Removing Shoes and Socks
Step 1: Your child should be seated so that he can reach his shoes.
Step 2: Say, "Undo laces," or "Unbuckle," and then take his preferred hand and physically move him through the motions of untying or unbuckling his shoes. Praise him.
Step 3: Say, "Shoes off," and then take his hand and place his index finger in the heel of his shoe and push down on his hand until the shoe drops off. Praise the child then repeat the procedure for the other shoe.

Step 4: Say, "Socks off," and place the child's thumb and index finger under the top of his sock and push his hand down until the sock comes off. Praise the child and repeat the procedure with the other sock.

Step 5: Once your child seems to be trying to cooperate and has the general idea of what is expected of him, start with the *last step* in the sequence first, and let him take off the last few inches by himself. Praise him generously for doing so.

Step 6: Once your child can remove the last few inches of sock by himself, have him pull it off his heel by himself and remove it the rest of the way. Be sure to praise him.

Step 7: Continue to fade your prompts (reduce your assistance) slowly, making sure your child has had several successes at each stage before requiring him to do a little bit more by himself.

Step 8: Work backward in this manner until your child can take off his shoes and socks independently.

Step 9: Once the child knows how to take off his shoes and socks, have him do it several times (you put the socks and shoes back on after each trial) in response to your instruction "Shoes and socks off." This is to practice undressing to your command, to help bring him under verbal control.

Removing Pants

Step 1: Your child should be wearing pants with an elastic waistband or pants that can be removed without being unsnapped or unzipped.

Step 2: Say, "Pants off," and hook your child's thumbs under the waist of his pants at the side and pull his pants down with your hands over his hands. Praise him for pulling down.

Step 3: Say, "Lift your foot," and, if he does not follow this instruction, prompt him by placing your hand behind one knee and lifting his foot out of one pant leg. Repeat the procedure with the other leg. Reward his cooperation with praise.

Step 4: If this step is too difficult for your child to do standing up, then have him sit down. Say, "Sit down," and, if necessary, prompt him to do so by pushing down on his back with one hand and on his stomach with the other. This will cause him to bend over. Pushing a little more on his back will help him get the idea that he is to sit down. Once he is seated, say "Leg out," or "Pull your leg out," and help him grasp the pants while lifting one leg out of the pant leg with your hand on his shin or behind the knee. Repeat for the other leg and be sure to praise him.

Step 5: As with the shoes and socks, begin to give less assistance starting with the last action. Allow your child to lift his feet the last few inches out of his pants by himself. You can ensure success here by pressing a little harder behind his knees just before you let go so the momentum will carry his foot out of the pants leg.

Step 6: Give less and less assistance until your child lifts his feet by himself when you say, "Lift your feet."

Step 7: When your child needs only occasional reminders to lift his feet, begin fading out your assistance for pulling his pants off. Again, start out by letting him pull down the last few inches by himself. Be sure to praise your child and allow him a few successes at each stage before going to the next.

Step 8: Continue to fade your assistance until your child can perform the whole sequence when you say, "Pants off." Remember to praise at each small step. Remember to practice often in order to gain verbal control.

Basic Self-help Skills

DRESSING

Dressing should be taught in the same manner as undressing, that is, from the last action in a sequence to the first. You should, however, wait to teach fastening skills such as snapping, zipping, and buttoning until later because these tasks require more dexterity and cannot be expected of very young children. It may help to teach fastening skills by attaching fasteners to a board and guiding the child through the skills while the fasteners are in front of him before asking him to perform them on his own clothing.

As with undressing, the skill of putting on each garment should be broken down into small steps. Provide verbal cues for each step, and physically prompt when necessary. Then fade out your assistance starting with the last step. However, don't move on to the next step until the child has succeeded a number of times at the previous step. Be sure to praise him at each step.

The following steps for each garment are suggested. They are listed in the order in which you would teach them, that is, in reverse sequence.

Putting On Pants

It is easier for children if they sit down while first learning to put pants on.

Step 1:   Position waistband of pants.
Step 2:   Pull up pants from buttocks to waist.
Step 3:   Pull up pants from knees to buttocks.
Step 4:   Pull up pants from ankles to knees.
Step 5:   Stand up.
Step 6:   Push feet through pant leg holes so pants are at the ankles.
Step 7:   Put pant legs over feet (one at a time).
Step 8:   While still holding pants, reach down to feet.
Step 9:   Grasp pants at side, holding front-side up.
Step 10: Pick up pants.
Step 11: Sit down.

Putting On Shirt

Step 1:   Pull body of shirt down to waist.
Step 2:   Put arms through sleeves (one at a time).
Step 3:   Hold shirt so that arms can go through sleeves (one at a time).
Step 4:   Pull shirt over head.
Step 5:   Place shirt on top of head.
Step 6:   Hold shirt in proper position so that it will go on correctly.
Step 7:   Pick up shirt.

Putting On Socks

Step 1:   Pull on top of sock.
Step 2:   Pull the heel of sock over heel of foot.
Step 3:   Pull sock up to heel after correctly positioning it on toes.
Step 4:   Position sock on the toes.
Step 5:   Hold sock correctly, ready to be put on.
Step 6:   Pick up sock.
Step 7:   Sit down.

Putting On Shoes

Step 1: Push heel of foot into heel of shoe.
Step 2: Pull heel of shoe almost over heel of foot.
Step 3: Push foot into shoe, after correctly positioning it on toe.
Step 4: Position shoe on the toes.
Step 5: Hold shoe, correctly, ready to be put on.
Step 6: Pick up shoe.
Step 7: Sit down.

In teaching undressing and dressing skills, you have been prompting the child by physically assisting him through the action. Another method of teaching these skills is through modeling. That is, try to teach the child by having him imitate your actions. Advantages of imitation training are that the child will learn more and more to imitate you and less time will have to be spent with the tedious shaping of each separate step. You may still need to shape his behaviors but to a lesser degree than before. You should try to prompt the child's behavior through imitation of your actions and then reinforce him, instead of relying exclusively on manual (physical assistance) prompts.

CHAPTER 17

BRUSHING OR COMBING HAIR

You must decide ahead of time how your child should brush, or comb, his hair and then break it down into a logical sequence of steps. Each step should contain a verbal cue. Choose a sequence of steps that is natural for your child and appropriate for your child's haircut. These steps can include: picking up the brush with the preferred hand, brushing the hair starting at the part and stroking downward on the left and right sides, brushing the hair on the back of the head, and brushing the bangs. Additional steps include brushing the underside of the hair for long hair, or using front to back strokes rather than downward strokes. You should teach your child while he is sitting in front of a mirror so that he can see what he is doing.

The following procedures should be followed when teaching how to brush or comb hair.

Step 1: Give the command for each step, for example, "Brush back."

Step 2: Model that step by performing the action yourself. You may want to say "Do this," to get the child ready to imitate you. Praise him for imitating you. Repeat the modeling procedure for each step, if necessary.

Step 3: Once your child has the general idea of what your command means, you may want to provide physical prompts if he cannot get the feel of performing the action properly. Give the command, then guide his hand through the appropriate motion. Provide only enough assistance to allow him to complete the action. Praise him.

Step 4: When your child can perform the action, but needs a reminder, provide a visual prompt. For example, point to the back of his head for the command, "Brush back." If this prompt is sufficient, provide no further assistance and praise him when he completes the action. If the visual prompt is not sufficient, then give a physical prompt (guide the action with your hand), but only the minimum prompt needed to remind him.

Step 5: Gradually fade out (decrease) your assistance by first gradually reducing the amount of physical assistance you provide. Next, gradually reduce the amount and frequency of visual cues and prompts you provide. Finally fade the verbal instructions for each step.

When the program is completed, your child should comb or brush his hair independently when you give one instruction, "Comb hair."

TOOTH BRUSHING

CHAPTER 18

The act of tooth brushing is composed of a long and complex sequence of actions. As is the case with any complex behavior, tooth brushing should be taught in very small steps. With such a complex act, it becomes quite clear how much the program in teaching imitation (Chapter 7) can help. It would be so much easier to just demonstrate the sequence, instead of having to hand-shape every step. We hope to be able to save as much time as possible through demonstrating (modeling) the right actions, using hand-shaping when modeling fails.

The following sequence of steps is recommended as a guideline for teaching your child how to brush his teeth:

1. Turn on the water.
2. Pick up the toothbrush by its handle.
3. Wet the toothbrush.
4. Turn off the water.
5. Grasp the toothpaste tube with the nonpreferred hand.
6. Remove the toothpaste cap.
7. Set the cap down.
8. Apply toothpaste to the brush.
9. Lay the toothbrush down.
10. Replace the cap on the toothpaste.
11. Lay the toothpaste tube down.
12. Pick up the toothbrush.

Much of the information presented in this chapter has been adapted from *Project More*, University of Kansas Bureau of Child Research, Parsons State Hospital and Training Center, Parsons, Kansas.

13. Brush the outside surfaces of upper and lower teeth.
14. Brush the biting surfaces of teeth.
15. Brush the inside surfaces of upper and lower teeth.
16. Lay the toothbrush down.
17. Pick up a cup.
18. Turn on the water.
19. Fill the cup with water.
20. Turn off the water.
21. Rinse the mouth.
22. Put the cup down.
23. Wipe the mouth.
24. Turn on the water.
25. Rinse the toothbrush.
26. Lay the toothbrush down.
27. Rinse the sink.
28. Turn off the water.
29. Dry hands.
30. Put the equipment away.

This sequence of steps is recommended, not required. It may be that rearranging the order of some of the steps will be more convenient for you and your child. However, make sure that the sequence you choose contains steps that follow in a logical manner.

Before beginning to teach tooth brushing, see if your child can perform any of the above steps on his own. Provide him with all the essential materials (toothbrush, toothpaste, cup) and ask him to brush his teeth. Sometimes you can save several steps because your child already can perform part of the task. You can simply indicate to him the appropriate time to perform that action.

Once you have established the steps your child can and cannot perform on his own, choose a verbal command to accompany *each* step. You should have as many verbal commands as you have steps. Your child may not need as many steps as are recommended here. For example, if your child already understands that wetting something requires that he turn on the water, put the object under the water, and then turn off the water, Steps 1 through 4 could be combined into one step, "Wet toothbrush." Choose the right number of steps for you and your child so that he understands exactly what is required of him when you give the command for that step.

As in other complex behaviors, the best strategy for teaching your child to brush his teeth combines the techniques of modeling, imitation, and prompting. The following method is recommended for each step:

Step 1: Give the command for that step, for example, "Wet toothbrush."

Step 2: If your child can perform the necessary action just by being asked, provide no further assistance. However, be sure to praise him when he completes that step. If your child can't perform the action, show him by modeling, that is, perform the action yourself. You may need to say "Do this" to get him to imitate you. Praise him for imitating the action.

Step 3: If your child is unable to imitate the action, then prompt him by guiding his hands with yours. Gradually, over successive trials, decrease your amount of assistance.

Step 4: When your child understands which action he must perform to your command, but sometimes needs a reminder, provide a visual prompt or instruction.

Step 5: If a visual prompt is not enough of a reminder, then provide a physical prompt by guiding his hands through the action. Provide only enough assistance as is necessary to get him to perform that step. Be sure to praise him.

Step 6: Fade out (decrease) your assistance by first gradually reducing the amount of physical assistance you provide. Next, gradually reduce the amount and frequency of visual cues or prompts you provide. Then gradually fade the verbal commands.

When the program is completed, your child should be able to perform his entire tooth brushing routine when you tell him only, "Brush teeth."

REFERENCES

Azrin, N. H., and Foxx, R. M. A rapid method of toilet training the institutionalized retarded. *Journal of Applied Behavior Analysis*, 1971, *4*, 89-99.

Baker, B. L., Brightman, A. J., Heifetz, L. J., & Murphy, D. M. *Steps to independence: A skills training series for children with special needs.* Champaign, Ill.: Research Press, 1977.

Watson, L. S. *How to use behavior modification with mentally retarded and autistic children: programs for administrators, teachers, parents and nurses.* Tuscaloosa, Alabama: Behavior Modification Technology, 1972.

RECOMMENDED READINGS

Bernal, M. E., & North, J. A. A survey of parent training manuals. *Journal of Applied Behavior Analysis*, 1978, *11*, 533-544.

Foxx, R. M., & Azrin, N. H. *Toilet training the retarded: A program for day and nighttime independent toileting.* Champaign, Ill.: Research Press, 1974.

UNIT V

INTERMEDIATE LANGUAGE

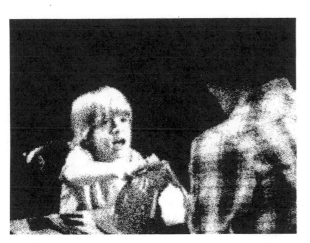

By this time your child has learned to follow certain simple instructions (Chapter 10), and is learning to imitate your speech (Chapter 11) and hopefully making some progress in both areas. It's time then, to proceed with more language training. The material in this Unit is a little more complex for your child to learn, but is not necessarily more difficult for you to teach. Programs are introduced that will help the child describe his environment more completely and his behavior more accurately.

There are two parts to language. One has to do with behaving appropriately to language as an input of information. This is receptive speech and it is illustrated in the section in which we taught the child to follow simple instructions. It is called *receptive* because the child is receiving language, and acting on it. The other part of language is called *expressive,* that is, the child himself will express in his own words what he sees, hears or feels (others may act on what he says). These two aspects of speech, receptive and expressive, are usually taught side by side, with the receptive part being presented initially, followed by the expressive counterpart. We begin by teaching a child to respond appropriately to an object (e.g., by pointing to a cup) when an adult says its name ("cup"). We teach him to *receive* what is said. Later, he is taught to *express* what he sees (e.g., he says, "cup").

Some children talk inappropriately, that is, they talk too much and when they do talk, it does not make any sense. For example, some children will echo what you say, either immediately or after a delay (they will repeat your question, such as "What's your name," instead of answering the question). Or, they will persist in repeating favorite sayings from TV commercials quite out of context, and apparently without knowing what they are saying. Or, some children will string together words in combinations that do not make any obvious sense (for example, a child who exclaims in any context, "Helicopter pillow pilot"). Although it is good that the child talks, such echolalic or psychotic talk often interferes with his social and educational adjustment. As far as we can understand, echolalic and psychotic talk is self-stimulatory behavior. Chapter 23 contains certain programs to help the child decrease such talk.

Some children have serious difficulty in both receiving and expressing vocal language. If you have worked with a child for several months and he is making no progress on verbal imitation, or on receptive (vocal) labeling, then consider teaching him to *sign* instead of vocalizing. Sometimes signing programs facilitate the development of vocal language, and other times they provide a good substitute. In any case, keep in mind that some children may have serious problems with understanding vocal (auditory) input and may do relatively better with manual signs (visual input). But try vocal training first, because it is most practical in our society.

The training protocols for intermediate language are presented in some detail. This may seem redundant, since they are similar to those in the earlier chapters, but we decided to present them in detail, to be on the safe side.

Giving names to (labeling) objects (with nouns) and simple actions (with verbs) are among the most fundamental of language skills. Your child must learn to comprehend and use the names of "things" and "actions" in order to interact and communicate with other people. This Unit describes a set of programs that can be used to teach your child to understand and use a variety of names or labels that will be necessary in his everyday interactions.

The first four chapters of this Unit cover the following areas: 1) understanding names of objects, or receptive object labeling, in which the child learns to respond to instructions such as "Touch *cup*," or "Touch *book*"; 2) learning to name objects or expressive object labeling, in which the child is taught to answer questions such as "What is this?" and "What do you want?"; 3) understanding names of simple actions, or receptive action labeling, in which the child learns to perform or indicate an action when given instructions to do so, such as "Walk," or "Show me jumping"; and 4) learning to verbalize the names of actions, or expressive action labeling, in which the child is taught to respond to the question, "What are you (or am I, or is he) doing?", using a verb to describe the action. Your child must learn a great number of names or labels in each category in order to interact effectively with other people.

Please note that the separation of receptive and expressive label training in this manual is somewhat artificial. After the initial stages of the program, receptive and expressive labeling should be practiced and trained concurrently. Receptive and expressive training should be intermixed particularly in the generalization portions of the programs.

Remember that the program on language in this book is an introduction to language; it's meant to get you going. If you feel you are making progress, and want to do more than what is suggested here, then you may want to read about the extension of this program in a book specifically on teaching language, *The Autistic Child: Language Development through Behavior Modification* (Lovaas, 1977).

RECEPTIVE OBJECT LABELING

CHAPTER 19

The procedure for receptive labeling is most easily carried out with objects placed on a small table between you and your child or with you and your child seated next to one another with the objects on a table in front of you. A large number of common, everyday objects should be used in this program.

FIRST LABEL

We chose a cup for a first object because it is frequently encountered. It is important to pick an object that is familiar and that he can handle. Any number of objects, such as a truck, a doll, or a ball, or foods, such as toast or cereal, can be used. You are particularly fortunate if your child can point to an object before he has received any formal training. If so, *start with the objects he can name already.* It is true in labeling, as it was in teaching him imitation and to follow instructions, that the child may already "know" some of these objects, but he does not use them that often. Your job now is to get control over these early labels, by rewarding correct responses, and punishing incorrect ones, as well as punishing the child's failure to cooperate. Determine at the start (by observing, or, if you are the child's teacher, by asking his parents) what the child already can name (even if he is unreliable at it) and get control over those labels first. It will save you a great deal of time.

Step 1: Remove all objects from the table, out of sight and reach of the child. Begin training by placing the cup, on the table about 1 to 2 feet in front of the child. Then present your instructions to the child, in this case, "Touch cup." If the child responds to criterion, go on to the second label. If the child responds incorrectly for five trials, go on to Step 2.

Step 2: *The visual prompt.* You can prompt the child's response by placing your hand on the cup so that the child will do likewise. If the child fails to imitate this action, follow the procedure given in Step 4, the physical prompt. A correct response has occurred when the child imitates you by reaching out and placing his fingers on the cup in response to the command "Touch cup." Reward the child with praise and food. When the child has responded correctly (imitated your action) for 5 consecutive trials, go on to Step 3.

Step 3: *Fading the visual prompt.* To fade the visual prompt, you first move your hand toward the cup, without actually touching it. Then you gradually reduce how much you move your hand in the direction of the cup, until you aren't moving your hand at all. Reinforce each correct response, and, when the child responds to criterion, go on to the second label.

Step 4: *The physical prompt.* A physical prompt may be necessary if the child fails to imitate you, or if, as previously noted, the child imitates so well that he fades his response as you fade your prompt. In either case, physically prompt the correct response by taking the child's hand and placing it on the cup. Then remove your hand and reinforce the child after he has kept his hand on the cup for 2 or 3 seconds. Gradually and systematically fade, or reduce, this prompt by pulling more lightly on the child's hand and releasing his hand sooner and sooner before it has reached the cup. Continue training until the child touches the cup on your command without any physical prompt at all (e.g., *your* hand stays in your lap or at your edge of the table). After the child responds to criterion, begin to teach the second label.

SECOND LABEL

In order to minimize the child's confusion, the second object chosen for label training should be quite different in physical form and in function from the first object. Thus, if a cup were the first object, a glass, similar in shape to a cup and also used for drinking, would be a poor choice for the second object. In addition, the labels or names of the two objects should be maximally different. For instance, if "Cup" were the first label trained, "Cookie" would be a poor choice as a second word, because both words start with a "k" sound. Also, they have very similar functions—both go in the mouth. A good choice for the second label would be a doll, for which the command would be "Touch doll." A shoe would be another good choice.

Step 1: Remove all items from the table except for the doll being used for training. Place the doll on the table in front of the child. Give the instruction, "Touch doll." If the child responds to criterion, go on to discrimination training using random rotation. If the child makes five consecutive errors, go to Step 2.

Steps 2-4: These steps are carried out in exactly the same manner as those in the first label. When the child has mastered this second label, go on to random rotation.

RANDOM ROTATION

Step 1: Once the child has reached criterion on the second object (doll), the first object (cup) is again presented by itself. Conduct several test trials to ensure that the child still responds correctly to the instruction, "Touch cup." If the child does not respond correctly, the correct response should be retrained.

Step 2: The second object is reintroduced. The trials are presented (following the procedure in Step 1, above) until the child responds correctly with no prompt for five consecutive trials.

Step 3: Steps 1 and 2 are repeated until little or no prompting is needed the first time that an object is presented.

Step 4: The two objects are presented in random rotation. The random rotation procedure is reviewed below to reduce any chance of misunderstanding.

Place both objects on the table about 1 to 2 feet from the child and about 1 foot apart. Present one command, e.g., "Touch doll," and reinforce the child with praise and food if he is correct. On succeeding trials, you must alternate your instructions in a random fashion so that the child cannot use the pattern of commands rather than your actual commands as a basis for responding. For instance, on a series of trials you might ask for: cup, cup, doll, cup, doll, doll, doll, cup, doll. In addition, the position of the two objects should be alternated in a random fashion during the series of trials in order to prevent the child from associating a command with a position (right or left) rather than with the object being named. A typical sequence of trials might show one object in the following positions: R(ight)-L(eft)-R-R-L-R-L-L-L-R. If the child responds to criterion, then he can discriminate between objects and you may go on to teach a third label. If your child responds incorrectly for five trials, go back and retrain both labels separately, then begin random rotation again.

THE PROMPTS

The simultaneous presentation of the two objects and the requirement that the child learn to select the correct item on the basis of your verbal cue may be quite difficult. There are several procedures for prompting a correct response, and you should try each one until you find one that is comfortable for you and successful with your child. Let us illustrate two procedures.

Proximity Prompting

This procedure involves placing the object named in your instructions closer to the child than the other object. On the first trial, place one object (the cup) 1 foot from the child and the other object (the doll) 2 feet from the child, then say, "Touch cup." On succeeding trials you continue to say, "Touch cup," as you gradually move the cup back into line with the doll. You must choose the side (left or right) on which the cup is placed in a random fashion as you fade the proximity cue. Remember to allow the child a few successes at each level of prompting before moving the cup closer into line with the doll. Continue to present trials until the cup is back in line with the doll. After the child has responded correctly to the command, "Touch cup," with no prompt for five consecutive trials, you begin to say, "Touch doll." On the first trial, place the doll about 1 foot from the child and the cup 2 feet away from the child. On succeeding trials fade the proximity prompt, that is, move the doll back into line with the cup, as you did before with the cup. Continue to present trials until the child has responded to "Touch doll" correctly without a prompt for five consecutive trials. Repeat the prompting procedure for cup, then for doll, and so on, each time decreasing the distance of the proximity prompt used on the first trial (from 6 inches to 4 inches to 2 inches) and fading until the child needs, at most, one prompted trial each time you present a command for the first time.

Now use random rotation when presenting the two commands. Some slight proximity prompting may be needed for several trials. Continue to present trials until the child has responded to criterion. Your child now has learned his first receptive label discrimination.

Modeling

This procedure is most appropriate for the child who readily imitates. Select a matching set of objects for yourself and for the child. Place the objects on the table so that your array is a mirror image of the child's. Give the instruction, "Touch cup," and prompt the child to touch his cup by modeling the response, that is, by touching your cup. On succeeding trials, randomly alternate the two commands and the left-right positions of the objects. Remember that the positions of the objects in your's and the child's set should always match. Over a series of trials, reduce the modeling prompt by coming less and less close to touching the objects in your set. Remember to allow the child to succeed at a given level of prompting a few times before reducing the modeling prompt further. Continue to present trials until the child has responded to criterion, without prompting. You now have taught your child his first receptive labeling discrimination.

LABELING OTHER OBJECTS

Once the child has learned to identify two objects, go on to teach him to identify other objects in his environment. You should always present a new object by itself and teach the child to respond to this object following the procedure outlined above for the first and second labels. Each time the child has learned a new object label in isolation, it should be presented simultaneously with two or more objects that he can already name. As the child builds a repertoire of receptive objects labels that he can discriminate, you should present many combinations of these items to be sure the child has learned each label well.

GENERALIZATION TRAINING

When the child has mastered six or more labels you should begin generalization training. The child must learn to identify other examples of an object correctly, not just the single item with which he has been trained. For instance, you want to teach your child to identify all cups, not only the cup with which he was trained. At first, training should be extended to items that are quite similar to the original object. Gradually, you should introduce objects that are more diverse. You may need to use prompts during generalization training. Follow the same procedure you used in teaching matching (Chapter 8). Continue training until the child can correctly identify a new member of a class (e.g., a type of cup that he has never been asked to label) the first time it is presented. When your child can correctly identify a member of a class the first time he is asked to do so, he has a "concept" of that class.

Once your child can easily label a variety of objects of different classes, you should begin to generalize his use of these labels to new situations. For instance, you should place items that he can label around the living room (e.g., a cup on a coffee table, a doll on the floor, a ball on a chair) and ask him to find them. You should regularly quiz your child on the names of objects he encounters in his environment (e.g., the cup from which he is drinking, or his shirt). In essence, you must extend your training into every possible part of your child's daily life. Only in this way will he become competent in generalizing skills he acquires in the more structured therapy sessions to the less structured real world.

The following list contains suggested items you may want to teach. You may want to add items not on the list or forego teaching others. Your primary consideration should be to choose items for training with which your child has frequent contact.

cup	doll	foot	juice	tummy
cookie	block	milk	pen	head
banana	shirt	shoe	eyes	sock
pants	book	knee	truck	car
apple	teeth	boat	bowl	cereal
toast	meat	ball	brush	ear

CHAPTER 20

EXPRESSIVE OBJECT LABELING

After your child has learned to identify (point to) approximately 10 objects receptively, you may begin to teach him to name these objects, that is, to use *expressive* labeling.

In this program, your child will learn to say the name of an object when he is shown that object and asked, "What is it?" A large number of common, everyday objects should be used in this program, starting with the same objects used in teaching receptive language (Chapter 19). Moreover, the child should now know how to verbally imitate you when you give the names of the objects chosen for training (through the verbal imitation training).

FIRST LABEL

Step 1: You and your child should sit facing each other across a table. Place an object on the table in front of the child. In the beginning, you may want to choose objects that your child wants, such as foods or a favorite toy, since you want to teach him to ask for these objects by name, and to get them when asked. For example, if you start with "Cookie," the child should be expected to say "Cookie" before you give it to him. This serves to make his speech practical and functional, which also strengthens it. Place a cookie on the table and as soon as the child looks at the cookie, ask, "What is it?" It is important that the onset of the trial, that is, the placement of the cookie on the table and your question "What is it?" be as distinct, succinct, or discrete as possible, so that it catches the child's attention. If the child answers to criterion, go on to the second label. If the child responds incorrectly or fails to respond for five consecutive trials, go on to Step 2.

Step 2: *The prompt.* Place the cookie on the table. Do *not* ask the child "What is it?" As soon as the child looks at the cookie, prompt the correct response by saying "Cookie." If the child imitates you accurately, immediately reinforce him and remove the cookie from the table until the beginning of the next trial. The interval between trials may be anywhere from 3 to 5 seconds, long enough to make the beginning of each trial discrete and definite, that is, the trial should have a clear onset, so as to catch the child's attention. If the child fails to respond correctly for five consecutive trials when you use the whole word as a prompt, you may suspend work with that object, and begin training a different object with a label that the child can imitate.

Step 3: *Fading the prompt.* After the child has correctly labeled the object for five trials with a full prompt (the entire word), you should begin to *fade or reduce the prompt.* Gradually reduce the amount of the word that is used to prompt the response and the loudness with which the prompt is spoken. For instance, "Cookie" might first be faded to "co" at full volume, then to "k" at intermediate volume, and finally to a whispered "k". The child should respond correctly with the full word "cookie" at a given level of prompting a few times before the prompt is further reduced. When the child has responded correctly at least five times to a minimal prompt, the prompt should be eliminated. At this point, the cue for the child to respond is the appearance of the object on the table in front of him. Control over his saying "Cookie" has been shifted from your saying "Cookie" to the sight of the cookie on the table. The training procedure is completed when the child correctly labels the object to criterion without prompting.

Almost always, if you now were to place *any* object in front of him, the child will say, "Cookie." It is not until he has a second label that he begins to learn that different objects have different labels.

SECOND LABEL

The second label is taught in the same way as the first. Remember that the second object chosen for training should be quite different in form and function from the first, and, in addition, the labels of the two objects should be maximally different. If "Cookie" was the first label, "Ball" may be the second. Teach him to label the second object to criterion, the same way as you taught the first label.

RANDOM ROTATION

Step 1: After the child has correctly labeled the second word to criterion, the first label is again presented by itself. If the child does not label the object correctly for five trials, prompt the response. The first prompt should be the weakest one used in training the word, for instance, a whispered "k" sound for cookie. If this prompt fails to elicit a correct response, a stronger prompt should be tried on the next trial. Continue to increase the strength of the prompt on succeeding trials until the prompt is strong enough to produce a correct response. After a correct response has been elicited, the prompt is then gradually faded in the same way as in the initial fading. Trials are presented until the child responds correctly, with no prompt, for five consecutive trials.

Step 2: The second object is then reintroduced. Trials are presented (following the procedure in Step 1, above) until the child responds correctly with no prompt for five consecutive trials.

Step 3: Steps 1 and 2 are repeated until little or no prompting is needed the first time that an object is presented.

Step 4: The two objects are next presented in random rotation. Slight prompting may be necessary on the first few trials. (If slight prompting is insufficient to elicit correct responding, return to Steps 1-3.) Training with random rotation should continue until the child responds to criterion.

Once the child has begun to label or name objects, and can identify several objects when asked to do so, you have made a good beginning on language. Much of the hard work is done because many of the later programs are elaborations on the two we just discussed. There is much work ahead, but it will not be as tricky as building verbal imitation and teaching the first meaningful words.

LABELING OTHER OBJECTS

The procedure for teaching other words is the same as that used to teach the first two words. After the child learns each new label, you should mix presentations of the new word with presentations of labels learned earlier until the child responds to criterion. Remember to choose objects that have already been used in receptive label training and whose labels the child can imitate.

GENERALIZATION TRAINING

Begin generalization training after the child has learned six expressive labels. The procedure for generalizing expressive labels is the same as that described in the section on receptive object labeling. Remember that this step is crucial in the child's language development because he must learn "concepts," not just labels of single objects and he must learn to use language all day, every day, not only in structured therapy sessions.

TEACHING "WHAT IS IT?"

After the child has mastered perhaps a half dozen labels, you should begin asking the question, "What is it?" when presenting the object to be labeled. This question is not asked in the preliminary stages of training, since it may block a good response to the prompt, and conceivably also block the child's attention to the training stimulus. In the early stages of training, if possible, you should say only the prompt word. In general, the less you say at first, the better.

If the child echoes the question instead of labeling the object or echoes the question just before giving the label, see the later section on procedures to control echolalia (Chapter 23).

TEACHING "WHAT DO YOU WANT?"

After the child has learned to respond correctly to "What is it?", training can begin on, "What do you want?" Place one object on the table. The object must be one that the child would like to have (a favorite food or toy) *and* that he can label expressively. When the child visually fixates on the objects, you ask, "What do you *want*?" If the child fails to respond, then you should prompt the response (e.g., say, "What do you want? (pause) *"Cookie"*). The prompt is then faded. In the beginning of this training, you may find it helpful to ask the question, "What do you want" at low decibel level and quickly, while saying the prompt, "Cookie," loudly and clearly. Later, raise the decibel level of the question and fade the prompt. When the child has mastered this phase of the program, you should begin to place two or more items that the child would like to have on the table before asking the child "What do you want?" The child is then given the object that he labels. Thus, in this phase of the procedure, the child learns that he must name the item that he wants. Once the child can answer the question correctly, he should be required to ask for (by labeling) any desired item or action (such as food, toys, hugs, "open door" to get out, "up" to get picked up, "down" to get off the chair) before he receives it.

Additional objects are introduced for labeling in the same manner as was suggested for other discriminations (such as the receptive labels).

CHAPTER 21

RECEPTIVE ACTION LABELING

Once your child has learned to identify and name objects, you can begin to teach him how to identify and name behaviors or actions. That is, after he has learned to point to and name objects such as milk, cookie, truck, and doll, he can learn to do the same with words that describe actions, such as standing, sitting, jumping, and laughing.

The program for teaching your child to perform actions in response to your instructions is similar to the procedure for teaching him to follow verbal instructions (outlined in Chapter 10). We describe the training program again here, with the intent of elaborating on some of the more complex behaviors.

"WALK TO (PERSON/OBJECT)"

This task teaches the child to walk to another person in the room (if one is present) or to walk to an object in the room (e.g., a table).

Step 1: You and your child should be seated approximately five steps from the person or object to be approached (for example, the child's father). Present the instruction "Walk to daddy" to the child. If the child responds to criterion, go on to the second behavior. If the child responds incorrectly for five trials, go on to Step 2.

Step 2: *The prompt.* This and similar behaviors are most easily taught by having the child imitate you. Thus, after saying, "Walk to daddy," you should say, "Do this," then stand up, turn in the direction of the person to be approached, and walk to that person. If the child fails to imitate you for five trials, use physical prompts to get the child to do what you have requested. For example, you can prompt the child to stand by placing your hands on his upper arms and pulling him up. You can then turn him in the appropriate direction with your hands in the same position on his upper arms. Finally, you can prompt him to walk to the specified person or object by taking him by the hand, or by pushing him from behind if necessary. When the child reaches the person or the object, he should be rewarded immediately with food and praise.

Step 3: *Fading the prompt.* Gradually and systematically fade or reduce any physical prompts you may be using. Begin by pushing the child more and more lightly and for fewer steps to get him to walk. Next, touch his arms more and more lightly to get him to stand and turn in the appropriate direction until you need not touch him at all. While you fade or reduce the physical prompts, continue to perform the action yourself. Thus, when the physical prompts are completely faded, the child should be imitating you. Now you must fade your modeling (demonstration) of the behavior so that the child can perform the behavior on his own in response to your instructions. As with most of the other training procedures we have described, you fade the prompts starting at the end of the behavioral sequence, that is, starting with the last step in the sequence. In this case, that step is walking with the child to the appropriate person or object. Thus, you should gradually walk a shorter and shorter distance with the child until he is walking the entire distance alone. It may be necessary to introduce and then fade (gradually eliminate) a push from behind to get the child going when you are no longer walking with him. Next, you should fade the prompt of turning in the desired direction by turning less and less. Again, the use of a light physical prompt to turn the child when you are no longer turning with him may be used and then gradually faded. Finally, you should fade the prompt of standing with the child by standing to less and less of your full height and by returning to a sitting position once the child is standing. Use a light physical prompt if necessary to get the child to stand when you are no longer performing the action, and to keep him standing when you are returning to a sitting position. Eventually the prompt may be so much faded that you only nod your head in the appropriate direction. When the child can stand, turn, and walk to the appropriate person or object unassisted and without a model (someone to imitate) to criterion, begin teaching the next receptive verb label.

"JUMP TO (PERSON/OBJECT)"

The second receptive verb label is taught in exactly the same manner as the first was trained. If you are using an object rather than a second person in the training procedure, be sure that you use the *same* object in teaching both behaviors. When the child has learned the second receptive label (e.g., jumping to the person or object on command), go on to random rotation.

RANDOM ROTATION

Step 1: Reintroduce the first command ("Walk to *Person/Object*"). If the child does not respond correctly for five trials, prompt the response. Begin by using a weak prompt, for instance, walk one or two steps. If this prompt fails to elicit a correct response, try a stronger prompt on the next trial. Continue to increase the strength of the prompt on succeeding trials until the child responds correctly. After a correct response has been elicited, fade the prompt in the same way as in the initial training. Continue to present trials until the child responds correctly, with no prompt, for five consecutive trials.

Step 2: The second command ("Jump to *Person/Object*") is now reintroduced. Present trials (following the procedure in Step 1, above) until the child responds correctly, with no prompt, for five consecutive trials. Make sure that the emphasis in your voice is on the word "walk" and on "jump," to help your child discriminate.

Step 3: Repeat Steps 1 and 2 until the child makes no more than one error the first time you give the instruction.

Step 4: The two instructions are presented in rotation. Slight prompting may be necessary on the first few trials. (If slight prompting does not produce correct responding, return to Steps 1-3.) Rotation should continue until the child responds to criterion.

LATER BEHAVIORS

The procedure for teaching other receptive verb labels in which the child performs the action is the same as that used to teach the first two labels. After the child learns each new receptive label, you should mix presentations of the new label with presentations of labels learned earlier until the child responds to criterion. Other beginning labels you may choose to teach in this manner are:

run	eat	throw (the ball)
lie down	drink	roll (the ball)
crawl	wave bye-bye	kick (the ball)

GENERALIZATION TRAINING

It is critical that your child use the labels he learns during structured therapy in nonstructured situations. Give your child commands using the receptive verb labels he knows whenever the opportunity arises in your daily interactions. For instance, ask your child to "Walk to car" instead of leading him by the hand, and ask him to "Open door" and "Wave bye-bye" to friends. Only through extensive practice will your child become proficient at using these labels. Let him do it, rather than your doing it for him.

PICTURE TRAINING

Next you may want to teach the child to identify the actions or behaviors of people in pictures. Pictures are useful teaching tools because they can illustrate actions that may be difficult for people to perform during therapy (e.g., sleeping or riding a bicycle). This task is taught in exactly the same manner as that outlined for receptive object labeling. However, pictures are substituted for objects. Initially each picture should show one person engaging in a single activity, such as eating or sleeping. Typical instructions used in this task would be "Touch eating" or "Point to sleeping."

When selecting pictures for labeling and discrimination training, be sure to select pictures that clearly illustrate the activity you want to teach the child to identify. You should select activities in which the child engages or that he sees others engage in frequently. Thus, in the early stages of training, you would probably not want to select a picture of a person skiing; a picture of a person driving a car would be more appropriate. As with object selection, initially try to select verb labels that sound maximally dissimilar to assist the child in discriminating the commands and to aid in later expressive language training. Finally, in the early stages of this training, try to present the various activities in pairs that are easily discriminated visually as well as auditorily. Thus, walking versus running may be a difficult discrimination early in training, as might be sitting versus eating (since eating usually occurs while seated). You should wait until the child can identify these pictures well when they are presented in combination with other activities before presenting them together. Just keep in mind, you want the child to respond correctly as often as possible. You can help this occur by presenting easy tasks first and *gradually* increasing the level of difficulty for the child. If the child is doing poorly, it is probably because you have proceeded too rapidly for him.

It is interesting to check and see the extent to which your child will be able to identify two-dimensional representations (as in pictures) of real-life three-dimensional behaviors. The question also arises as to whether he will be able to identify real-life three-dimensional behaviors, after having learned to identify these behaviors in pictures. With some training back and forth he should learn.

The list below contains examples of actions you may want to teach:

walking	driving	frowning
waving	sitting	kissing
jumping	standing	brushing teeth
cooking	reading	combing hair
eating	writing	swinging
sleeping	smiling	throwing

EXPRESSIVE ACTION LABELING

CHAPTER 22

You may begin this program when your child has learned to identify eight to ten behaviors. Your child will now learn to say the name of a behavior that he has just performed or has seen you perform. He also will learn to name behaviors illustrated in pictures. The first behaviors you choose for training should be behaviors he has already learned to label receptively. Continue to work on the preceding programs while you work through this program.

Essentially you will teach your child to name actions that you or he perform. The procedure for teaching expressive *action* labeling is quite similar to teaching expressive *object* labeling. There are only two main differences: 1) instead of showing the child an object you show him an action (which you or he performs), and 2) you ask him, "What am I doing?" instead of, "What is it?"

FIRST LABEL

Step 1: You and your child should sit facing each other. You stand up and simultaneously ask, "What am I doing?" If the child answers correctly, by saying "Standing" to criterion, go on to the second label. If he answers incorrectly or fails to answer for five trials, go on to Step 2.

Step 2: *The prompt.* To prompt the correct response, stand up and say, "Standing." Do *not* say, "What am I doing?" If the child imitates you accurately, immediately reinforce him. Sit down and stand up again, making the stimulus discrete. If the child fails to respond correctly for five trials when you use the whole word as a prompt you may either teach the child to imitate the label "Standing" (as in Chapter 10) or suspend work with this action and begin training with an action the name of which the child can imitate.

Step 3: *Fading the prompt.* The prompt (presentation of the correct response, "Standing") should be faded or gradually eliminated in the same manner as in earlier procedures. When the prompt has been eliminated, the cue for your child to respond will be your performance of the action (standing).

SECOND LABEL

The second label is trained in the same way as the first. Remember to choose an action that has been mastered as a receptive verb label. Waving the hand is a good behavior to pick.

RANDOM ROTATION

Present the first action to the child. If the child names it correctly, then present the second action. If he names the action incorrectly for five trials, go back and retrain that label, before presenting the other action. Alternate the presentation of the two actions until the child is consistently making no more than one error the first time an action is performed. At this point, you should begin random rotation of the two actions.

LABELING OTHER ACTIONS

The procedure for training other expressive verb labels and discriminations is the same as that outlined above.

TEACHING "WHAT AM I DOING?"

After the child has mastered labels for three or four actions, you should begin asking the question "What am I doing?" when performing the action to be labeled. If the child echoes the question instead of labeling the action or along with the label, see Chapter 23 for stopping echolalia.

PICTURE TRAINING

It is difficult to perform certain actions, such as riding a bicycle or sleeping, during a therapy session. For these actions, you should use pictures instead of live demonstrations in the initial stages of training. In all other respects, training is the same as described above. Remember to choose actions for training that have been mastered as receptive verb labels.

GENERALIZATION TRAINING

Generalization of expressive verb labels should be carried out in a variety of ways. First (and easiest for the child) persons other than the therapist should perform actions that the child can name and ask the child, "What am I doing?" Later you should ask, "What is he (she) doing?" while pointing to a second person who is performing an action that the child can label. In addition, you should have the child perform behaviors that he can name and then ask, "What are you doing?" Once the child has mastered these variations of the basic task, you should ask him to label actions that he can name as they occur in his everyday life and as they are seen in pictures. As noted before, in the early stages of each phase of generalization training, some prompting may be required.

CHAPTER 23

STOPPING ECHOLALIA AND PSYCHOTIC TALK

Many developmentally disabled children are mute (do not verbalize) when you start to work with them; that is, their language or verbal output is nonexistent, or is restricted to occasional vowels or consonants that appear in a random or meaningless fashion. Some children may evidence a great deal of speech, even though the speech appears to have no immediate meaning or significance for social communication. A child's speech may be echolalic when he repeats, either partially or completely, sentences that he hears other people say. The echolalia may be *immediate,* as when he echoes within seconds what an adult just said, or *delayed* in the sense that the child echoes words or sentences that he heard the preceding hour, or morning, or even weeks ago.

Other children have relatively elaborate speech, which does not appear to be echolalic. Instead the speech may be unusual word combinations ("word salads") that do not make any sense, such as "partridge hammock cake down eyelash," or the speech may be meaningful but it occurs out of context. An example of the latter is the case of a child who spends a great deal of his day describing elevators, clocks, or dates and calendars to anyone he meets and independent of what is actually happening at the time. Such inappropriate statements have been called psychotic talk.

Psychotic and echolalic talk directly interfere with the child's ability to generate appropriate speech. This is seen very clearly when you try to teach a child a simple question and in so doing block his opportunity to generate the right response. There will be many other reasons why you will want to help a child overcome echolalic or psychotic talk; for instance, the presence of such speech can delay cognitive development by interfering with learning processes. Echolalic and psychotic talk, and procedures to overcome them, are described in more detail below.

ECHOLALIA

Echolalic talk is not restricted to autistic children or to psychotic children, although it is often considered an indication of those conditions. Echolalia occurs in normal language development; it peaks around 30

149

months of age, then decreases. Echolalic speech can also be observed in children who have experienced recent traumatic brain injury.

The presence of echolalic speech in a child who is beginning therapy gives the child a better prognosis for learning language than if he were mute. Even though the child may not know the meaning of the words and word combinations he is echoing, he knows how to talk. If the child didn't have echolalic speech, then a great deal of time would have to be spent in teaching him to form sounds and words and word combinations. So, for no other reason than that time is saved, the echolalic child is far ahead of his mute peers. Children who are mute, but who later become good at speaking with language training, do so after they have passed through a stage of developing echolalic responding. The previously mute children who do not enter an echolalic stage rarely become good at using language, at least not vocal language. Therefore, it is to the child's advantage to learn to echo, even if he doesn't do so before you begin working with him. The child clearly has to go beyond echolalic (or psychotic) talk in order to function more adequately on an interpersonal level, to problem solve, and otherwise to improve in his cognitive functioning.

Why children echo is hard to say. It is unlikely that they echo because they are rewarded or reinforced for doing so by people who listen to them. In other words, echolalia is probably not operant behavior based on socially controlled *extrinsic* reinforcement, but instead it may be operant behavior based on *intrinsic* reinforcement, like self-stimulatory behavior. The child's reinforcement may consist of his matching what he hears himself say to what he has heard other people say. In other words, the reinforcer is to match, and in that sense the child gives himself his own reinforcement. Notice how closely and how beautifully some children track the nuances of other people's speech; in fact, some children have several voices, imitating their mother's intonations, their father's, and perhaps also their teacher's. Echolalia can be viewed as storing or otherwise preserving in the brain the auditory input from one's surrounding environment. In that sense echolalic speech would be analogous to a visual afterimage. So, it may be useful to retain certain aspects of it, as an "internal" rehearsal. Procedures for helping the child move past overt echolalic responding are described below.

OVERCOMING ECHOLALIA

An echolalic student is likely to echo statements that he does not understand. For example, if you say, "Point to your head," and if the child knows how to follow that command, then he will not echo that command. On the other hand, if you were to say, "Point to your cranium," then it is likely that the child would echo the statement and not follow the command. This means that you should observe some decrease in echolalic responding as the child acquires meaningful language. In any case, you may observe considerable echolalia even if the child is learning a great deal of language because he will remain ignorant of correct answers to most questions.

One procedure for stopping echolalic speech to unfamiliar statements (commands, requests) has been provided by Schreibman and Carr (1978). Echolalic children were taught to answer "I don't know," as a general nonecholalic response to questions or statements they did not comprehend. The procedure can be outlined as follows:

Step 1: Have the child sit in a chair facing you, perhaps opposite you at a small table. As usual, have the child sit quietly, without self-stimulating, and visually attending to you. Select four or five questions to which the child does not know the answers: for example, "Why do birds sing?" "Where is London?" "How many brothers and sisters do you have?" or "Why do sailboats move?" There are many similar "How," "Why," "Who," and "Where" type questions that you might find more appropriate for your particular child. You should also select some questions to which you know your child already knows the answers, for example, "What's your name?" "How old are you?" "Who is that?" (while pointing to his mother). Now present the first question, for example, "Why do birds sing?", very quickly, and at a low decibel level (in a whisper). Then immediately state the answer, "I don't know," very loudly. Try experimenting with the volume of your voice until the child echoes the correct answer and not the question. Reinforce him heavily for a correct response.

Step 2: In very gradual steps, begin to raise the decibel level (loudness) of your question while gradually lowering the decibel level of the answer. If the child begins to echo the question during this process, give him a sharp "No" and backtrack a little by decreasing the loudness of the question.

You do not want him to echo the question; in fact, you prevent this by rewarding him for being quiet, for withholding his response in the presence of the question. This very promising technique of presenting the cues for the wrong answer at a very low intensity teaches the child to tolerate or not to respond to the presence of the wrong cue.

Step 3: Eventually, ask the question "Why do birds sing?" in a normal voice, and withhold the answer. The child has mastered the task when he withholds echolalia and gives the correct answer, "I don't know," without prompt and to criterion.

Step 4: Once you have trained the response "I don't know" to questions such as "Why do birds sing?", then introduce a question to which he already knows the answer, for example, "What's your name?" (The child says his name, and is reinforced.) If he fails to respond, or responds incorrectly, prompt the correct answer, then reinforce to reestablish correct responding. The importance of introducing questions to which he already knows the answer and intermixing them with questions to which he does *not* know the answer is to retain the discrimination between what he knows and does not know. It should help him avoid learning to say "I don't know" to all questions.

Step 5: Present another question, such as "Where is London?", and train the correct response, "I don't know," to that question, continuing to intermix questions to which he knows the answer.

If you continue this procedure using questions that start with "how," "why," "when," and "where" intermixed with questions to which the child does know the answer, you will find that after a while the child will spontaneously answer "I don't know" to a question to which he does not know the answer even when you present this question for the first time (that is, without prior training). You may say now that he knows what the "rule" is. In any case, through this procedure you can help a child terminate his echolalic responding in a variety of situations.

PSYCHOTIC TALK

In general, it is probably safe to assume that psychotic talk is self-reinforcing and will not disappear or decrease markedly if you place it on extinction or use time-out. Many children will persist in expressing psychotic talk, even though they can also talk appropriately, apparently because psychotic talk is so reinforcing to them. There should be some replacement of psychotic speech by appropriate language, since appropriate language gives the child access to many of the self-stimulatory reinforcers previously available to him only through psychotic speech. That is, appropriate speech may come to substitute for the (self-stimulatory) properties of psychotic speech. In most instances, however, psychotic speech will stay at a high level, and in those instances we must actively intervene to eliminate the psychotic talk.

OVERCOMING PSYCHOTIC TALK

The treatment rationale behind programs to stop inappropriate and psychotic talk is that the presence of a great deal of psychotic talk socially isolates a child. It makes him stand out like a sore thumb with his friends at school or in the community. You want to help him suppress psychotic talk just as you help him suppress other kinds of self-stimulatory behaviors.

Start by giving the child a sharp "No!" (or other kind of disapproval) immediately after his psychotic production. You may want to say "No, no silly talk," in an attempt to help him discriminate why he is being admonished. (However, there is no guarantee that he will make the discrimination.) A better way might be to teach a child to talk "silly" (that is, psychotic) on cue. Teach him to talk "silly" or to echo when you say "Talk silly and echo," and reinforce him for talking psychotically or echoing at that time. Then switch and say, "*Don't* talk silly and *don't* echo," and reinforce him for withholding his response at that time. The main justification for going through such a procedure is to teach the child to discriminate between appropriate and inappropriate speech. Although we as adults clearly know the discrimination, it is obvious that psychotic and retarded persons do not.

CHAPTER 24

SIGN LANGUAGE
Edward G. Carr

A *significant* number of developmentally disabled children show marked improvement in their receptive and expressive verbal ability when they are trained using the techniques described throughout this manual. However, some children show only minimal gains. For them, sign language is a useful alternative to verbal language. In addition, there are children who acquire fairly good receptive verbal skills but whose expressive verbal behavior remains so poorly articulated that no one can understand them. These children, too, can profit from being taught to express themselves through signs.

A word of caution is in order concerning who should *not* be taught sign language. Signing should not be taught to very young children (less than 4 years of age) whose language simply may be delayed or to children who have not yet received very much verbal training. Try verbal training first. Signing should not be taught to echolalic children or to children who have otherwise good verbal imitation skills. These groups of children can profit most by being started on a verbal language training program such as that described in earlier chapters. In short, parents and teachers should resist the impulse to try to teach sign language just because it is new or because they feel that a child is not learning verbal language quickly enough.

ADVANTAGES OF USING SIGN LANGUAGE

There are several reasons why signing is considered useful for nonverbal children. First, some professionals believe that if an adult communicates with a child by pairing signs with spoken words, a method referred to as *simultaneous communication*, the appropriate use of *speech* will be facilitated, or trig-

Preparation of this chapter was aided by U.S.P.H.S. Biomedical Research Support Grant 5 S07 RP07067-11 at Stony Brook. Thanks are due to my students, especially Eileen Kologinsky, Paul Dores, Margie Pelcovits, Cathy Pridal, Sheila Parris, and Jody Binkoff, for their help in developing the training procedures and to Dr. Martin Hamburg, Executive Director, Suffolk Child Development Center, for his generous support.

gered. This expectation is quite controversial. While some nonverbal children do begin to talk following simultaneous communication, a great many others do not. What is clear, however, is that most nonverbal children can learn at least some signs and therefore show improved communication with adults. Second, it has been known for some time that although many developmentally disabled children have a great deal of difficulty understanding spoken words, they appear somewhat better at comprehending gestures. Perhaps this is based on the greater ease with which many developmentally disabled children discriminate visual, as compared to auditory, stimuli. Perhaps visual stimuli are inherently easier to discriminate, or many disabled children attend better to visual stimuli rather than auditory stimuli. Since sign language is primarily a visual (gestural) system, it offers the promise of facilitating language acquisition. A third consideration is that a teacher or parent can easily mold (i.e., manually prompt) the child's hands into the appropriate sign configuration. This advantage is particularly beneficial during the difficult period of initial sign acquisition when much prompting is necessary. Fourth, for many signs, there is a concrete relationship between the sign and its referent. For example, the sign for banana consists of "peeling" the extended index finger of one hand with the fingers of the other hand. The iconic or pictorial quality of many signs is likely an additional teaching advantage. Some illustrative signs are presented in Figure 24-1. Fifth, and finally, a child who has acquired sign language potentially can be mainstreamed into a classroom and/or community for the deaf, thereby providing additional opportunities for academic, vocational, and social development.

MILK

COOKIE

APPLE

BANANA

CANDY

Figure 24-1. Iconic or pictorial quality of signs. Reprinted by permission from: Carr, E. G., Binkoff, J. A., Kologinsky, E., & Eddy, M. Acquisition of sign language by autistic children. 1: Expressive Labelling. *Journal of Applied Behavior Analysis,* 1978, *11,* 489–501.

WHERE TO START

Before beginning any sign training activities, the adult should ensure that the child has the basic learning readiness skills described in earlier chapters, especially those in Unit II. That is, the child should have been taught to attend to an adult on command and to sit still in a chair for 10 minutes or more at a time. It is important that self-stimulatory behavior be suppressed. Not only does self-stimulation act to block learning, but it may also make it very difficult for an adult to discriminate the child's signs. A child who is flicking his fingers intermittently while signing is less likely to be understood by adults who must grapple with the task of "weeding out" the self-stimulatory behaviors from the signs. A child should have also shown some progress in nonverbal imitation (Chapter 7). If a child is good at imitating nonverbal (motor) movements, an adult can use this skill as an aid for teaching new signs. However, even here, some manual prompting initially may be required in order to refine the signs so that they more closely resemble the specific signs being taught.

The next step is to acquire a sign language dictionary. We have found two dictionaries particularly useful. *Talk With Me*, by Jeanne Huffman and colleagues (1975), explains the origins of each sign, thereby providing a useful mnemonic for the adult who must master this new language in a short period of time. For example, the sign for an orange consists of making a squeezing motion with the hand positioned near the mouth. Another desirable feature of this dictionary is that the signs are combined into convenient groups, e.g., clothing, body parts, and colors. *The Signed English Dictionary for Preschool and Elementary Levels* by Harry Bornstein and colleagues (1975) lists all the signs in alphabetical order, thereby allowing for rapid retrieval of information. In addition, there is a clear and detailed explanation of how to form each sign. This feature is often poorly set out in other dictionaries. Both dictionaries are written for elementary level signing and are therefore appropriate for use with developmentally disabled children. A brief description of where the reader can go for additional information on sign training is given in the reference list at the end of this Unit.

Finally, the adult must decide to use either signing alone or simultaneous communication, that is, signs accompanied by spoken words. We have found that the best way to decide is to teach the child first using the simultaneous communication method. If, after a period of 6 to 8 weeks, the child appears confused (i.e., shows inconsistent responding or fails to respond at all), we have reverted to signing alone. Apparently, some children are unable to attend to both the spoken words and signs when they are presented simultaneously. Often such children will show increased rates of learning when the adult drops the speech component of communication. For simplicity, our sign language training program is described as if we were using signing alone. In practice, if we were employing simultaneous communication, the only change we would make would be to speak each word as we signed it.

CURRICULUM FOR TEACHING SIGN LANGUAGE

There are many similarities between teaching a child to speak and teaching a child to sign. More specifically, the procedures necessary for teaching receptive sign language are almost identical to those described earlier in this book for teaching receptive verbal language. Instead of the adult vocalizing the label for the object she wants the child to touch, he or she signs the label. So, to avoid repetition, we limit our discussion to the problems of expressive sign language. By training nonverbal children to produce signs, one gives these children a direct and effective means for communicating with others.

Labeling Objects

Labeling objects is the first skill to be taught. It makes little sense to begin by trying to teach the child the labels for clothes or parts of the body since these labels will have minimal significance for the child. Instead, we begin by selecting a number of foods that we know the child likes. In addition, the first few signs chosen for training should be visually and motorically distinct from one another. The signs for apple and orange are similar to one another, but the signs for apple and milk are not. Therefore, one may best begin by training the latter two signs.

During training sessions, the child and the adult should sit facing one another as in the early phases of other programs. A trial should start only when the child is sitting quietly and attending to the adult. Inattentiveness and self-stimulatory behaviors must be suppressed. The training itself is carried out in three steps. Consider the procedure for teaching the label for apple:

In Step 1, the adult holds up the apple in front of the child's eyes. Since the child will not respond at this point, a prompt is given. That is, the adult lifts the child's hand and molds it into the correct sign configuration. The correct prompted response is followed by social reinforcement (e.g., the adult signs GOOD), and primary reinforcement (e.g., a piece of the apple).

In Step 2, the adult repeats Step 1, except that the prompt is gradually faded out until the child can make the sign unaided. By the end of Step 2, the adult merely has to hold up the apple and the child may sign correctly. Run this first sign to criterion.

Once the sign for apple is acquired, consider training the sign for milk. This sign consists of slowly closing the outstretched five fingers to form a fist while moving the hand in a downward motion, a pictorial representation of milking a cow. In Step 1, the adult would prompt the sign by lifting the child's hand from the lap, spreading the fingers, and then placing his or her hand behind the child's hand so as to squeeze it into a fist while forcing the hand downward. In Step 2, the adult would fade the prompt, first by squeezing and pushing down the child's hand with less and less force, and then by reducing help with spreading the fingers, and finally by eliminating the aid provided in raising the hand from the lap. If the child signs incorrectly after all the prompts have faded, the adult should vigorously shake his or her head "No" and sign NO. The trial would be repeated, reinstating prompts if necessary. Of course, on these prompted trials, the child would not receive any food reinforcers, although social reinforcers would still be given. Run the second sign (milk) to criterion.

Once the child has mastered two signs, place these signs in random rotation and run to criterion. Now practice teaching a third sign, and then intermix the third sign with the other two signs to facilitate the discrimination between the three signs.

After a child has learned five or six (sign) labels using the above procedures, the adult can begin signing WHAT? before showing the child the object. It is best to keep the signed question simple at first (like WHAT?) and not to introduce extra signs, such as WHAT IS THIS? or WHAT AM I SHOWING YOU?, at the start of training since the child is likely to become confused when there are too many signs because he may not know to which stimulus to attend.

When beginning this kind of expressive label training, approximations to a given sign can be accepted. That is, it is senseless to spend weeks shaping a perfect exemplar of a given sign. The idea is to begin by teaching the child the general concept that "different things have different names (signs)." Once the child has mastered this concept, then one can sharpen the topography of the various signs. There is a parallel here with spoken language. When an infant labels a cookie "oo-ee", we do not dismiss the vocalization as inadequate. Instead, we reinforce the attempt and only later do we try to sharpen the topography.

Another point worth noting is that after a child has learned five or six signs and therefore understands the task, new signs can be taught primarily through (nonverbal) *imitation*. That is, in Step 1, the adult would model the correct label for an object (i.e., give an imitative prompt rather than a manual prompt) and reinforce the child for imitating correctly. Then, over many trials in Step 2, the adult would gradually fade out the imitative prompt. At first, the child's imitations of a sign will be very poor and some manual prompting will be necessary. However, after a dozen or so signs have been acquired, many children become quite adept at learning through imitation and therefore require only a minimal level of manual prompting. If a child is at first not capable of nonverbal imitation, then this skill could be taught concurrently with signing by using the procedures described in this book. Eventually, the newly acquired imitative skill should be integrated with the sign training procedure.

The data on one child, Darrick, are representative of the results we have obtained using the above techniques. Darrick's learning rate is not dramatically different from many children learning expressive labels by verbalizing them. Darrick was 10 years old and had been institutionalized for 5 years. His vocal behavior was limited to infrequent and meaningless sounds and he showed a variety of autistic behaviors including self-stimulatory hand movements, social withdrawal, and lack of toy play. He was functioning in the profoundly retarded range. Over a 3-year period he had made no progress in his use of vocal language. Darrick required over 7000 trials in 1 week to learn his first three expressive labels (cookie, milk, and candy). In contrast, he acquired his twelfth sign (ball) in only 18 trials. It is important to note that not every child requires so many trials to learn the first few discriminations. Individual differences aside, however, we have obtained one finding consistently, namely that all children show a "learning set." That is, they require fewer and fewer trials to master new discriminations as more and more discriminations are taught. Thus, adults should not give up sign training efforts if progress is difficult at first. Even the slow child will eventually show a rapid increase in the rate of learning.

Spontaneity

A child may know the sign for an object, for example, a cookie, and yet never use that sign spontaneously in order to request a cookie. The problem seems to be one of *narrow stimulus control*. That is, the sign will be made only when an adult holds up a cookie in front of the child and asks, "WHAT DO YOU WANT?" The purpose of this section is to discuss some techniques for broadening the stimulus control of sign language so that the mere presence of an adult will be sufficient condition for a child to spontaneously initiate requests. Problems in spontaneity will arise in any program, and the suggestions presented here can be extrapolated to vocal language as well.

We begin training for spontaneity by selecting a strong reinforcer. The child's favorite food could be used. In this case a cracker is used. The adult approaches the child and gives an imitative prompt (i.e., the adult signs CRACKER). When the child imitates the adult's sign, the child receives a piece of the cracker. Over trials, the adult gradually fades out the prompt and *waits* for the child to initiate the sign before delivering the reinforcer. At this point, it may be necessary for the adult to "look expectantly" at the child before the child will make the sign but after a while even this prompt can be faded out. At the end of this stage, the child will spontaneously initiate a request for cracker whenever the adult appears.

We continue training by recycling the above procedure with a variety of other food signs. Later still, we compile a list of favorite toys and activities and add them to the spontaneity training as well.

We would like the child to sign in a variety of contexts and not merely in one training room. Therefore, once the child has been taught to sign spontaneously for three items, training is carried out in a variety of different situations (e.g., classroom, playground, kitchen, and bedroom) and in the presence of a number of different adults in addition to the original adult teacher. Following such training, the child will exhibit a variety of spontaneous signs to many different adults in many different situations. In short, child initiated signing will be under broad stimulus control.

The final stage of training consists of making the child's spontaneous signing contextually appropriate. In the beginning stages of the training described above, we would reinforce the child's spontaneous signing irrespective of whether it was appropriate for a given context. We did this in order to strengthen spontaneity. However, once the behavior is established, we begin to refine it further. Thus, if the child is in bed ready to go to sleep, we do not want him to sign CRACKER, PLEASE even if we initially reinforce him for doing so in this context. Instead, we would choose to reinforce a request for KISS or HUG. The best way to ensure appropriate spontaneity is to observe what reinforcers are available in a given context. Having made this determination, we would imitatively prompt the appropriate signs for these reinforcers and then gradually fade the prompts. Now, when the child makes a contextually inappropriate sign, he is simply ignored. Of course, when he makes a contextually appropriate sign, he receives the specific reinforcer requested. Soon the child's spontaneous signs will be appropriate for each given context.

When we carried out the above training, we found that after a while a child would display high rates of spontaneous signing. In addition, the child would sign appropriately to many different adults in many different settings. Interestingly, the spontaneity was quite natural in character. Thus, a child who had been signing for potato chips (and presumably was getting thirsty) would inevitably begin signing for fluids. A child who had eaten a lot and, therefore, was not interested in food any more would start signing for various toys and activities. An important side effect of this training was that as children showed higher and higher levels of spontaneous signing, they gave up much of their self-stimulatory behaviors. Such a shift away from self-stimulatory behaviors, as appropriate behaviors are acquired, can be observed in most teaching situations. Perhaps when we teach children that they can have an effect on adults and can get things that are of value to themselves, self-stimulatory behaviors become less important ways of gaining satisfaction and are therefore decreased.

Descriptive Sentences

Programs for teaching early phrases and sentences are presented in more detail in Chapter 28, but sentence structure for children who sign is introduced at this point.

Once a child has been taught to use sign language to label objects and to make requests, the next step is to teach the child to combine signs to form simple sentences. One particularly useful sentence type to teach involves description. The goal is for the child to learn to describe ongoing events using simple verb-noun combinations. For example, an adult might pour a glass of milk and ask the child, WHAT AM I DOING? The child would then sign POUR(ING) MILK. (It is not necessary at this stage for the child to sign the "ing" ending on the verb; the goal is simply to teach verb and sign combination skills.) By teaching descriptive sentences, what we are in fact doing is broadening the basis for conversational communication between the child and the adult.

When we begin to teach description, we find that the child has a strong set (due to prior training) to label everything as a noun. For example, the adult might move a toy truck across a table and ask the child WHAT AM I DOING? The child will likely respond by signing TRUCK only; that is, the child has not yet learned to attend also to the behavior or action which was performed on the truck. To overcome this deficit, we would initiate the following training program.

In Step 1, the adult teaches the child to attend to and label behaviors. For example, in order to teach the verb POINT TO, the adult begins by making an exaggerated motion that involves moving the extended index finger in a large arc which culminates in touching the surface of a table. No object is present on the table, however. The purpose of this step is to draw the child's attention to the behavior involved in pointing. The absence of all objects prevents the child from being distracted from the adult's pointing activity. When the adult completes the pointing motion, the child is asked WHAT AM I DOING?", and is then prompted to make the sign for POINT TO, and finally, he is reinforced for doing so. Over trials, the prompt is faded and eventually the child makes the POINT TO sign whenever the adult performs the exaggerated pointing motions. Next, a second verb (e.g., "pick up") is introduced using the same procedures just described. The standard random rotation procedure is employed; that is, trials involving the previously mastered verb are intermixed with trials involving the new verb until the child has acquired a discrimination between the two verbs. Finally, a third verb (e.g., "hold") is taught in the same manner as the other two verbs. At the end of Step 1, the child will correctly sign POINT TO, PICK UP, and HOLD in response to the adult's making exaggerated motions representing these three verbs.

Once a child has learned to attend to and label three different actions on the part of the adult, Step 2 is initiated. In this step, objects are reintroduced and the child is required to describe what the adult is doing using a simple verb-noun sentence. For example, the adult might point to a toy truck on a table and ask the child WHAT AM I DOING? Typically, at this stage, the child will sign only the verb (i.e., POINT TO) and omit the noun (i.e., TRUCK). Therefore, the adult must prompt the noun sign immediately after the child makes the sign for the verb. Over trials, the adult fades out the prompt. Next, a second verb-noun combination is taught (e.g., PICK UP TRUCK) via the stimulus rotation procedure. Following this, the third verb-noun combination (e.g., HOLD TRUCK) is taught as above. Once the child has mastered the three different sentences, the exaggerated motion for each verb is faded out. For example, consider the action representing point to truck. The adult will have been demonstrating this action by moving his index finger in a large arc prior to bringing the finger into position a few inches above the truck. During the fading sequence, the adult would begin to decrease the size of the arc until it gradually approximated a normal "point to" gesture. A similar procedure would be carried out with respect to the PICK UP and HOLD verbs. At the end of Step 2, the child would be signing POINT TO TRUCK, PICK UP TRUCK, and HOLD TRUCK in response to the corresponding adult actions.

In Step 3, new nouns are taught in conjunction with the above three verbs. At this stage, exaggerated movements are no longer used. The adult simply demonstrates a new combination (e.g., the adult might point to a spoon on the table) and repeats the procedures described above. Once the three new verb-noun combinations have been acquired, trials based on the old and new nouns are intermixed (e.g., PICK UP SPOON, POINT TO TRUCK, and HOLD SPOON) until the child has mastered all the combinations. Step 3 is recycled with a number of new nouns using the same procedures just described. In the end, the child will be able to use a two-word sentence to describe the three actions that the adult performs with respect to a variety of objects.

Finally, in Step 4, new verbs (e.g., throw, run, and jump) are introduced for appropriate objects. Generally, at this point, the adult needs only to use exaggerated movements for a small number of trials and to prompt the signs corresponding to the verb-noun combination only a few times. After this relatively brief training period, the exaggerated movements and the prompts for the signs can be faded out and the procedures of Step 3 can be followed. At the end of Step 4, the child will know how to describe a great number of events involving many different nouns and verbs.

When we have used the above procedures, we found that during Step 3, the child became able to sign new verb-noun combinations that had *never been taught* to him. For example, after training only five or six nouns (e.g., truck, spoon, shoe, pencil, and towel) with the initial three verbs, we found that we could present a new situation (e.g., PICK UP BOAT, POINT TO BOAT, and HOLD BOAT) and the child would correctly sign the new verb-noun combination even though we had never trained that particular combination. This skill is referred to as *generative signing;* that is, the child generates or creates new combinations from signs he already knows in order to describe new situations. This skill is commonly seen in the verbal language of young normal children and is highly desirable because it means that a child does not have to be taught *every* possible combination of words. Apparently, the children themselves become capable of rearranging what they already know in order to meet new communication challenges. The fact that this skill can be taught to developmentally disabled children bodes well for their continued language growth.

Abstract Sign Language

Verbs and nouns are concrete parts of language. Although they are useful to know, a child must learn abstract language forms as well in order to function adaptively. Abstractions define relationships among people, objects, and events and include prepositions, pronouns, and time concepts as well as a host of other concepts such as color, size, shape, "yes" and "no", and "same" and "different." These relationships are shared by many different objects, and therefore, before a child can be said to have mastered such concepts, he must be able to "abstract" or discriminate what all the objects have in common. Thus, "brown" can be characteristic of wood, chocolate, cars, leaves, and many other objects. The child must learn that brown is not a characteristic of one specific object but rather a characteristic of a wide variety of objects otherwise differing in many dimensions such as height, weight, and volume. Concepts represent one of the greatest challenges in teaching language to developmentally disabled children.

Programs for teaching abstract relationships, using signs, are quite similar to programs described in the next unit (Unit VI) for teaching advanced verbal language. Therefore, they will not be presented in detail here. The reader can easily substitute the appropriate sign for a particular vocalization in the programs that follow. Incidentally, children who have to use signs can be taught complex abstract relationships, just as vocal children can.

CONCLUSION

We have reviewed a number of procedures designed to teach sign language skills. Clearly, many areas were not discussed. For example, we did not talk about building more complex sentences or advanced conversation, nor did we discuss storytelling or recall. In a preliminary way, we have begun to teach these more sophisticated skills as well. It is likely that the techniques described in Unit VI for teaching advanced verbal skills will also prove useful for teaching advanced signing skills. In any event, we have now made significant inroads in teaching nonverbal children to communicate.

REFERENCES

Bornstein, H., Hamilton, L. B., Saulnier, K. L., & Roy, H. L. (Eds.). *The signed English dictionary for preschool and elementary levels.* Washington, D.C.: Gallaudet College Press, 1975. (Available from Gallaudet College Bookstore, Gallaudet College, Washington, D.C. 20002.)

Carr, E. G., Binkoff, J. A., Kologinsky, E., & Eddy, M. Acquisition of sign language by autistic children. I. Expressive labeling. *Journal of Applied Behavior Analysis,* 1978, *11,* 489-501.

Huffman, J., Hoffman, B., Gransee, D., Fox, A., James, J., & Schmitz, J. (Eds.). *Talk with me.* Northridge, Calif.: Joyce Motion Picture Co., 1975. (Available from Joyce Motion Picture Co., 18702 Bryant St., P.O. Box 458, Northridge, Calif. 91324.)

Lovaas, O. I. *The autistic child: Language development through behavior modification.* New York: Irvington Publishers, 1977.

Schreibman, L., & Carr, E. G. Elimination of echolalic responding to questions through the training of generalized verbal response. *Journal of Applied Behavior Analysis,* 1978, *11,* 452-463.

RECOMMENDED READINGS

Bonvillian, J. D., & Nelson, K. E. Sign language acquisition in a mute autistic boy. *Journal of Speech and Hearing Disorders,* 1976, *41,* 339-347.

Carr, E. G. Teaching autistic children to use sign language: Some research issues. *Journal of Autism and Developmental Disorders,* 1979, *9,* 345-359.

Creedon, M. P. (Ed.). *Appropriate behavior through communication.* Chicago: Michael Reese Medical Center, Dysfunctioning Child Center Publication, 1975.

Fulwiler, R. L., & Fouts, R. S. Acquisition of American Sign Language by a noncommunicating autistic child. *Journal of Autism and Childhood Schizophrenia,* 1976, *6,* 43-51.

Longhurst, T. M. (Ed.). *Functional language intervention: Readings* (Vols. I & II). New York: MSS Information Corp., 1974.

UNIT VI

ADVANCED LANGUAGE

Programs for introducing the child to more difficult language are described in this Unit. The child is taught not only to label discrete and simple events (such as the objects that he sees around him), but he can also be taught more complicated language, such as that used in describing the attributes or properties of objects (size, color, and form), describing the relationships between objects and events (using prepositions such as in, beside, under), identifying the persons to which objects and behaviors belong (using possessive pronouns such as your, my, his, or hers), as well as many other concepts, including time. As you begin to teach the child how words are combined into simple phrases or sentences to enable him to describe more completely something happening around him (teach him to say not only "Mommy," but "Nice Mommy") and to use sentences to express his wants ("I want some milk.").

When a child understands the concept of time, it will be easier for him to learn to wait for something without becoming too upset. As the child learns to more accurately describe his experiences, you will acquire a more thorough understanding of what he is all about, and will then be in a better position to help him.

Language is a very complicated behavior to teach, and this Unit only suggests some programs that can help your child get going. Should your child have some talent for learning speech, then you may want to familiarize yourself with more elaborate language programs.

Chapter 25 gives programs for teaching the concepts of color, form, and size because these are relatively easier to teach than prepositional concepts (under, inside, in front), which are introduced in Chapter 26. Pronouns (you, I, her) are introduced in Chapter 27, followed by programs for teaching the child to understand temporal concepts such as first and last in Chapter 28. A program for teaching the child the appropriate use of yes and no can be found in Chapter 29. Unit VI concludes with Chapter 30, which presents programs for teaching appropriate use of sentences—the beginnings of grammar.

SIZE, COLOR, AND SHAPE

CHAPTER 25

The programs for teaching size, color, and shape are illustrative of the approach for teaching many concepts of advanced language. The procedure for teaching each of these abstract concepts is similar to that described earlier for teaching simple labels. The following instructions serve as examples of how this procedure may be adapted for the teaching of many kinds of simple abstractions.

TEACHING SIZE

Receptive Training

The program for teaching size may be the easiest for your child to understand. As in teaching labels, you should begin with receptive speech because it is generally easier than expressive speech. You should place on the table in front of the child two objects that differ only in size, and *not* on any other dimension (such as shape, or color). For example, place one very large (10 inches or more in diameter) ball on the table, and next to it place a rather small ball (1 or 2 inches in diameter) of the same material and the same color. You then present the command for size, that is, ask the child to point to (or give you) a particular size. You may say "Give me big," or just "Big," which means the child has to give you the big ball. In any case, the word "big" should be the dominant cue, being pronounced very loudly and clearly. Since the child most likely does not know what to do, you should prompt the correct response, that is, you should point to the big ball, or otherwise guide the child's manual response toward the correct object.

You may find it necessary to present some "ready signal" (such as, "Look here") while gesturing toward the table in the direction of the stimulus objects, before presenting the command. Some children will learn to attend to and visually fixate on the object without such a ready signal; others, however, do not look at the objects they are asked to identify, and obviously need to visually attend. In any case, you should wait for a child to look at the objects before presenting the command. In this way, your command may serve as the child's reinforcement for visually attending to the object. On the other hand, your child could associate this reinforcer with the undesirable behavior in which he has just been engaging. For example, let's say the child is inattentive, or he is throwing a tantrum, and you wait until he

165

becomes attentive and looks at the objects on the table before you say "Point to big." Your verbal instructions, possibly serving as a reinforcer for the child, could strengthen the child's inattention or tantrums.

Once you have prompted the correct response, then fade the prompt as you have done in other programs. Continue presenting the command, and remember to change the positions of the objects on the table randomly so that sometimes the large ball is on the child's left, sometimes on his right. Once the child has responded to criterion, you may introduce the second size concept by saying "Small," or "Give me small." Again, you should prompt, if necessary, and fade the prompt until the child responds to criterion without prompting. Now reintroduce the first command, "Give me big." When the child makes three or four correct responses in a row, switch to the second command, "Small," or "Give me small." Again, prompt if necessary and then fade the prompt until the child responds to criterion. Now intermix the two commands using random rotation as you have done in all the discrimination training programs discussed in this book.

Once the child can reliably identify a large ball versus a small ball, you can teach him to discriminate between the sizes of other objects. The child has learned the concept of size if he responds correctly on the first trial, without any prompting, when you present a new pair of objects (a pair that he has not been trained on).

Some children learn to discriminate size very easily, and others are slower. If your child has made no progress on this task after 1 week of training (1 or 2 hours per day) then put it aside and reintroduce the task a month or two later. You may try teaching some other concepts in the meantime. If the child continues to have difficulty, you may also want to go back and pretrain him on the matching size program, explained in Chapter 9. In teaching the child to match sizes, place two objects on the table in front of the child and give him a third object, which matches one of the two objects on the table. The child is then asked to place the object in his hand with the object it matches on the table ("Put it where it goes," or just, "Match up"). In this way the child may learn to match size, and in so doing he may have learned to attend to size as a cue and to discriminate.

Expressive Training

So far you have been teaching the child a receptive understanding of size, that is, you label the object (like "Big") and teach the child to respond appropriately to *your* label. Now, you may want to teach the *child* to use the correct label himself, so that he verbalizes "Big" in the appropriate circumstance. (This training in the expressive use of concepts is taught in the same fashion as the expressive labels of simple objects in Chapter 20.) Place two balls on the table in front of the child, then ask him to point to one (e.g., "Big"). Then, once the child has his hand on the appropriate object, ask "Which size?" (For the first few trials you may simply delete the question and just pause, in order to avoid any interference that may be caused by the question.) The desired response is then prompted, the prompt is faded, new stimuli are added, and so on.

You can help the child by indirectly prompting the correct response when expressive labeling follows receptive labeling. That is, when you first asked him to identify a particular size, you said, "Point to big," and when you then asked him, "What size?" his answer, "Big," was actually contained in your earlier command. Later, to make certain that he is not merely repeating your words, skip the command ("Point to big"); instead prompt him to touch the big object, and then ask him, "Which size?"

You may want to begin speech training on the expressive use of size labels after your child has mastered the receptive use of size labels. Or, you may want to go on to first teach other abstractions at the receptive level, waiting to teach expressive abstractions. There is no good reason for choosing one approach over the other. You should choose the approach that works best for your child.

TEACHING COLOR

The program for teaching colors outlines a way to teach recognition of colors and to label them appropriately. As in teaching size and other more concrete labels, receptive speech training is generally useful as a pretraining for expressive speech. You should teach color concepts the same way you taught size. That is, place on the table in front of the child two objects (blocks, plastic chips, or the like) that differ only in color and *not* in any other dimension. The child is to identify a particular color when you give the command for that color, such as "Red" or "Give me red." He has to give you the red object when two objects of different color are placed on the table in front of him. You should prompt and fade these prompts, then present the colors in random rotation, the same way you did when teaching size. The expressive use of color labels is taught in the same fashion as the expressive use of size labels. Remember to generalize the use of color labels by using different objects. (See the section on generalization training at the end of this chapter.)

TEACHING SHAPE

The program for teaching shape is carried out in the same way as teaching size or color. Merely select two objects that are alike in all dimensions except shape, and place them on a table in front of the child. You may want to select a circle and a triangle. Prompt, fade, and rotate as you did in other programs. Remember to teach generalization, such that when the child has learned to tell a plastic circle from a plastic triangle, you then present him with forms made of different materials and in different colors and sizes. For example, present him with a pair of objects, both rather large and made from yellow cardboard paper, if the first objects he encountered were small and made from white plastic.

We usually teach shape after color, but there is no good (data-based) reason why we do so. Children differ quite a bit in the ease with which they learn different kinds of concepts, so it is best to be somewhat flexible and to try to figure out the particular training sequence that best suits your particular child. Usually, you can do that by keeping a program in operation for a certain time (about a week or so). If the child makes no progress, you should be willing to set aside that particular program for a while, and then come back to it at a later period. For all you know, your child may be color-blind (there is no easy way to diagnose this with disabled children), and it would be a pity to stay with this one concept, exposing your child to lots of frustrations, when there are so many other concepts left to teach.

Once the child has learned two or three abstractions, then the training program can become quite interesting and very complex. The good part of a complex program is that the child is asked to pay attention to increasingly fine details in his surroundings. For example, you may place a blue square, a red circle, and a yellow triangle in front of the child. Then tell the child "Hand me the *blue square*," or "Hand me the *red circle*." Using even more complex instructions, ask the child to discriminate the dimensions as in the request to "Hand me the *small blue square*." However, as the program becomes increasingly complex for the child, it does not necessarily become that much more difficult to teach (thank heaven).

GENERALIZATION TRAINING

As in all the other programs, the child's training should be taken outside the teaching situation in order to train and test for generalization. The color of a person's eyes, hair, or clothing, and pieces of furniture may be used; the shapes of tables, containers, and toys may also be included. Once mastered, color and form discriminations are often quite useful in facilitating new learning. For example, one will find many programmed learning materials for teaching reading in which color is initially used to help the child form the correct discriminations between words. Keep in mind that you should teach the child in his everyday surroundings in an attempt to expand his understanding of these concepts, once you have helped him learn them in a controlled training environment. The only reason that you start with a controlled training environment is that it is easier to teach a child in a simplified situation than it is to teach him out in the real world, where there is so much going on. Learning to label objects in the controlled teaching environment is of little importance unless the child can learn to use these labels appropriately in his daily activities.

CHAPTER 26

PREPOSITIONS

The purpose of the program for prepositions is to teach the child to label spatial relationships between objects, such as under, above, and inside. Later, you will attempt to teach the child about his own position in space, such as *on* the bed, and *inside* the house. The program for prepositions is an example of a program that always begins with receptive speech training.

RECEPTIVE TRAINING

You and your child are seated at a table on top of which is a small container, such as a cup, and a small object, such as a penny. You instruct the child to place the object in the container by saying "Put penny *in* cup," or by simply saying *"In."* If necessary, the correct response is prompted by taking the child's hand, placing the penny in it, and helping him put the penny in the cup. Reinforce the child and fade the prompt in the usual manner by gradually diminishing your participation in the child's response. (The choice of a penny may not be ideal for some children who have a problem with fine finger dexterity because it is so difficult to pick up. Pick an easier object for the child to handle; you do not want to distract the child.)

When the child is responding to criterion with "in," then begin to train a second preposition; we usually choose "under." You could have chosen "beside," or some other preposition, that sounds and looks maximally different from "in." In teaching the second preposition the same object (the penny) may be utilized; however, a *different* container (e.g., a small box) can be used. You can say, "Put penny *under* box," or simply, *"Under."* The response is prompted and the prompt is faded. When the child has mastered "under," "in" is reintroduced and the first response is retrained, and then "under" is retrained and so on until the child is making no more than one error each time you switch the training stimuli.

During the entire training program thus far, one container has been used for "in" and another for "under." In all probability, the child is now learning that when one container is present, he is supposed to place an object *under* it, and when another container is present, he is to place an object *in* it. That is, the child is probably not learning much about prepositions. The two different containers are

169

employed to facilitate the child's discriminations; they serve as a prompt. Preposition training is difficult; that is our reason for using such prompts. Some children may be able to catch on using the same containers; others may need different kinds of prompts. Keep in mind that it is a difficult concept to learn, and that you need to be able to improvise.

To keep the child from relying on such prompts, and to bring him under the control of the prepositions you verbalize; you must teach the child to make both responses using only one container (e.g., to put the penny "under" or "in" the cup). This procedure consists of two steps.

Step 1: •You first place *both* containers on the table at the same time, tell the child "in," and, if necessary, prompt the child to place the penny in the cup. When the child reaches criterion on this response, you introduce the command "under," and if necessary, prompt the child to place the penny under the cup. When the child reaches criterion on this response, "in" is again introduced and retrained. Then retrain "under" until the child consistently makes no more than one error with each change in command. Then, randomly rotate the commands as before.

Step 2: Remove one of the containers so that the child will make both responses using the *same* container. You may want to fade the other container farther and farther away from the child, so that it will be easier for him to use the same container for both "in" and "under."

When the child can respond correctly to "in" and "under" using the same container, and with rotated trials, generalization training may be instituted using new containers. New prepositions and prepositional phrases, such as "beside," "on top of," "behind," and "in front of," may be taught using the same procedures, omitting any steps that seem unnecessary for your particular child. Thus, for one child it may be necessary to train a new preposition in isolation, then alternate training the new preposition and a previously mastered preposition, and finally presenting the new preposition in random rotation with previously mastered ones. For another child, it may be sufficient to simply bring in new prepositions without concern for first training them in isolation.

EXPRESSIVE TRAINING

When the child has mastered five or six prepositions at the receptive level, you may begin expressive speech training. The procedure is exactly the same as that for receptive speech except that now you place the object *in* or *under* the container and then ask the child "Where is it?" The desired response, e.g., "In" (or "In the cup") or "Under" (or "Under the box") is prompted, and the prepositions are taught in the same manner that expressive labels were trained. Note that a receptive trial may serve as a prompt if it is followed by an expressive one. For example, if you say "Put *in* cup" (and the child responds correctly), and if you then ask "Where is it?", your instruction contains the prompt for the child's answer ("In"). This may or may not be helpful for your child.

GENERALIZATION TRAINING

As with the other programs described in this manual, once the child has completed the initial training phase of the program, generalization training is carried out in the child's everyday life. Your goal now is to teach the child about his own position in space and the spatial relationships between major everyday objects, for example, hiding "behind" the dresser, sitting "inside" the closet, putting the books "on top of" the bed, and placing his slippers "under" the bed. Teach the child the correct response to the most common prepositional relationships in the home and/or school so as to later facilitate the day-to-day interactions you have with him.

Once the child can carry out the most common demands involving prepositional relationships, you may begin generalization training on expressive speech. For example, you may first instruct the child to sit *on* a chair, and then present the question "What are you doing?" The child is then prompted to reply "I am sitting *on* the chair." You may ask the child to "Sit on the bed" or to stand "On the chair," and then prompt the child's correct verbalization of these behaviors. You also may ask about other objects or persons ("Where is the baby?" "Where is the milk?"). We must repeat again that the generalization phase is the most important part of the program for teaching prepositions. Your child must use the prepositions that he learns regularly and in a variety of situations for them to become a functional part of his vocabulary. Our experience has been that the children do not transfer learning to everyday life unless they are taught to do so.

PRONOUNS

CHAPTER **27**

The goal of the program for pronouns is to teach a child to understand language that deals with personal relations. It attempts to teach the child the beginning meaning of terms such as "yours" and "mine," what a person means when he talks about "I" versus "you," and what is meant by "we" and "us" as compared to "they" and "them." One could speculate on how important it is for the child to learn such terms— for example, how important it is for him to learn "I," in order to achieve a sense of identity—but such speculations are beyond the scope of this book. Let's just agree that it is of some value for the child to learn pronouns. The program introduces pronoun training, giving the adult and the child a "feeling" for how such a training program is constructed.

RECEPTIVE SPEECH TRAINING FOR "YOUR" AND "MY"

Training in the receptive use of the genitive case of pronouns, such as "my," "your," "his," or "hers," requires that a large number of common personal possessions (such as clothing, and jewelry) and body parts (nose, eye, ear, and arm) be used as basic stimuli. The child should already know how to label these possessions and body parts. That is, training for words like "your" and "my" implies that the child now will learn to correctly identify the *personal referent* of your statement, i.e., the child must discriminate not only an object (a nose or an eye) but the pronoun related to that object ("your nose," "my eye").

Step 1: Begin with the instruction "Point to *your* nose" (or some similar body part), or you may simply state "*Your* nose."

Step 2: At the same time that you give this instruction, you should prompt the correct response by moving the child's hand to the child's nose and having him touch his nose.

Step 3: Training is continued until the child responds to criterion with no prompts.

Once this behavior is established you then introduce a second instruction, "Point to *my* nose," or just "*My* nose," and train the behavior to criterion. When the child has mastered "My nose," then begin random rotation with these two commands, as you have done in all previous training. The child has mastered this discrimination when he can respond correctly to criterion with these two commands randomly intermixed.

Once this initial learning is established, then the training is broadened to introduce other body parts. The discrimination for each new body part (e.g., "my ear" versus "your ear") should be mastered first, then the newly mastered instructions are intermixed with those already trained. A series of trials at this stage in the training might go as follows: "Point to *my* nose," "Point to *your* ear," "Point to *your* nose," "Point to *my* ear." The child has mastered this phase of pronouns when, on the first trial, he can correctly point to a particular possession or body part that was not used in an early training. For example, he can correctly point to his head or to your head even though he was not specifically trained to do so earlier.

Pronouns are difficult to learn and some children experience major difficulty in training at this level. One way to ease the difficulty is to pretrain using the child's name and your name. If that needs to be done, change your instructions and ask the child to "Point to (child's name) nose," and "Point to Mommy's nose." Once this discrimination is established, you can then use this command as a prompt and superimpose the pronouns "your" and "mine" on the proper names, gradually fading the latter. For example, you ask the child to "Point to Billy's *your* nose," making the pronoun "your" quite loud and pronounced, and then gradually fading the loudness of the child's name ("Billy") so that it becomes inaudible and only the command with the pronoun ("your") remains. This same kind of pretraining, using proper names, could be used for many kinds of pronouns.

Once the receptive use of pronouns such as "your" and "my" is established, you might try expressive speech training for these same pronouns. This is a very difficult discrimination to learn because the child has to learn to reverse pronouns. Such pronoun reversal is complicated. For example, suppose that the child had just been taught "Point to *your* nose," and his correct response was to point to his own nose. Then you taught the child "Point to *my* nose" and the child's correct response was to point to your nose. In *expressive* training, when you say "Point to *your* nose" the child must now point to his own nose, and he must verbalize "*My* nose" (even though the label "my" was previously taught in relationship to your nose, and not his). However, pronoun reversal can be mastered. Try to make the situation (the cues or stimuli) very succinct, help the child identify the referent of the question. For example, if you ask the child, "Point to *my* nose," you should ask him to do this *while he holds his hand on your nose*. As an additional cue, ask "Whose nose?" The movement and the position of the child's hand helps provide action cues for him.

You may want to teach personal pronouns using a large number of ordinary, common activities that a child can already label. Start this kind of training by asking the child to perform some activity, such as waving his arm. The child is then prompted to say, "*I* am waving." At this stage you may also ask the question, "What are *you* doing," although the presence of "you" in that question may temporarily confuse the child. In either case the prompts are faded as we have done in other programs. You may then go on to some other activity (such as standing, pointing, jumping, smiling, or laughing) for use in training of the pronoun "I."

Once this phase of the training is accomplished, that is, the child can now verbalize correctly "*I* am standing," "*I* am pointing," and so on, you may engage in some behavior and ask the child "What am *I* doing?" It may be helpful during these early stages if you point clearly to the *child* when you ask the question, "What are *you* doing?" and point clearly to *yourself* when you ask, "What am *I* doing?" It is probably easier for the child to come up with a correct pronoun to a visual cue (pointing) compared to finding the correct pronoun to your question without other cues. The visual pointing prompt can then be gradually faded. In subsequent training it is possible to use pictures for teaching pronouns such as "he" and "she."

If the child has some difficulty with pronouns such as "I" and "you," you may begin this kind of pronoun training using proper names, so that the child will be initially taught to correctly label "Billy is waving." Use the proper noun as a prompt to be faded and superimposed by the pronoun "I."

The pronoun training described in this chapter can serve as an example of pronoun training in general. Pronoun training is tedious work and clearly emphasizes the need for a large group of people to work with the child. This implies that people without formal speech training can, in fact, help the child's language development. No doubt such is the case, and no doubt it is critical for the child's language development that a large number of people do, in fact, work with him.

CHAPTER 28

TIME CONCEPTS

The goal of this program is to teach your child to understand simple time concepts, such as "first" and "last," and "soon" and "later." You may begin the teaching of time concepts by teaching "last." As usual, begin this kind of training under controlled circumstances. This means that you and your child sit facing each other, a small table between you, with a set of distinct and relatively discriminable objects placed in a row on the table.

TRAINING FOR "LAST"

We suggest that the training begin with "last" as a temporal and spatial cue because this concept is most recent in the child's mind. You should place two objects that the child can now label (such as a key and a ball) on the table in front of him about 1 foot apart. It is advisable in this program, like all the others, to select objects that look somewhat different. You then tell the child to touch the two objects in a certain order. For example, you may ask the child to "Touch key *first*" (or simply, "Key first"), prompt the response, reinforce, and then ask the child to "Touch ball *last*," and again prompt and reinforce. On any one trial the order in which the objects are touched and their position on the table may both be changed. Ask the question, "What came *last?*" Once the child has mastered this discrimination, introduce a new pair of objects (such as a penny and a glass) and repeat the training on this new pair of objects. As in other programs, the learning is considered complete when the child can correctly verbalize the concept "last" on the first trial on a pair of objects he has not encountered before.

It may be helpful in this training to have the child verbalize your command. That is, when you tell the child to touch one object "first," and some other object "last," you should encourage the child to repeat these instructions. For example, in the trials given above you say "Key first," have the child give the correct response, *and* have him repeat "Key first." The same thing happens with the command "Ball last"; when you ask "Which did you touch last?" the child has available (stored) the correct response ("Ball last").

You may also consider working with more than two objects at a time. If you work with sets of five objects, asking the child to touch any two of those, you may avoid the child's response becoming associated with a particular object, rather than the temporal order in which an object was touched.

TRAINING FOR "FIRST"

In training for "first," the same sets of objects are used, the instructions are identical to those for training the concept "last," but the question, "What came last?" is replaced by the question, "What came first?" The child is prompted and trained as before.

Once he has performed to criterion on the concept "first," then the two labels, "first" and "last" are randomly rotated as in all previous training.

GENERALIZATION TRAINING

Many opportunities are available to generalize the use of time concepts to everyday life. As always, *gradually* move away from the original training situation, and begin to include more general behaviors, such as touching head first, touching table last, then standing up first, and turning around last. Slowly, training can be generalized to more elaborate sequences of activities that the child must perform (e.g., "Hang up your coat *before* you go outside," "*First* eat your vegetables"). You may move from teaching the child to interact with simple objects to having the child explicitly engage in a set of behaviors that can be sequenced, such as standing up, closing the door, and then sitting down. In any case, the generalization of these concepts to everyday life will benefit the child, and all significant language training should take place in his everyday environment.

YES/NO TRAINING

CHAPTER 29

Let us mention one more training program involving a different kind of instruction, one that is perhaps not all that difficult to learn. This concerns teaching the child to appropriately use the terms Yes and No. This is a very useful part of language, but developmentally disabled children may have problems with such language and may need explicit instructions. Yes/No training can be divided into two procedures, training for personal feelings and training for factual matters. Generally we begin with personal feelings because they seem easier to teach.

YES/NO TRAINING FOR PERSONAL FEELINGS

Select two behaviors, one that your child definitely prefers and one that he definitely does not prefer. For example, you may ask a question such as, "Do you want candy?", as contrasted to the question, "Do you want a spanking?" Ask one of these questions, and then prompt the correct response. For example, ask "Do you want some candy?", while holding a piece of candy clearly in front of the child; then prompt the child to verbalize "Yes" before you actually give the child the candy. You then say, "Do you want some candy?" (pause) *"Yes."* The prompt ("Yes") is then gradually faded, and you end up with a situation in which the child is verbalizing "Yes" to your question, "Do you want some candy?" Once this is established you then raise your arm and ask the child the question, "Do you want a spanking?" and prompt the answer "No." In gradual steps this prompt is faded. The critical training comes when these two questions are intermixed using random rotation.

It is probably wise for you to let the child experience the consequences of his using the terms yes and no correctly, as well as the consequences following an incorrect usage. That is, if the child says, "Yes," when you ask, "Do you want a spanking?" then the child should probably be given a swat (just enough for him to feel a little uncomfortable). You can help the child formulate the correct answer by grossly exaggerating your gestures when you ask "Do you want a spanking?" That is, raise your arm so it is clear to the child what may be in store for him. Similarly, hold the candy clearly in the child's line of vision when you ask, "Do you want candy?"

Initially, the child is probably responding to the *visual* cues of your raising your arm as compared to holding forth some candy. These visual cues must then be faded, over trials, leaving the child to respond to the question only. For example, you end up asking, "Do you want candy?" without showing that candy is available.

YES/NO TRAINING FOR FACTUAL MATTERS

You may want to teach Yes/No in relation to factual matters. Start with some simple situation, such as holding a book in front of the child and asking, "Is this a book?"; then prompt and fade the prompts for the correct response, "Yes." Then hold up a phone, or some other object, and ask "Is this a book?" and prompt and fade "No." Then present the two stimuli in random rotation. Refer to earlier chapters for an outline of random rotation presentation. Generalization training, described earlier, should also be undertaken.

CHAPTER 30

TEACHING PHRASES AND SENTENCES

As the child begins to learn the meaning of complicated words, such as the concepts underlying pronouns and time, you will increasingly feel the need to teach the child how to use these newly acquired words in a correct form. That is, after he has learned the concept of color, you may want your child to use his color terms when he expresses himself, as in the case of "the red truck." The child has to learn to put together words in the right order so that they make sentences.

Some people feel that the ability to express and formulate sentences is an innate capacity, and others feel it is learned. Since many developmentally disabled children do not talk in sentences, many professionals have thought that they lack this innate ability, or that some part of the brain is damaged and therefore it is difficult or impossible for your child to speak in sentences. Others say that the child may have problems talking in sentences because he has some brain damage. Even the experts don't agree on the causes. Therefore, it is probably best if you yourself take charge of the situation and see what you can teach your child.

Actually, teaching the child to speak in sentences is not all that difficult. It is quite possible for you to teach your child grammar, or what others call syntax. As with all other kinds of learning, it is best to break the behavior down into smaller sections, then teach those smaller sections one at a time. One of the smallest word combinations is a noun with a modifier, denoting a quality or attribute of that noun. For example, an object such as a truck has some attribute, such as a size, color, or form. In other words, you want to teach your child to describe objects in more detail so he ends up saying not just "Truck," "Cookie," and "Mommy," but that he describes them in more detail, such as "Red truck," "Big cookie," and "Nice Mommy." Later in the program he may describe these objects in even more detail, as in the case of "My big red truck," or "His nice Norwegian teacher."

Start the training by choosing a set of objects your child can label, such as a truck, a cookie, a cup of coffee, a big ball, a little ball, and a square block. Have these objects differ on specific dimensions so that the truck is red, the cookie is brown, and the coffee warm. If your child can now label not only the name of these objects but also their attributes (such as their color, size, or shape), then you proceed by indicating some object (e.g., a truck) and asking him the question, "What is this?" If he answers "Truck," then you correct him and prompt him to say, "Red truck." As in all the other training you have taught so far, repeat the question, "What is it?" and proceed to fade your prompt ("Red") so that he eventually ends up saying, "Red truck" to your question "What is it?"

Repeat this training with a large set of objects, say 10 to 20, and you will quickly observe that one day you will hold up an object, such as a green turtle, or a blue butterfly, or a square piece of cheese, and your child will use the correct combination of the adjective and the noun without your having trained him on this particular phrase. That is, he will say, for the first time in his life, "Green turtle," "Square cheese," and so on. When the child can construct a phrase, as in combining an adjective with a noun, he is, in fact, beginning to understand grammar.

In a similar way you can teach a child to combine nouns and verbs. Consider the phrase, "I want _____." There are a lot of things your child wants, such as cookie, juice, cup, out, car, or music. When he was first taught to use these words correctly, he was merely required to state the label of the object or action he wanted. If he wanted juice, then all he had to say was "Juice." Now you may want to change the rules and ask for a little more; ask him for a complete sentence, such as "I want juice." If this is done consistently, across a large range of wants ("I want _____") then at some point he will be confronted with a behavior or object that he desires, and will then be able to state, without having been specifically trained, the correct combination of words to express a want. For example, after he has learned 10 or 20 "I want _____" phrases, then some day, faced with a bite of ice cream (which he can label), when he is asked "What do you want?" he may say, "I want ice cream," even though he has never been trained to express this particular request. Again, he is moving closer to understanding the correct use of language.

It may be necessary to use the backward chaining procedure in teaching phrases and sentences. You start training the behavior closest to the reinforcer, for example, the last word in the sentence. If you are training him to express the sentence, "I want cookie," then you would start with the word "cookie." Then you move backward to the next-to-last word, "want." In the final step of the teaching sequence you would add the first word in the sentence, "I want cookie." The sentence is a "chain" of words. You teach these words separately to the child and then teach the child to chain (combine) these words into a sentence by working backward.

It is true in teaching phrases and sentences, as in all other kinds of language learning, that the most meaningful part of the learning occurs in day-to-day living, and takes place several hours a day. It is very unlikely that your child will ever learn to speak grammatically correctly if all the learning he experiences takes place in one hour a week with his speech therapist. The following dialogue illustrates how you can teach your child to expand his use of grammar at any time during the day (Lovaas, 1971, p. 53).

Teacher: "What do you want?"
Billy: "Egg."
T: "No, what do you want?" "I..."
Billy: (no response)
T: "I..."
Billy: "I want..." (T's "I" cues Billy's "I want" on the basis of prior training)
T: "Egg." (pause)
       "O.K., What do you want?"
Billy: "I want egg."

Advanced Language

T: "Good!" (feeds Billy)
      "What do you want?"
Billy: "Egg."
T: "No, what do you want?" "I. . ."
Billy: "I want egg."
T: "Good boy!" (feeds Billy)
      "What is this?" (shows Billy bacon)
Billy: "Bacon."
T: "Good, what do you want?"
Billy: (no response)
T: "I. . ."
Billy: "I want bacon."
T: "Good! What do you want?"
Billy: "I want bacon."
T: "Good!" (feeds again)
      "What is this?" (shows milk)
Billy: "Milk."
T: "Good!" "I. . ."
Billy: "I want milk."
T: You want what?"
Billy: "I want egg."
T: "O.K." (feeds)
Billy: "I want egg."
T: "Good!" (feeds)

REFERENCES

Lovaas, O. I. *The autistic child: Language development through behavior modification.* New York: Irvington Publishers, 1971.

RECOMMENDED READINGS

Carr, E. G. Teaching autistic children to use sign language: Some research issues. *Journal of Autism and Developmental Disorders,* 1979, *9,* 345-359.

Carr, E. G., Binkoff, J. A., Kologinsky, E., & Eddy, M. Acquisition of sign language by autistic children. I. Expressive labeling. *Journal of Applied Behavior Analysis,* 1978, *11,* 489-501.

Longhurst, T. M. (Ed.). *Functional language intervention: Readings* (Vols. I & II). New York: MSS Information Corp., 1974.

Lovaas, O. I. *The autistic child: Language development through behavior modification.* New York: Irvington Publishers, 1977.

Schreibman, L., & Carr, E. G. Elimination of echolalic responding to questions through the training of a generalized verbal response. *Journal of Applied Behavior Analysis,* 1978, *11,* 453-463.

UNIT VII

EXPANDING YOUR CHILD'S WORLD

Unit VII is the last unit in the book, and it contains some very interesting programs. By this time you have worked through some very tedious lessons, and Unit VII can be considered your reward; it is fun to teach at this level.

The Unit starts out with programs in Chapter 31 on how to better manage your child in community settings, such as stores and restaurants. This is followed by four chapters teaching rather general but extremely important behaviors. Chapter 32 deals with teaching the child to better express and understand feelings. Chapter 33 addresses itself to helping the child develop ways to expand and use his fantasy life, as in pretending and imagining. Chapter 34 teaches the child to learn by observing others learn. This should help him move away from relying on strict one-on-one teaching situations, which he will not receive in most public school settings because teachers rely on (observational) group instruction. Various programs on increasing spontaneous behavior are presented in Chapter 35 because the authoritative procedures presented in the earlier programs in this book have probably created a student who is too dependent on adult directions.

Chapter 36 contains programs for preparing your child for the classroom instruction that he will receive in school. Chapter 37 gives suggestions to classroom teachers on how to construct a more behavioral classroom. Finally Chapter 38 summarizes some of the more common problems in teaching developmentally disabled children; an awareness of these problems is essential for optimal teaching.

CHAPTER 31

MANAGING THE CHILD IN COMMUNITY SETTINGS

Parents come to us with tales of horror about a recent trip to a supermarket, a restaurant, or a neighbor's home. Although sometimes amusing in retrospect, incidents in which a child has knocked down a store display, has begun to tantrum, or has thrown food in a restaurant are very disturbing and embarrassing to a parent. Other incidents, such as running into the street in front of a car or getting lost at the beach, may even jeopardize the safety of the child. In any case, a child who is too unruly imprisons himself and his family. You are unlikely to return to a restaurant or some other public place if all eyes were glued on you and your child as he screamed, threw food, pulled the tablecloth off the table, and knocked the dishes on the floor the last time you were there. Similarly, you become reluctant to invite other people to your house if you remain fearful that your child might disrupt a dinner party. Even mild misbehaviors, such as his incessant masturbation in front of your guests during dinner, are likely to seriously inhibit your party mood. You and your child end up being prisoners, so to speak; his misbehavior is your jailer. But it doesn't have to be that way at all. Instead, your child could actually become a most attractive and charming person in any crowd. This chapter suggests some simple techniques for making exposure to the community safe and enjoyable for both parent and child.

PREPARATORY TRAINING

Most people agree that the best way to handle a problem is to prevent its occurrence. The major part of a child's community training should be completed *before* the child is even introduced to a particular community setting. A child should learn something about a setting and how to behave in that setting while in the more familiar and controlled circumstances of his home or school. He should not expect to learn new ways of coping in an environment that is at once new, strange, and perhaps even frightening. On the other hand, good *preparatory* training will ensure that the child, with your help, need only transfer already well-established behavior to new conditions.

Visiting A Store

Preparatory training may be best illustrated by using a concrete example of an intended trip to the store. Begin by practicing "store" in the house. Create a little grocery store at home by placing some cans, jars, and boxes on a shelf, as in a grocery store display, and get a shopping cart. Have someone play the part of the storekeeper who operates a toy cash register. Have some money ready to pay for the food. Starting with the easiest step, simply teach your child to help you push the cart in a straight line, and to go and stop on your command. Prompt, reward, and punish as in other programs. (Use cereal as a reward for good behavior, and whacks on the rear for bad behavior.) Have the child stop the cart while you put in the items, and later have him put the items in the cart as you ask him. Always proceed in gradual steps. For example, at the check-out counter first you should give the cashier the money; later teach your child to do it.

You will be greatly expanding his receptive vocabulary in this training: "Stop," "Put in the green beans," "We need some cat food," "Give the money to the man." At the same time you will be teaching him control: "No, don't run, walk," "Hands down, no stimming," "Take my hand." You want to be reasonably certain that your child does not drop or throw grocery items, does not scream when pushing the cart, or misbehave in other ways *before* you go to the store.

In planning the first visit to a community setting, design the trip to be short and simple and to focus upon the child. Do *not* take him on a long shopping trip to a large, bustling supermarket where there are many people and where you may be caught in a long line at the checkout counter. A small, local grocery store where you might shop for 15 minutes or so would be a much better choice. You want as few witnesses as possible, in case things go wrong, or if you have to admonish him for acting up.

The first trips should also emphasize the child's active participation, which can make a visit not only an enjoyable occasion but also a meaningful learning experience. The parent's role should be one of prompting and helping the child to employ successfully in this new environment the skills learned at home and of praising the child lavishly for attempting to do things properly and for acting appropriately. If the child is busy acting appropriately, the chances of misbehavior occurring are greatly reduced and the chances of a successful subsequent trip are greatly enhanced.

While the training and planning might sound formidable and time-consuming, this is not the case. One or 2 hours over three or four evenings will probably suffice to accomplish the pretraining at home. The child should be graduating from short visits to small stores to longer visits in larger stores over a 1-week period, with store visits scheduled for *every second day*.

Visiting A Restaurant

What has been said about managing the child in stores is equally applicable to restaurants. If your child has problems managing himself in restaurants, start teaching good table manners at home, and make home look like a restaurant for a while to give your child the necessary experiences. For example, one of the most difficult behaviors for children to learn is to wait. At home everyone sits down when the food is served, and almost immediately starts eating. In restaurants one sits down, waits, orders, waits some more, and then begins to eat. So, start teaching sitting and waiting, for increasingly longer periods.

When you do decide to go out to eat, go to a fast-food restaurant first, and gradually expand to more elaborate establishments. If your child acts up very badly, you may want to warn him sternly and give him a pinch on the bottom under the table. If that does not work, you may want to leave the table with him and give him a stronger reprimand outside. When he has stopped misbehaving, and you and he have both regained your composure, then go back inside the restaurant and return to your meal.

PROBLEMS IN NEW SETTINGS

There are some unusual problems that may occur when the child is taken out of the house and placed in different settings. Often the child fails to generalize or transfer what he has learned at home to the new situation. He may be obedient and respond correctly to instructions, such as "Come to me" and "Hold my hand," at home, but this control may completely vanish in a store or a restaurant. This seems particularly true of the older children. In such instances the child probably thinks that he will not be punished for misbehaving in public; that is, he has the adult "over the barrel" so to speak, and he thinks he can get away with murder. We recommend that you take a little bit of "home" into the outside world, and that little thing from home may be the paddle. If he has been hit on the behind a couple of times at home for misbehaving, then all he has to see is the paddle in Mom's purse while they are in the market.

Running Away

Sometimes there is a lot of excitement and distraction in a store that may interfere with the child retaining good manners. Particularly, if he is some distance (like 20 feet or more) away from you in a store, or at the beach or in the park, he may not come when you say, "Come here," if he has been taught to respond to that command while being only 5 feet away from you at home. The child may even try to "leave" you by running away upon hearing the "Come to me" command. There are several ways of remedying this problem. For example, start teaching "distance responding" at home, so that the child is taught to respond to you, even though he is far away. Another method is to have a second adult (a cohort or a collaborator) present in the beginning, to "bait" or "test" the child on purpose, while you are in contact and are calling the shots. For example, let the child wander away, then when the distance is 20 feet or more, call him to come back; if he does not come immediately, your "collaborator" quickly emerges from an inconspicuous position near the child and administers the appropriate consequence (a stern "Go" or a slap on the bottom) *before* the child has an opportunity to experience the rewards he gets from ignoring you or from running away.

A child may sometimes run when excited, or will try to play a game of "chase" with you. Under these conditions you must use consistent and total discipline. As the child begins to run away, you should sharply say "No!" and then *walk slowly* toward the child, even if he continues running. Under most circumstances running toward a child will only make him more excited and hence run faster. Upon reaching the child, you should firmly state "No! Don't run away!" Repeated incidents of running away should be consequated with physical discipline or a time-out condition in addition to verbal chastisement.

There should be no leeway allowed in cases of running away once the first "No!" has been exclaimed. It is simply too dangerous for developmentally disabled children to run away, since they could be hurt (for example, most of them do not understand the dangers involved in traffic). The "No!" is your signal to the child that he has done something wrong, and will be at least verbally disciplined. The statement "No!" helps to bridge the gap in time between this initial exclamation and whatever follows (further verbal discipline, physical discipline, time-out). A pattern that often emerges is the child's tendency to stop suddenly upon hearing "No!" and then to hastily return to you with the expectation of forthcoming praise. While the child's approach is desirable in this context, praising him at this point will only encourage future repetitions of the entire running away-coming back pattern. On the other hand, following through with discipline at this point will help to discourage such a game-like pattern from forming. After disciplining your child, you can then immediately say, "Hold my hand" or "Stay by me" in order to provide a positive learning experience, that is, an occasion leading to praise or reward for appropriate proximity behavior.

FRUSTRATION TOLERANCE

One very useful program that we sometimes teach explicitly is *frustration tolerance*. Most readers can probably construct one at this point. Present a frustrating situation (e.g., food on a plate to a hungry child), then reinforce the child heavily for a short (5-second) delay before he starts eating. Prompt "holding back" behavior if necessary by giving him instructions ("Hands quiet," "Look at me") or by asking him questions ("What kind of food are we eating?"). Then gradually increase the delay to 1 or 2 minutes before he is allowed to eat. (Note how you could use this kind of program to teach him to better cope with all kinds of frustrations. For example, if your child can't handle criticism, start with a mild criticism, then gradually increase it to more and more serious criticisms, all the time reinforcing the child for "keeping his cool.")

Unless you already have good control over your child at home (or in some similarly limited situation), it is just wishful thinking to believe that the child will act appropriately in larger, more stimulating environments. The child has to first be taught to act appropriately at home; then he can be introduced to the community.

TEACHING ABOUT FEELINGS

Teaching about feelings has, of course, been part of our teaching method from the very beginning of the first program. The child has learned about feelings during interactions where emotions were expressed or withheld. For example, when the child received rewards, he probably experienced happiness and expressed this feeling in his interactions. As the child's environment expands, he is able to acquire more and more rewarding properties; his feelings of happiness or unhappiness increasingly come under environmental control. Likewise, the more the child's environment expands, the more there is to lose, and therefore there exist more opportunities to feel and express feelings such as sadness and grief. We have repeatedly observed the gradual emergence of genuine and elaborate human feelings in children (such as autistic or schizophrenic children) who were supposedly incapable of expressing such feelings. Quite possibly, the environment did not initially possess reinforcing properties for the autistic or schizophrenic child, hence the corresponding lack of appropriate affect. When the child learned which behaviors would elicit reward or punishment from his environment, he no doubt experienced a feeling of relief or happiness at being able to control a potentially threatening situation. In other words, as the child acquired rewarding and aversive qualities from the environment, he experienced more natural, human feelings. One of the most gratifying experiences in working as a teacher with developmentally retarded children is to see and discover these newly found feelings in the children and to help them cope better.

There are certain aspects in the child's emotional life, however, that will not develop constructively unless the child is taught about feelings more directly. This is particularly the case with some children who do not know how to identify and describe feelings. We constructed programs that would help children talk about the feelings in themselves and in others. Although a child may feel very happy and perhaps grateful, he may not know how to naturally or spontaneously express those feelings. Therefore, from the very first day we see a child, all through the programs, we teach him to express affections in an appropriate manner. Similarly, children have to be taught appropriate ways to assert themselves. Some children who are too assertive and endanger the welfare of other children have to be taught more appropriate ways of asserting themselves. Other children who are too passive and quiet have to be taught to become more assertive. Finally, some children show a great deal of unusual fears, sometimes referred to as "irrational fears," so we developed a program for helping them overcome fears.

IDENTIFYING FEELINGS

You may find that using this program to teach the child to discriminate and label feelings of happiness, sadness, anger, and fear adequately covers the main emotions. It is important during this program to make certain that the child enters into the interaction with the attending adult as actively as possible to allow him to describe his own feelings and the causes behind them.

Begin the program by teaching the child to label facial expressions as happy or scared. You should have two adults present to help teach the program. Have one adult tickle or feed the second adult who would then smile and give signs of happiness. You then ask the child, "How does he (she) feel?" Prompt the child to respond with "Happy:" or "He (she) is happy." Once the child can respond appropriately to the question without prompting, then a second emotion, scared, is introduced. Now, the first adult will behave as if he or she is going to hit the second adult, who cowers and shows signs of being scared. As before, you ask the question, "How does he (she) feel?" and prompt and reinforce the child to answer appropriately, "He (she) is scared." Notice that there are several cues in this situation that prompt or otherwise signal the feeling state. Most noticeable is the context of the feeling, such as the first adult threatening to strike the second adult. Gradually, these cues should be faded so that the child can answer appropriately by merely looking at the second adult's face. In other words, the child will have learned to read the cues of the emotional state by attending to the facial cues only.

One useful way of expanding the above program would be to gradually replace the second adult with pictures of people who look scared, or happy. As in all other programs, the more pictures you have and the more diversified they are, the more effective the program will be.

Another useful expansion of this program is to teach the child to match facial expressions with their corresponding emotions. For example, once the child has learned to correctly label various facial expressions, such as smiling, the child could then be taught to match the facial expression with the emotion it expresses. In this way, the child will be able to describe a picture of a happy person as, "He is smiling and he is happy."

After the child has learned to label feelings, it is appropriate to begin teaching the child to make statements about the causes of feelings. The program on labeling facial expressions, with its heavy emphasis on contextual cues, would provide ideal teaching material. After the child sees the second adult being fed and learns to respond, "He (she) is happy," the child can be taught to respond to the question, "Why is he (she) happy?" In this instance, the appropriate response would be, "Because he (she) is being fed." Similarly, the child could be taught to identify being hit as a cause of fear.

In general, the more explicit the context of these various feelings, the easier it will be for the child to discriminate among them. Going back to the original situation in which the child observed one adult hitting the other, the person who is getting hit (receiving punishment) would be afraid while the person who does the hitting (administering punishment) would have a facial expression showing anger. While the child previously had learned to label the feelings of the recipient as "afraid," the child would now be asked to describe the feelings of the adult who is doing the hitting (and who looks angry).

Another important program is one that teaches the child how to apply these emotion labels to himself. The child will learn to make happy and sad faces. In devising more elaborate programs for the identification of the child's own feelings, it may be wise to closely parallel the programs we already described for teaching the child to label emotions in others. For example, the first program could be modified so that the child is the one who is tickled or fed. When the child had been made to look happy, he would then be asked, "How do you feel?" Once the child can reliably discriminate between two feelings (such as happy or afraid), he can be taught to describe the causes of his feelings.

A third emotion, such as anger, can be introduced when the child can adequately discriminate between two feelings, such as happiness and fear. You might find it easier to begin the program by having the child discriminate between happiness and anger, rather than happiness and fear, because it is easier to visually display anger than fear. The third emotion, whether anger or fear, would be placed into the training routine using random rotation, such as was done in the training of receptive and expressive labels for objects and/or behaviors in Unit V.

The feeling of sadness usually occurs in the context of some sort of loss, so the person who teaches sadness should create a situation where someone loses something. An example would be a situation where one adult takes a toy away from a second adult, and the second adult mimics sadness by making crying noises and pretending to wipe the tears from his face. The child is then asked to label these feelings, is prompted ("He is feeling sad"), and is reinforced as before.

Note that this kind of training eventually becomes problematic because the cues of the more complex feeling states are very subtle and difficult to discriminate, such as the distinction between sadness and guilt. Furthermore, the cues that distinguish many emotional states are sometimes internal. Nevertheless, good progress can be made on identifying the basic emotions of anger, fear, happiness, and sadness.

TEACHING AFFECTION

The extent to which a child's feelings are a product of his heredity or are derived from his environment (are learned) is a matter of debate. It is our experience in working with many children that, except for the most elementary and rudimentary expression of emotion, such as anger, feelings have to be taught; at the least, their expressions have to be shaped by the people who care for the child. Feelings such as affection, appropriate assertion, and showing kindness, concern, and consideration for others all have to be shaped in careful steps. Otherwise, the child would not express any of these emotions, to the detriment of himself and of those around him.

From the very beginning of the program, perhaps from Day 1, we have placed a great emphasis on the children's being affectionate and kind to the adults who care for them. Being kind means many things; to many it means to express affection, such as by kissing and hugging, which are easy to learn. Begin by prompting (manually guiding) and reinforcing the child for touching his cheek to yours, as you instruct him by saying, "Hug me." Then gradually fade the prompt while you provide reinforcement for more and more elaborate and longer hugs, such as those lasting for 5 or 10 seconds, with his arms around your neck. In our program, particularly through the first several months or year, hardly 5 minutes go by in a teaching situation without the child being expected to show affection to the adults who deal with him directly, and he is prompted and requested to do so if the behavior does not appear spontaneously. In general, our philosophy is that in these programs, where the adult gives so much of himself or herself to the child, the adult deserves affection, and the child is expected to offer affection to show his gratitude. Children who are nice had to be taught to be nice, to a certain extent.

ASSERTION TRAINING

Asserting oneself appropriately is a very complex skill that requires, in most instances, a lot of training, even for average persons. We have found developmentally disabled persons to be markedly lacking in appropriate assertion skills. One of the first behaviors we teach in this regard is taught in a teacher-student relationship where the teacher will purposefully place the child in an uncomfortable situation and will prompt the child to say, "Stop it," "No, thank you," or some other appropriate response.

We usually begin such training by having the teacher mess up the student's hair or engage in some frightening behavior, such as shaking the child or lifting the child high in the air. Once the child has learned to terminate these kinds of interactions with the appropriate assertive response, the adult progresses toward more subtle stimuli, such as taking favorite toys away from the child or removing food from his plate. Later, the adult may feed the child food he really doesn't like, tighten his belt too tight, put his hand in cold water, or perform some other action. We have been astounded at the extent to which a developmentally retarded person will seem to accept, or fail to reject, stimulus situations that are very aversive to him, or at least that seem aversive from the adult's point of view. For example, we have seen children eat food that has been much too hot for them, almost scalding their mouths. We have seen children in the shower when the temperature of the water has changed to what most would consider uncomfortably cold or hot, and they did not object. And we have seen children not able to refuse food, who would simply eat everything that the adult had given them, no matter how full or stuffed they became. Similarly, we have many stories of children who have broken an arm or a leg or who have experienced toothaches or high fevers without being able to communicate their state of discomfort. Needless to say, you would probably begin teaching such children to express their feelings in simple situations first, in which the adult knows (and can vary) their feeling states.

Some of our children needed a lot of attention when they were placed among peers in an everyday environment because they were too aggressive and would totally dominate the group and deprive other children of valued items, such as toys and food. In such a situation, we trained appropriate assertive behavior (like asking for favors) in a one-to-one situation with the teacher, and then put adults into the child's everyday environment to stop the aggressive behavior and to prompt appropriate assertive behavior when necessary.

Most developmentally retarded individuals have a general impoverishment of affective expression of almost any kind. They appear very stoic and bland. A great deal of prompting and display of appropriate affect, through playing and generally "horsing around," is a necessary and important supplement to any teaching program. Perhaps the ideal ratio of work to play (the teaching of intellectual functioning to emotional expression) would be a ratio of five to one. That is, for every 5 minutes that the child is taught intellectual, social, and self-help skills, he would be taught 1 minute of affective expressions. The 1 minute of teaching affect could well be used as a reward that would be contingent upon 5 minutes of intellectual and social work.

Note again that a lot of the proper expression of affect has to be creatively prompted, as in the use of nonverbal imitation with mirrors to teach various facial expressions. A great deal of concern and care should be placed on helping the child to discriminate the appropriate stimulus or environmental conditions for expressing the various feelings. For example, giving a hug and a kiss should occur with a smiling face, and statements of assertion should occur with a stern or serious face.

We have constructed a number of other assertion or "conviction" programs. One program is called the "Alternatives Program," in which the child is taught to respond correctly to choices like, "Do you want a tickle or a slap?" and then gradually faced with more difficult choices, such as, "Do you want to work or play outside?"

You may have to teach your child *convictions*. For example, some programs may help the children defend their answers and discriminate misinformation. The training may proceed as follows:

Step 1: Have the child label an object: "This is a cup."
Step 2: After the object is labeled correctly, tell the child, "No, it is a book." Help the child by making the choice as absurd as possible. For example, he labeled a cookie correctly, but you called it a horse.
Step 3: Now teach the child to defend his answer by restating the correct label.

A program that may facilitate the development of the child's "convictions" is one that teaches him to label and consequate incorrect behavior in others. (This could be an addition to the "Playing Teacher" program that is outlined in Chapter 33.) In other words, one attending adult is instructed to give incorrect answers or to act inappropriately (such as engaging in self-stimulatory behaviors) and the child is taught to correct and admonish such behaviors, as he is taught to reward others for acting appropriately.

Again, these are only examples of the programs you may need to build appropriate feelings. Enough has been said by now that you should be able to construct your own programs to "fill out" all the necessary behaviors.

OVERCOMING FEARS

Some developmentally disabled persons show irrational fears. We have two criteria for inferring that a fear is irrational: 1) the fear persists for months and is expressed consistently (such as daily), and the fear does not seem to diminish despite repeated exposures to the feared object(s); and 2) the fear is unreasonable given the child's age or level of functioning. By unreasonable fear, we mean that the fear interferes with the child's level of functioning. An example of an irrational fear is a fear of the noise generated by vacuum cleaners, which persists over months or years and totally absorbs the child whenever he is anywhere near a vacuum cleaner. Other fears include fear of dogs, open doors, heights, bubbles, balloons, and cracks.

The presence of irrational fears is used by some people to diagnose childhood psychosis. Irrational fears are not present in all psychotic and retarded children, but interestingly, fears will often emerge in a child who is getting better with treatment. Thus, the child who improves substantially will develop a large range of fears. Why these fears exist or come about as a child improves is an open question; it might be because the child becomes more aware of his environment. It is important to note that a child who has irrational fears, or who in general seems quite anxious, does much better in the kind of teaching program we have developed. Some children are quite void of any anxiety, and their prognoses appear less favorable. The presence of fear in the child provides him with an additional source of motivation. To some extent teaching can become a way of helping the child to cope with his fear, or to "get a handle on it." It is important to distinguish between fears that the child can learn to manage and that can be used therapeutically, and fears that directly interfere with the child's learning.

There are two programs in helping a child overcome fears: modeling and "working through."

Modeling Program

In the *modeling program* (Bandura, 1967), the teacher first makes certain that the student's fears are not reinforced (they are not *operant,* such that the child uses his fear to obtain a desired result). For example, it is entirely possible that a person may use his fears to escape or avoid certain demands or unpleasant situations, thereby learning to become fearful. It is also possible for a child to learn to become fearful in order to get lots of attention from adults, who try to comfort him whenever he is fearful. The extent to which such fear is "real" (fear generated by painful situations) or shaped as operant behavior is hard to say (watch a good actor acting a frightening scene and try to tell the difference).

Once it has been determined that rewards, such as escape or attention, have been removed and that the fear is not decreasing, the adult may want to model appropriate behavior in relation to the feared object or event, and perhaps verbally describe the situation as not fearful. For example, if the child is afraid of dogs, the adult would model approach behavior toward the dog, including petting the dog, while reassuring the child, "See, I'm petting the dog. Gee, that wasn't hard." Of course, the child's approach behavior to the feared object should be immediately rewarded.

It is surprising, in view of all the modeling and gradual exposure to the feared objects, that most of the children with whom we worked still remained very fearful. That is, we were unable to desensitize them and almost invariably we had to force them into contact with the feared object.

"Working Through" Program

This program resembles a "flooding" program used in treating adult fears. When the fears persisted after a modeling program, the child was placed into the fearful situation and kept there until he gave signs of extinguishing his fear. This lasted anywhere from 5 minutes to several hours. At any one session, no more than one-half hour went by without taking a break of 5 to 10 minutes, and then the child was reintroduced to the fearful situation. "Flooding" the child in this way with the fearful object, that is, ensuring prolonged exposures to the feared object, ensured extinction of the fear. The procedure has been markedly effective. For example, the child may be very afraid of going into the swimming pool, or even afraid of going into water in the tub or shower. He screams and fights whenever he is near water. In that situation, we eventually may end up placing him in a tub, or in the swimming pool, for anywhere from 15 to 30 minutes, despite the fact that he screams and kicks. We may take a short break after 15 to 30 minutes, and then place him back in the pool again for another exposure, so that during one afternoon he may be in the pool for 3 hours, and out of the pool, for 10- to 20-minute breaks, for a total of 30 minutes. Most of the child's fears of water should be extinguished within a half-day session like that, and it is probably safe to say that if the fear persists despite two or three sessions of 3- to 4-hour durations, then the technique does not work. Also, it is important to note that if the child gives signs of diminishing fear after the first day, then the sessions must be continued the second day. Do not allow too much time to elapse between trials.

Other fears are extinguished in similar ways. For example, if the child is afraid of heights you would purposely put him on top of chairs and tables 30 to 40 times an afternoon, or carry him piggyback with you, so as to help him extinguish the fear. If he's afraid of vacuum cleaners, then purposely run vacuum cleaners around him several hours a day for however many days are necessary to help him overcome that fear.

We have observed a very interesting effect, *counterphobia,* in children who have successfully lost (that is, mastered) their fears. Essentially the children who previously were afraid of an object, once their fears reach manageable levels with regard to that object, become quite attached to and obsessed with the previously feared object. For example, the child who was afraid of heights now insists on jumping off of chairs and tables, and the child who was afraid of the water now insists on spending all his free time in the pool.

CHAPTER 33

PRETENDING AND IMAGINING

The programs in this chapter teach the child how to pretend and to imagine—how to use his fantasy. Essentially, these programs involve teaching the child to construct in his imagination a reality that may not be there, and to act as if that reality is present, which it is not. Such behavior is considered to be the most advanced attribute of language. For developmentally retarded children to be able to learn such behavior would seem particularly encouraging since many theoreticians have written on the "inability" of developmentally retarded persons to abandon what many consider their basic concrete attitude and engage in more abstract and creative behavior. As you will see when you teach these programs, children with developmental retardation are quite able to learn to pretend and to fantasize, with some help on your part, and will show signs of enjoying this kind of activity as much as any average person.

Obviously, since these programs on pretending and imagining require a considerable amount of language, it is best to start these programs after the child has become proficient in his use of abstract language, after he can easily identify and describe events and behaviors around him, and after he has developed some conversational skills. In other words, the programs on pretending and imaginative play are best suited for higher-functioning children. The child should have mastered the basics of nonverbal imitation, as well as intermediate language (Unit V).

The programs offered in this book are intended largely to serve as guidance for the teacher's construction of more complete programs. Thus, we use a number of programs that are not presented in detail here. In the "Predicting Program" the child is taught to predict what will happen in the future: you ask the child questions such as, "If I drop this glass, what will happen?" or "What are you going to do after lunch?" Another program, the "Tell a Story Program," starts with the child completing statements already begun by the teacher in reference to a picture. For example, you start the "story" by saying, "This boy is wearing a _____." Gradually drop such prompts while moving on to more elaborate accounts with decreasing cues ("Who are they and what are they doing?"). Finally, you may reduce your part in the story to the following request, "Tell me a story about the picture," and your child takes it from there.

BASIC PRETENDING

In this program the child will be performing an action in relation to some object that is not present, or pretending to be an individual or organism that he is not.

Begin the program by teaching the child to engage in some behavior that he finds entertaining, but without using the "props" that are necessary in reality to complete the act. For example, face the child and say to him, "Do this, pretend you are drinking juice." In most of these "imagined" or "fantasized" behaviors it is critical that the child has some prior gratifying experience "in reality," and that he has already described the behaviors "in reality" before you start them "in fantasy." Model the action for the child, holding the (imaginary) cup in your hand, smacking your lips, and making slurping noises, while "drinking" the imaginary juice. Prompt the child to imitate you if he doesn't do so spontaneously and provide all the necessary contextual cues, such as saying "ah" and "um" to communicate your pleasure with the exquisite juice you are drinking. In other words, "ham it up" and prompt the child when necessary to do likewise. Over several trials, fade out the modeling prompt, so that by the end of a series of trials you can simply ask the child to perform the action ("pretend you're drinking juice") and then reinforce him heavily for acting appropriately. Your joy over his creative and imaginative efforts should be a part of the reinforcement he receives. The other part of his reinforcement should be that which is intrinsic to the behavior. That is, by choosing a behavior that he likes, such as drinking juice, the acting out of the behavior is very likely to elicit the kinds of positive feelings in him that are rewarding, hence maintaining the imaginative behavior.

Once this first behavior has been acquired, you will want to introduce another pretend action, and mix it in with the first action (randomly rotate) in order to help him form a discrimination. Choose actions of pretending that he enjoys and that are associated with some discriminable and clearly identifiable behavior. For example, if drinking juice is the first behavior, then "eating a cookie" might be the next behavior that he pretends, followed by "kissing baby," "going to sleep," or "driving a car." For each of these behaviors the teacher has to become quite creative in order to bring in all the nuances of the act. For example, driving a car would entail more than just holding the hands on the steering wheel. It involves shifting gears, sounding like an engine, and moving to the left and to the right as the car negotiates different turns. For children who like to ride in cars, imagining being in a car should become very pleasing. If your child does not like riding in a car, pick some other behavior.

Basic pretending also includes teaching your child to pretend to be something which he is not, for example, a dog, a cat, or a bird. Hearing the expression, "Let's pretend we are birds," and then watching an adult and a child running around the room with arms flapping is quite a sight to behold. Many actions of dogs can be imitated: they bark, they scratch their heads for fleas, they eat out of a dish on the floor. Pretending makes teaching fun.

Some children become extremely gratified by learning to use their imagination. One slight problem which then may occur is that some children become so involved in their fantasy that it takes on inappropriate or psychotic proportions. For example, once the child is taught to pretend to be a dog, some children may become so involved in playing the part that they would rather be a dog than a human being. They spend the entire day barking, eating off dishes on the floor, and even smelling the legs of adults or tree trunks. Adults have to provide the child with feedback when he becomes too involved in some behavior. That is, he is just plainly told, in harsh terms if necessary, "That's enough dog, let's play something else."

ADVANCED PRETENDING

After the child has mastered "simple" pretending, that is, once he can act out several simple pretend actions with little or no prompt from the adult, then he is ready to learn larger sequences of actions, such as "Getting ready for bed." This sequence of pretend actions may include getting undressed, taking a bath, brushing his teeth, climbing into bed, putting head on pillow, closing his eyes, and sleeping. You should state the action, "Pretend you are getting ready for bed," and prompt the child, which will be necessary in the beginning. Also ask the child to label the behavior that he "performs," so that he may describe his actions, such as "I am taking my clothes off," or "I am closing my eyes." Prompt him to express these verbal descriptions of "getting ready for bed" activities. These prompts should be as "light" as possible.

Once the child has mastered any one sequence, other sequences of behaviors should be trained, such as "cooking breakfast," and "getting ready for school." Again, select those behaviors the child finds most reinforcing in everyday life.

In order to build your child's imagination, the child must learn to label more and more of his behaviors in everyday life. For example, if the child goes to a store, or to the beach, or to some place he enjoys, have him label his behaviors (that is, give a verbal description of each act) as he goes through them. Behaviors that have been labeled or described as they actually occur in the real world will be easier for the child to remember and to use in fantasy at a later stage. Too many developmentally retarded children will engage in some pleasurable activity, but, since they do not conceptualize or verbalize the behavior at the time, they are less able to draw upon these experiences for subsequent gratification in fantasy.

The programs in basic and advanced pretending are tied to experiences in the child's "real" life. "Going shopping," "playing in the park," and "eating breakfast" are all behaviors that are closely tied to the child's daily life. It is possible to stretch these behaviors a little and to introduce new material that does not strictly correspond to what the child may already have experienced. For example, playing "mama bear" and "baby bear" are certainly behaviors that the child has never seen or had contact with, and they would be proportionately more difficult to build or shape up. Because of that we prefer to start with pretend behaviors that the child encounters in everyday life. Pretending that involves events that are totally constructed in imagination should nevertheless become important for facilitating peer play (one peer becoming mama bear while the other peer becomes baby bear), or play with many toys, such as dolls, where one doll is "mama doll," another is "baby doll" who is fed and bathed by "Mama."

PLAYING TEACHER

"Playing Teacher" is a program that many children find *very* rewarding. This program is less complicated than the other programs and can be started quite early in the child's training. The teacher takes the role of the child and prompts the child to take the role of the teacher. The program is designed to teach the child an explicit form of control over his environment. He becomes boss, so to speak.

It might be easiest to start this kind of interaction with a second adult, who stands behind the child and prompts the child to give the teacher orders. Fade this second adult as soon as possible. For example, the child is prompted to say, "Stand up," "Sit down," "Clap your hands," and so on going into increasingly complex commands where the teacher immediately performs the actions. Later the child is prompted to reward the teacher for complying ("Good standing," giving the teacher food and kisses), or to admonish the teacher in a stern voice ("No, pay attention!") if the teacher does not comply.

"Playing Teacher" in this way is probably a very important part of a child's play and should facilitate socialization. We frequently observe a great deal of joy in the child as he takes command. We also see a substantial improvement in the clarity and volume of his diction. "Playing Teacher" may serve as a good procedure for helping children who typically are inaudible and poor enunciators to enunciate clearly and loudly.

When a child has been on the receiving side of a teaching program such as we have outlined, all effort should be made to help the child "take command" of the situation as soon as possible. The important message in all teaching, whether one is working with developmentally retarded or normal children, is that the child has to submit himself to some control at one time in order to become a free person at a later time. The program "Playing Teacher" is one small step in that direction.

CHAPTER 34

OBSERVATIONAL LEARNING

The child learns much by merely observing and then doing what other children do or what adults do with other children. Perhaps quite suddenly and without a great deal of practice, the child may show that he has learned through the mere observation of the behaviors of others. He does not have to be explicitly shaped through successive approximations. This is called learning by observation, or observational learning. Sometimes observational learning goes hand in hand with the kind of shaping that we have already described in this manual. For example, the child will be prompted to act in a certain way by observing someone else behave, but since the behavior may at first be imperfect, the behavior gradually will be shaped to criterion. It can be argued that observational learning is critical for a child's normal development, that learning through direct shaping is not enough. This becomes particularly true when the student starts to interact with his peers. Most of what a child learns from peers will be learned through observation, and that learning is critical for his full development.

In any case, it would be extremely helpful for a child to learn behaviors by merely observing those behaviors in others. The importance of learning by imitation is a good illustration. The child watches the behavior of somebody else and then tries the behavior on his own. When a child cannot learn by this kind of observation (and most developmentally retarded children seem unable to do so) perhaps he could be taught to do so. This is exactly what we attempted to do when we set up programs for teaching verbal and nonverbal imitation in the earlier sections of this book. This chapter expands on these programs, largely by teaching the child to become more observant of what is happening in his environment.

Note that some of the programs in this chapter (such as "What's Missing?") may be started relatively early, for example, after the child has completed Unit V. As we present these programs, keep in mind that you have to work out the details on your own. The order in which these programs are presented does not have to be the order in which you teach them. Observational learning is vastly more complex than what we have outlined here, but the intent of the chapter is to provide a beginning in teaching the child to learn by observation. You have to construct more elaborate programs on your own. The variations that may be introduced on these programs underscore the need to be aware of the child's level of functioning, and to be aware of possible mistakes in one's teaching. It is easy to see how one could be teaching behaviors that lead nowhere.

THE "WHAT'S MISSING?" GAME

The purpose of this program is to help the child pay more attention to the things he sees around him. Start in the usual position, with you and the child sitting across from each other at a table.

Step 1: Place one common object on the table (like a set of keys, or an ashtray, or a watch) and ask the child to label it by saying, "What is this?" (The child must know these labels by now.)

Step 2: After you have pointed to the object and he has labeled it (e.g., "watch,"), tell the child, "Cover your eyes" (a response you should practice independently), or cover his eyes for him with your hand. As soon as his eyes are shut, remove the object, or cover the object with a napkin. Then tell him, "Open your eyes," or remove your hand from his eyes and let him look.

Step 3: Point to the table where the object was last visible and ask your child "What's missing?" If he answers incorrectly, you may want to prompt the correct answer by showing him parts of the object you are hiding.

Step 4: Once he has mastered the task with one object (the watch), try different objects, one at a time (e.g., keys, glasses, or candy). When he responds to criterion, go on to Step 5.

Step 5: Place two common but distinct objects on the table (e.g., keys and a watch). Point to each object and ask the child "What is this?" If the child responds correctly (e.g., "Keys"), then point to the second object and again ask, "What is this?," reinforcing the child's correct label. The child is then asked not to look while one of the two objects is removed. If the child has problems here, just cover the object with the napkin, without actually removing it. He is then asked, "What's missing?" With two objects present, the child is forced, or enabled to learn the concept, "What's missing?" since he has to remember what was there before but is not there now.

In gradual steps, make the task more difficult by adding more objects (some children will be able to detect what is missing from as many as eight or more objects on the table), increasing the amount of time the child looks away, and skipping the labeling of the object (say "Look at these," while moving your finger slowly behind the objects, facilitating the child's scanning).

Generalize this program to the everyday environment by removing dishes or eating utensils from the table, by removing familiar pieces of furniture from his room, by removing your shoes, or by taking a picture off the wall. At the risk of being redundant, let us reiterate that it is crucial to teach the child to generalize these tasks to his everyday environment. It is of no particular benefit to the child to learn to detect objects on a table if he remains oblivious to the rest of his environment. You merely *start* the training on the table to help the child learn to look and identify changes around him.

Expanding Your Child's World

THE "WHAT IS IT?" GAME

Unlike the "What's Missing?" game, the "What Is It?" game requires a fairly sophisticated use of language. Essentially, the child is given a verbal description of an object or a behavior and is required to identify the corresponding object or behavior in his environment. This game is usually played as part of preschool preparation training with several adults (playing the part of children) sitting in a group with the child, but it could be taught in a one-to-one situation as well. In a group situation (the adults are seated in a circle so everyone can be seen), each person holds up an object (such as a yellow cup, a blue cup, a black book, a black comb, a white shoe, or a square block). The teacher then asks a question, such as "What do you drink from?", and the child is prompted to answer and is reinforced as before. A target response may be the child pointing to the object and correctly verbalizing. The questions gradually are made more difficult, such as, "What is yellow and you drink from it?" or, "What's big and white and goes on someone's foot?" At some point, different persons in the group "take turns" answering different questions. The answers should become prompts for the child when he cannot respond correctly. Remember, the purpose of the program is to teach the child to learn by observing and listening.

In the case of identifying behaviors, the members of the group may demonstrate some action, or the adult may want to use pictures. A beginning step may be for the child to identify who is smiling when one of the persons in the group is smiling (e.g., the child responds "Laurie is" when asked, "Who is smiling?"). A more complex question would be "Who is smiling and has a yellow sweater?" This helps the child listen to the question and scan his environment for the appropriate cues. Needless to say, successful answers to a task like that forces (or enables) the child to "turn outward," or to become aware of his surroundings.

THE "I DO/I AM" GAME

The "I Do" game is very similar to the "What is it?" game. The purpose of "I Do/I Am" is to teach the child to learn by listening and looking at people around him and by comparing himself with others.

Arrange a group of people in a circle and then begin with a question like, "Who has the yellow cup?" The person who has the yellow cup would be required to say, "I do." The child is then given the object (e.g., the yellow cup) and is prompted to respond correctly to the question. Later, the cues that are required for correct responding may be more subtle, such as, "Who is wearing jeans?" or "Who is wearing a yellow sweater?" Later, the teacher may ask quite difficult questions, such as, "Who is smiling and has blonde hair?" or "Who has brown eyes and white shoes."

An interesting variation of this game, which makes it more certain that the child is in fact learning the rule, is to have an adult answer incorrectly. The child should then be taught to say, "No, you are not," and to correct the adult. It is the child's ability to discriminate at that level that allows you to infer that he has acquired the task.

An interesting variation of the "I Do/I Am" game involves the introduction of competition. For example, the teacher may ask, "Who wants ice cream?" and then reinforce whoever says, "I do," with a spoonful of ice cream. Once this behavior is established and the child is answering appropriately, change the question to, "Who wants a spanking?" Needless to say, correct responding to these questions necessitates that the child listen carefully rather than learning to say, "I do," to whatever is asked.

Observational Learning

THE "LISTENING AND FINDING" GAME

The "Listening and Finding" game is very similar to the games we have already described and involves only a slight variation, underscoring the fact that developmentally disabled persons need explicit teaching. In this particular game a group of people is not essential. It may be played by having just a teacher and a child present, but since it is a typical preschool game, it is probably wise to include other people, especially children, in a group-like format at later points. Essentially, the teacher describes a picture that only she can see, and, once this picture is described, then that particular picture, along with another similar picture, is placed in front of the child. The child is then required to identify (point to) the picture the teacher has described. In other words, the child is asked to identify a picture based on *someone else's* description of it.

For example, the teacher may hold the picture of a boy eating ice cream and describe this picture quite simply in the beginning: "The boy is eating ice cream." The teacher then shuffles that picture with another one, places the two pictures face up in front of the child, and tells the child "Point to the correct picture." To make it easy, perhaps the first time one picture would show a boy eating ice cream while the other picture would be blank. When scenes come to be included in the second picture, they might be clearly different from the first one.

Gradually, the description is increased in complexity, with a corresponding complexity in the choices between the pictures. For example, it is entirely possible that the teacher eventually present a very lengthy description of the picture in which the key element, such as a boy riding a bicycle, is a relatively small part of the story. Then, the child is presented with two quite similar pictures, for example, one picture may include a boy riding a bicycle while the other picture merely shows a bicycle as part of a scene. Again, note that you want to move from the simple to the complex, and to make it simple in the beginning so that the child gets a chance to exhibit the correct behavior.

"STORY TIME"

"Story Time" is particularly useful for students who are about to enroll in preschool, or in classrooms where students have to listen to the instructions of the teacher and then respond appropriately. The goal of such a program centers on increasing the child's knowledge of the world and thereby helping him to be more useful and entertaining with his social group.

It is perhaps best to "play school" in this program by having the child sit on the rug, like children do in school, either alone or with other persons, and listen to the teacher offer "Story Time." You may want to proceed as follows:

Step 1: A very simple and easy book is selected. One adult serves as teacher and reads one or two sentences from the book. The second adult is then asked a simple question based on the material read and provides a simple answer. This adult is then reinforced. The material is then reread and the child is asked the *same* question. This is to facilitate the child's listening to other members of the group and to get prompts from them when necessary.

For example, the teacher may read, "The dog does not say, 'cluck cluck,' the dog says 'bow-wow.'" The teacher then asks an attending adult "What does the dog say?" This adult then answers "The dog says 'bow-wow.'" The teacher then reinforces the adult for "good listening." At that point the teacher faces the child and asks "The dog doesn't say, 'cluck cluck,' the dog says 'bow-wow.' What does the dog say?" If the child now says the right answer, he is reinforced; if not, he may be prompted. His prompt may be given by repeating the question to the first adult.

Step 2: The child may now be asked the question directly by the teacher without the teacher first asking the attending adult. If the child fails to answer the question or answers incorrectly, the material may be reread and the teacher may ask the first adult for the correct answer. What the program attempts to do, in part, is to help direct the child's attention to other members in the group as providing information about correct responding in addition to helping him attend to what the teacher is reading.

In subsequent steps, the level of difficulty is increased by the teacher reading longer sentences and including references to the character's knowledge, feelings, and so forth. Note the importance of reading material that directly relates to the child's own experiences, that is, material that is meaningful to the child. If you can't find such a book (many books for children are written at an unbelievably difficult level and from the framework of an adult), you obviously can make up your own story. Make certain that it fits the child's experience, dealing with activities that he clearly understands and can conceptualize.

As training progresses, the material becomes more demanding and the child may now expect to listen to a story, for example, for 3 to 5 minutes, before questions are asked about that story. The story could deal with people's feelings, reasons for their feelings, and what they were thinking. Note also that "Story Time" provides an opportunity for the child himself or other children to present their own material to the story. In other words, as soon as the child has mastered the early steps, make learning more demanding, and more interesting.

THE "GETTING INFORMATION" GAME

In a program very similar to, and complimenting "Story Time," the child is taught to seek information by addressing attending persons.

Step 1: Start by asking the child questions that he knows the answer to, such as "What's your name?" or "Where do you live?"

Step 2: Then present a question he does not know how to answer, such as, "How old is he? (pointing to a particular adult)" or "What are you going to have for dinner?"

Step 3: Prompt your child to ask someone else in the room, who then gives the child the correct answer.

Step 4: Repeat your question to the child and prompt the correct answer if necessary. Also, you may occasionally ask him questions from Step 1 at this point.

Step 5: Repeat Steps 1–4 with new questions until the child learns to ask attending adults for answers to questions he cannot answer.

An important extension of this kind of program is to have persons in the child's environment make certain statements (initially offering simple facts, later more subtle descriptions) and then ask your child to tell you about what was said. Repeat, prompt, and fade the prompt as before in order to get this kind of behavior under appropriate control. It is a critical skill for your child to learn if he is going to benefit from group instruction in school or from most other situations in life.

CHAPTER 35

BUILDING SPONTANEITY VERSUS CONTROLLING BEHAVIOR

Many teachers who become familiar with the kind of behavioral teachings we have discussed throughout this book wonder about the extent to which children taught by these procedures lack spontaneity. They may have a valid concern because any authoritarian and controlling atmosphere such as the one we employ may well curb spontaneity. This chapter presents definitions of spontaneity, and describes ways of encouraging and building spontaneous behavior.

Spontaneous behavior is behavior that is not explicitly taught, but is in a sense "free" and unpredictable. This definition of spontaneous behavior relates to generalization as discussed in Chapter 13.

In *stimulus generalization*, spontaneous behavior can be viewed as behavior that occurred in new situations, that is, in situations not explicitly associated with teaching. *Response generalization* can be viewed as the appearance of new and novel behavior. Generalized behavior change refers to behaviors not explicitly taught.

FOSTERING SPONTANEOUS BEHAVIOR

The following set of procedures has been designed to foster spontaneous behavior.

1. As many persons should work with the child as possible. This will facilitate stimulus generalization so that the child will behave spontaneously in the presence of new persons. *Avoid* situations where the child has only one teacher because this will probably teach him to discriminate between persons, and cut down on spontaneous behavior. Be sure to include children as "teachers" in the beginning; otherwise the child may learn to discriminate between adults and children and remain passive with the latter.
2. Teach your child in as many physical locations as possible: in school, at home, in the car, on walks, in the park, in stores. You want as many situations associated with his new skills (language, play, social interactions) as possible. *Avoid* teaching programs where the child is taught in a limited environment, like sitting in a chair in a particular room in a particular school.

3. As early as possible, change to natural, everyday rewards and use as many different kinds of rewards as you can, including rewards that are available everywhere in people, in his own behavior, and so on. *Avoid* teaching programs that rely on a limited set of powerful rewards, like foods or candy. In such programs the child will learn to behave appropriately when he is hungry and food is present; otherwise he will not. You may have to use such artificial rewards as food in the beginning, but only to initiate certain basic behaviors.

4. Associate yourself with the delivery of powerful reinforcers, like giving or removing food and aversives, or providing the child with new opportunities to play. That way *you* will acquire increasingly complex rewarding value for your child, and so will other aspects of his behavior and environment in general. When that occurs, you will have to do less explicit shaping and teaching. He will begin to shape himself (that is, spontaneously change) in order to enjoy those new rewards.

5. As much as possible, reinforce appropriate behaviors that occur *without* the adult prompting or otherwise asking for it. In particular, be sure to fade out adult assistance, in the form of prompts and instructions, as soon as possible, and reward behaviors that occur in the absence of adult control.

6. The larger a child's behavioral repertoire, the more spontaneous he will seem. Clearly, a child who has only mastered one verbal response would not manifest a great deal of spontaneous verbal behavior when compared to a child who has a more extensive verbal repertoire. In other words, keep on teaching new behaviors to expand the child's repertoire. This will facilitate response generalization.

7. Teach as many "pivotal" responses as possible. That is, strengthen behaviors that allow the child access to a large range of powerful reinforcers. Make his language *functional*, teach him *practical* skills. For example, teach him to ask for favors, like food and play, rather than just teaching him to label body parts. Teach him to go to the toilet, to dress himself, and to eat appropriately, instead of just tracing lines or coloring inside a boundary. In the same manner, teach new behaviors that substitute for already established, less adaptive behaviors. For example, teach appropriate play and art to replace more elementary forms of the same, such as less elaborate, more stereotyped motor self-stimulation. Suppress the primitive forms of self-stimulation and hope for a behavior substitution of more appropriate behaviors.

8. Try to suppress the stereotyped, repetitive self-stimulatory behaviors, since these apparently block the development of new, more adaptive behaviors and reduce the child's responsiveness to his extrinsic environment.

9. Avoid prolonged use of aversives (generalized fear and anxiety) because aversives suppress spontaneous behaviors such as vocal language and play.

     Points 8 and 9 above may seem contradictory in that aversives may have to be used to suppress self-stimulatory behavior. Even so, once self-stimulatory behaviors are suppressed and replaced with more appropriate behaviors, aversives should be withdrawn to allow spontaneous behaviors to appear.

10. Create situations throughout the day in which you and your child can act as "free" as possible. Create situations in which he is physically very active in play, or he is rewarded for being active. Gradually introduce these situations over the first year of teaching as he learns to discriminate between situations in which he can play and those in which he has to work. In general, as the child is acquiring the basic behaviors necessary for more adequate functioning, the adult needs to back off a bit on teacher control so as to help the child assume more independence and freedom.

                                                       Expanding Your Child's World

CONTROLLING BEHAVIOR

When to control and when not to control is a basic and difficult question for both parents and educators alike. There are two types of control, control that is used constructively and control that is used to enslave. Constructive use of control provides children with the basic behavioral repertoire necessary to be free. Anyone who has visited a state hospital (or state school) for the developmentally disabled and emotionally disturbed has seen how behavioral impoverishment leads to enslavement. People are "stored" in those places because they do not have the behavioral skills to make it on the outside.

On the other hand, every dictator and oppressor has enslaved his people through the use of behavioral control procedures. The main steps involved in enslaving someone may read as follows:

1. Select a set of powerful, but limited, reinforcers, such as food, guilt, and anxiety. Allow only one or a limited number of persons to manipulate those reinforcers. Discourage the development of reinforcers the individual himself can manipulate, such as sex or personal creativity.
2. Build a limited set of behaviors only, and make certain that these behaviors are under the control of a limited set of easily identified persons or situations (build narrow stimulus control).
3. Strengthen incompetence, as in rewarding dependent behavior and interpersonal failures.

The list could be lengthened, but this is probably sufficient to alert the reader to the dangers of unchecked behavioral control. Remember, although control can be used to free persons and to build spontaneous behavior, it can also be used to enslave.

From what we have said, one obviously needs to exert considerable control in the beginning. It is the same with normal children—adults exert considerable control over them in the early years. That is, young children do *not* decide whether to go to school, whether to cross a street in heavy traffic, or whether to be freely aggressive toward their siblings. Adults make those decisions. As the child becomes behaviorally more competent, adults should reduce their control. When to stop harping and pestering, and, for the child's sake, when to let him make his own decisions are very difficult decisions for all parents. For example, one of the most difficult decisions any parent faces is to ease up on their control even though they are certain their children will make mistakes. Eventually children have to face reality on their own, and learn from the mistakes they make. It is hard for parents to face that, but it is better to make small mistakes as a child than big mistakes as an adult.

Easing control is a gradual process. We have learned to begin experimenting with lessened control some time after the child has mastered most of the programs in this book. The child's behaviors provide the guidance to us—if he continues to learn and function adequately, we lessen the control a bit more. If he regresses, stops learning, becomes inattentive in class, starts to self-stimulate, or begins some other inappropriate behavior, then we reintroduce the control, in order to lessen it again at a later date when he can "handle" it.

CREATIVE SPONTANEITY: INTRINSICALLY VERSUS EXTRINSICALLY CONTROLLED REINFORCERS

Many puzzling questions remain regarding spontaneous behavior versus controlled behavior. At this time we do not know how to raise an individual to come under the influence of personally controlled "creative" reinforcers (and, accordingly, to lessen the control of social, extrinsically controlled reinforcers). If we argue that *exposure* to already existing social behaviors is necessary (but not sufficient), we are not providing a teacher of creative students with much help. How, then, can a behaviorist deal with creative spontaneity, behavior that contributes to the individual's growth and our understanding of man? Let us try to conceptualize such creativity.

Consider the behavior of creative artists who clearly escaped from the control of their social environments. People like Van Gogh and Stravinsky are good examples. They created art that was "ahead of the times"—future generations were to appreciate their work more than the present. They may also have exercised a profound effect on culture, science, and politics. What shaped Van Gogh's paintings? He did *not* match his pictures to an "outside" reality, as painters had done before him. There is no way that his behavior could have been shaped by the social rewards (his public), which, of course, he didn't have in the first place. (In other words, there was not a group of people around Van Gogh who said, "Good painting, Vince.") In fact, Van Gogh and persons like him seemed quite independent of such social control. Most likely, then, Van Gogh shaped himself. He must have experienced, at the very moment he had put down a particular stroke on the canvas, that the form and the color were "just right"; the color and the form he created reinforced him.

In these instances, one may talk of *perceptual reinforcers,* which we introduced earlier in conjunction with sensory reinforcers. We said earlier that *matching* one person's behavior against some other person's behavior must have become reinforcing, as in imitative (echolalic) speech. In the case of Van Gogh, however, the matching did not occur against some external referent, because that external referent was not available. That is what makes Van Gogh's behavior so particularly *original* and *creative.* Instead, Van Gogh must have matched against some internal "template." In other words, the behavior of artists like Van Gogh is probably determined by internal, personally controlled reinforcers. Such personally controlled behaviors are the essence of creative spontaneity.

Much behavioral writing has attributed all of man's behavior to social control. B. F. Skinner, who is the best-known living spokesman of modern behaviorism, does not extensively discuss such personally controlled perceptual and conceptual reinforcers. Yet we might find it necessary to postulate such reinforcers in order to account for truly creative and autonomous behavior.

It would also be interesting to speculate on the emergence of creative behavior in developmentally disabled persons, and to speculate on the relationship between creative and psychotic behavior. Note, for example, how creative persons such as Van Gogh and Stravinsky were relatively free of social control. However, this relationship must await clarification through future research. For our purposes here, let us describe a more mundane and concrete program to initiate spontaneous behavior in developmentally disabled children. The program is known as "poster training."

A PROGRAM TO INITIATE SPONTANEOUS BEHAVIOR

Poster training starts with a set of ten posters, each having one picture of an object that the child has already been taught to label, such as an apple, a tree, a dog, or similar objects. The child is simply instructed, "Tell me about the poster." He is immediately shown the poster, and reinforced after he has made a correct response. The teacher then goes on to the second poster, and so on until the first set of ten posters has been completed. He is then shown a set of ten new posters, each having *two* familiar pictures, such as an apple and a dog. The child is reinforced after correctly labeling both objects. He may need prompting on the first few posters, and this set of posters may have to be repeated before he labels *both* pictures on the posters without prompts when asked to "Tell me about the poster." The teacher may want to help the child monitor his performance by teaching him to first point to one of the objects, and then the other, in the poster, perhaps moving from left to right, as in reading. After the child has mastered posters with two objects, he is shown ten posters with three pictures each, and so on until he can tell about posters with ten different objects on each poster.

The child is probably learning two things at this time. First he is learning to give longer and longer descriptions before he is reinforced, and his behavior is probably becoming less tied to explicit teacher control. Second, he may be learning to systematically scan or search his environment for necessary cues in order to come up with adequate behavior. Both these events serve to "separate" the child from explicit teacher control and to facilitate the beginning of spontaneous speech.

Once the posters are mastered, move the child on to more ordinary but complex pictures depicting heterogeneous scenes (dog, house, man, woman). You may then go on to ask the child to label everyday events around him, such as objects he sees in his house. For example, ask him to "Tell me what you see in this room," to which he may respond, "light, door, table, picture, floor." You should prompt his response when necessary, and gradually withhold the reward in order to get longer and more detailed descriptions.

Another exercise may be for the child to "Tell me about yourself," in which the teacher may start the child off by describing his head ("hair, eyes, ear") and moving down his body (to shoulders, arms, stomach). The goal in this training is to arrange for larger and larger behavior repertoires with less and less adult guidance. Remember that in these as in all other programs the teacher and the child are learning a procedure that works best when it is extended to the child's everyday environment.

These and similar procedures may well help the child to be more "free" and spontaneous. There are many other such practices, including teaching the child to be more physically active, as in play and sports, and to become more assertive. Remember to gradually fade out the explicit and strict control that you needed to get learning started in the beginning.

We have found physical aversives and fear to be inhibitors of spontaneous play and language. This implies again that the teacher needs to "back off" a bit on her control as the basic learning requirements have been met.

In summary, then, a number of different events help produce spontaneous behavior, and many of these involve the adult becoming *less* controlling of the child as the child becomes increasingly competent. A happy, anxiety-free environment seems to facilitate the child's creativity. Other aspects of spontaneity are less well understood. This is particularly true of our lack of information on the subject of how to create a teaching environment in which the child is helped to acquire intrinsic but socially meaningful rewards, such as in creative art.

PREPARING THE CHILD FOR SCHOOL

CHAPTER 36

Just as a parent of a normal child never relinquishes total responsibility for a child's education when he enters kindergarten or the first grade, neither would a parent of a developmentally disabled child. Active and close collaboration between parents and teachers of developmentally disabled children is critical; without close collaboration, the child will suffer. The kind of programs that developmentally delayed children are likely to encounter in school are often similar to the programs outlined in this book, such as programs for teaching the children abstract language, teaching appropriate play with toys and peers, and teaching listening and attending. Since the programs in school and at home are quite similar and because developmentally disabled children learn more slowly than average children, it is necessary that parents and teachers collaborate on the child's educational program. In a sense, parents become teachers, and teachers become (to some extent) parents.

SELECTION OF A SCHOOL

Once a parent has had some experience in teaching his or her child the kind of programs outlined in this book, the parent should have gained many teaching skills and should be in a position to evaluate and select the kind of school that is optimal for the child. Similarly, such a parent should be in a position to identify school programs that would be particularly detrimental. The following suggestions should help parents select a school for their developmentally disabled child.

First, try to enroll your child in a classroom where there are as many normal children as possible, or where there is a mixture of children, some of whom are perhaps more advanced than your child, others less so. Try to avoid classrooms or schools where your child is among equals, since he will not have many superior behaviors to model. Developmentally disabled children, placed among other disabled children with the same or worse status, tend to imitate or model the peculiar and bizarre behaviors of their peers. A disabled child placed among more normal children will improve simply because the opportunity to model more appropriate behaviors is more available.

You need to find a peer group for your child where your child's existing intellectual and social behaviors will match as closely as possible the behaviors of his peers. If the child is with a group of children of the same chronological age who are mentally advanced, then it is likely that he will be isolated and excluded from his peers because his behavioral skills are too immature. If he has to go to classes with other children who also have lots of behavior problems, make sure that those classes are at a minimum, and in schools with many normal children.

Second, try to place your child in a class with normal children who are functioning at a mental level similar to your child's. For example, if your child has a chronological age of 5, but in fact functions mentally at the 3-year-old level, then he is better off with children whose chronological age is younger than his. Younger normal children do not show much bizarre behavior, yet they are more likely to play with your child, and thereby make more demands on him for appropriate interaction because their mental ages are about the same.

Some parents of developmentally disabled children may want to state that the age of their child is anywhere from 1 to 3 years younger than it in fact is. This is somewhat believable, since developmentally disabled children often look younger than average children of the same chronological age, and, of course, their mental development (such as play and language skills) is more appropriate to a younger child. For example, in some cases, a parent of a child who is 6-years old and who normally should be entering first grade may assert that the child is 4 years of age and enroll the child in preschool, allowing the child to have an additional 2 years of teaching before he enters first grade.

Third, avoid bringing to the school's attention any mention of your child's diagnosis. For example, if your child has been diagnosed as autistic or brain damaged, the mere mention of such a diagnosis to school personnel and neighbors will very likely result in some very peculiar programming for your child by that school. It is sad but true that the diagnosis of a psychological problem *is* very likely to lead to a detrimental environment for the person being diagnosed. Most diagnoses cause a peculiar "hands off" attitude on the part of most teachers, and the calling in of experts who are particularly inept at adjusting your child to school. This does not mean that you lie or withhold information from the school personnel because you consider them naive or misinformed. Rather, do not provide them with misleading information, as you do when you label your child with a particular diagnosis (unless that diagnosis is well understood, such as PKU or Down's syndrome). They will obviously see that your child behaves differently from other children, which is all they need to know. When you achieve a mutually confident relationship with the school personnel you may want to mention your child's diagnostic past. Remember that if you had visited several diagnostic centers, your child probably has had more than one diagnosis. Tell the teacher that, if she doesn't know already.

Fourth, try to find a classroom that has a structured curriculum. Developmentally disabled children are unlikely to benefit much from a situation in which the child prescribes his own curriculum, or a system that is marked by a lot of finger painting and playing with clay. Such classrooms may at times be useful for normal children, but developmentally disabled children are not able to use their free time as well as others; consequently they need a clear definition of what is required of them. In this regard, it is safe to mention that you should be cautious about classrooms that have a very heavily one-sided theoretical orientation, such as a heavy emphasis on sensorimotor training, muscle patterning, or psychodynamic theory. The reason that we can post this warning to you is that, as of this writing, there are no facts or data that show that children treated with programs such as sensorimotor training, muscle patterning, or psychodynamics do better than children who did not receive such training. All too often, one meets parents who have had children enrolled in such programs and, after much work and money, their children are no better off than before they started. In general, consult educators and psychologists (e.g., at a local university) about programs for your child. Be prepared to make the final decision yourself.

Fifth, evaluate the teacher. Teachers are not all alike; some are better than others. Similarly, the teachers do not necessarily follow the philosophy of the school principal or whatever public relations person you first encounter. Therefore, it is essential that you see the teacher work with the children in her classroom, and come to know her and understand what *her* philosophy and teaching style are like. Another very important, perhaps essential, criterion is that the teacher allows you to visit her classroom and discuss your child's experience with her. Our experience has been that teachers who do not want to talk to the child's parents, or do not want the parents to observe the classroom, are often incompetent. Either they are incompetent because they are poorly trained and simply do not know what to do (they are afraid to be observed), or they perceive themselves as extremely knowledgeable to the point that outside advice and counsel are not sought. Since there are no such experts in the field of developmental disabilities at this time, you can safely assume that their contribution to your child will be limited.

TRANSFERRING BEHAVIOR FROM HOME TO SCHOOL

The most common reason for which children are dismissed from school is that they constitute a nuisance or hazard for the teacher and for the other children. That is, a child who disrupts other children at work, or who is aggressive toward other children and the teacher, is likely to have his dismissal requested. Surprising as it may seem, this common reason for dismissal is perhaps the most easy one to correct. As a parent, you should, by now, have considerable experience in handling the child's tantrums and disruptive behavior. The main problem for you now is to transfer the kind of control you have over the child's good behavior at home to the teacher at school. Do not assume that just because the child behaves appropriately around you that he will behave in the same way around the teacher. In fact, it is best to assume beforehand that he will "test" the teacher to see what he can get away with. Make sure that you help the teacher acquire the control that you have over the child. Since children differ markedly in the kind of problem behaviors they show, and differ markedly in the kind of ways they respond to discipline, you have to help the teacher by telling her and showing her (when the occasion does arise) how to handle your child.

Keep in mind that some teachers have learned a lot of techniques and philosophies of treatment that may be detrimental for your child. For example, a teacher has learned that the child is acting out because he has a deep sense of underlying anxiety about the teaching situation, and to top it off, you have caused it, you have traumatized your child; or the teacher has been told that your child is brain damaged, and that he has these tantrums and angry outbursts because the nature of his brain doesn't let him do what he wants to do and he is frustrated. The end product of all that misinformation is that the child is left to act inappropriately. In such cases, you will have to actively intervene on behalf of your child so that the teacher does not make your child worse. Most teachers will drop their misconceptions and follow your advice if it works. You may or may not find that this effort of working with your child's teacher pays off. When faced with the long and difficult task of reeducating your child's teacher about your child, it is possible that you would be better off transferring your child to another classroom. This will differ across school districts and across teachers, and there is no rule that one can reach at this point. Perhaps it is easier to advise a younger teacher than an older one, because a younger teacher may be more curious and more flexible. It is important to keep in mind, however, that teachers are people, too, and that the teacher is the boss in the classroom. You have to get your point across while being pleasant, playing to your teacher's strengths. It is difficult at times, but you should remember that, if things are handled well and the teacher is receptive and well-trained, he or she will become your child's most important helper. In fact, your child won't make it without a good teacher.

Parents can help the teacher to control a child's disruptive behaviors. You can also help the teacher with teaching. Teachers like children who learn in the classroom and show the kinds of appropriate behaviors that teachers try to teach. Therefore, some weeks before your child starts school, visit the school and find out what kinds of behaviors the teacher requires from the children. Make a list of these behaviors and teach them separately to your child at home *before* he goes to class. Some of the behaviors children should acquire are sitting on the rug and listening to stories, playing appropriately with play equipment, participating in group activities like playing ring-around-the-rosey, and singing songs like "The Wheels on the Bus Go Round and Round." A student who is ideally prepared for school is a student who already knows many of the tasks the teacher wants to teach. Therefore, you should practice many of these behaviors at home to perfection and then later help transfer these behaviors from your home to the school.

This "pretraining" can be done in gradual steps. Play school with the family and adult volunteers at home first. Later, try to teach your child in the presence of siblings or other children from the neighborhood. Although you initially teach the child in a one-to-one situation, gradually increase the number of children around him until you approximate the size of the group he is going to meet in school. Do not assume that, just because the child can behave very well at home with you in a one-on-one teaching situation he will transfer this behavior to the school or to a group of other children. By building the right steps, you can be sure the child is generalizing his behavior.

PARENT AT SCHOOL

It is essential in most successful placements of developmentally disabled children that the parent (or some adult who knows the child equally well) be present in the classroom as an assistant teacher during the early stages of the child's adjustment period. The parent (or parent assistant) may gradually leave the group and sit at some distance from the child and then slowly begin to fade out of the classroom for short intervals at a time. "Peek in" on the child to observe him when he does not expect you to be there. If he misbehaves without you there, consequate effectively for his survival in that class.

It is very likely that your child will "test" the teacher in your absence, if not before. For example, your child may begin to whine or tantrum, if his demands are not met. Or he may be "lazy" with his behavior and not behave as clearly or succinctly as he is able. Remember that you can minimize such problems by being present at first and, with the teacher's approval, consequating these behaviors the way you did at home. It is really best if you discipline him and get him under control, because most teachers feel reluctant to be as strict as is necessary. Ask the teacher to place your child in the front row where he or she can reach over and intervene the way that you do. Do not take generalization for granted. Make sure you do not hide from the kind of problems that may occur but are present during any important transition, such as going from home to school.

Throughout your contacts with the teacher, remember to heavily reinforce the teacher with positives for any behavior that you consider helpful. Most teachers are responsive to your approval. (Since they don't make as much money as their colleagues in psychology and psychiatry give them presents and do special favors for them at times.) If your child can't be all that nice to his teacher at this time, make sure that you are.

TEACHER AT HOME

Just as parents have the opportunity to visit the school, the teacher should also be able to visit the child at home. The ideal teacher is one who knows the child's family, (the mother and father and other siblings), who knows exactly how the child is capable of performing in optimal situations and who knows what the optimal intervention is. In many instances, this information can only be obtained by the teacher actively consulting with the parents for advice.

WORKING TOGETHER

The ideal teaching situation exists when several people work with one child, so as to spread the work and responsibilities around. Weekly or bi-weekly staff conferences should be held. Such "staffing" should include the teacher, the parent, and other adults actively working with the child. Make sure that each member of the staff actually works with the child in front of the other staff members, so as to get feedback on how they are doing, and to teach others. It is also extremely helpful for the teacher and the parent both to know what the child did in any one day. This can be done by exchanging brief written notes about problems or progress the child has made.

It is our experience that the kind of healthy separation that exists between teacher and parent in the case of normal children is very counterproductive when it exists for developmentally disabled children. School for developmentally disabled children is different from other schools, and segregation between parent and teacher only works to the child's detriment. Needless to say, achieving the kind of collaborative effort between parents and teachers, where both are considered equal and both possess important information from working with the child on a day-to-day basis, requires a great deal of time, tact, and patience on the part of both parties. It is rare to see parents and teachers work together in harmony, yet it is quite possible to achieve such a harmonious group.

LEARNING WITH SCHOOL FRIENDS

When a child goes to school, part of what he learns will come from his teacher. A *very* large part of his learning will be provided by his peers. Other children will teach him either directly by interacting with him or indirectly by being observed by him as they interact with the teacher.

If the developmentally disabled child already receives satisfaction from playing with other children, then, to some extent, the problem is already solved because the child will play with others and learn from them. However, many developmentally disabled children are socially very isolated and feel no particular satisfaction from playing with peers. A child has to learn to appreciate and enjoy the company of friends. One solution to this problem may be in building up the reinforcing properties of other children.

There are several strategies that you may use to help develop more adequate peer interaction. Remember that it is best to start building social interactions at home, either by working with the child's normal siblings or by helping children in the neighborhood to play constructively with your child. (Chapter 12, "Appropriate Play Skills" outlines programs for building peer play.) It will be easier to develop peer play at school if your child already possesses some basic language skills, is able to participate in cooperative play with adults, and is able to participate in social games with siblings and peers, such as running, climbing, and playing ball. The children he meets in school will be much more responsive to him if he can participate in some of their games.

There are three basic strategies that can be used to increase social interaction between a developmentally disabled child and his peer group:

1. *Teacher reward strategy*. The teacher (or some other adult present at the school) directly reinforces the children for interacting with each other. Thus the child may be reinforced for talking to other children, for sitting next to them, for playing with them, or helping them in some task.

2. *Peer group reward strategy*. The children themselves will, as a group, be rewarded for playing with a particular child. The teacher may inform the group that if the group plays with and helps a particular child interact more, the group as a whole will gain some particular privilege or recognition for such work.

3. *Peer reward strategy*. The teacher selects a particular child who seems very capable and competent in interacting with others and specifically asks that child to model, prompt, and reinforce the developmentally disabled child for interacting socially. In the beginning, it is best if the peer is told exactly what to do, which means that he acts just like a teacher-therapist: he instructs, rewards, and prompts. This is to help develop some interaction, because without such explicit instruction, there may not be any interaction. In the process of becoming familiar with each other, the peer will probably become more flexible and inventive, without losing contact with the disabled child. This strategy also has the advantage that it requires less of the adult's attention, and the end product resembles more closely a normal social interaction.

A DIFFERENT KIND OF SCHOOL

A classroom for many developmentally disabled children, at least initially, and in many cases permanently, only bears a slight resemblance to a classroom for average children. This becomes obvious when one considers the ideal teacher-to-student ratio in such a special class. Ideally, this ratio should not exceed two students per one adult. In most instances, a school is ideal when initially there is one teacher or adult for every child. It is clear that the disabled child's school experiences have to overlap with his everyday home activities. Developmentally disabled children are very slow learners and they simply don't learn enough in a 3- to 6-hour teaching environment, hence the need to extend school to all hours of the day. It is pointless to teach skills in school if the child does not transfer and use those skills at home, and vice versa. Many developmentally disabled children have problems in transfer, so you have to make it happen. The transfer will occur when part of school is at home, and part of home is at school. It is also true that the teaching curriculum for the developmentally disabled child should be different. For example, there seems to be little sense in having a child learn to read or do arithmetic if he cannot dress himself or behave in a store or travel on a bus. That is, the kind of academic behavior we should expect of a normal first grade child probably has no real usefulness for many developmentally disabled children. The teacher has to teach different skills, in most instances.

IF HE FAILS

Some children will succeed in school, that is, they will be promoted from one grade to another. Other children will stay somewhat at the same level of functioning for many years, neither advancing nor regressing. Many children will not be able to adjust to a particular school, and need to be placed in classes or schools with a less demanding curriculum. Remember that if your child "levels off," or starts to slip, and you have done your best, then say to yourself that such is life at this time, and, to some extent, so life will always be. Excellence is relative.

The point of this book is to help the adults who care for disabled children to work better with their children, but, once a good effort is made, to accept whatever limitations the child and the situation have. Once the effort is made, and the demands imposed, at some point one must accept the child's achievement, even though it is limited. This is a basic lesson of life that everyone has to learn. The disabled child shares that with all of us.

CHAPTER 37

SCHOOL
Crighton Newsom

The passage of the Education for All Handicapped Children Act (PL 94-142) in 1975 has resulted in access to publicly funded educational services for large numbers of developmentally disabled children who were previously denied these services. Educational programs have proliferated to the point where special education now constitutes the most common form of "treatment" for developmentally disabled persons. Therefore, an understanding of the major characteristics and problems of special education is essential, both for parents and professionals who interact with schools and for teachers who work in them. We draw attention to some of the characteristics of special education by contrasting them with features of the home treatment model that is presented in previous chapters and, subsequently, by discussing some essential characteristics of behaviorally-oriented special education programs.

DIFFERENCES BETWEEN HOME TREATMENT AND CLASSROOM EDUCATION

There are a number of differences between the home treatment model, described in other chapters of this book, and the classroom education model found in most schools with programs for developmentally disabled persons. Some of these differences are very basic and we discuss those that seem most important, because they go to the heart of the problem of using in the classroom many of the procedures that have proven successful in clinic and home settings.

One-to-One versus Group Instruction

School classrooms are, by deeply-ingrained tradition, if not by definition, group instructional settings. Instead of the one-to-one teaching format that is the basis of the home treatment model, the classroom teacher must work with a group of four to ten, and sometimes more, students. Even if an assistant is present to improve the adult-student ratio somewhat, the effect of group instruction is to spread instruction thinly and thus dilute its impact on the individual student. Although it is commonly felt that classroom instruction provides opportunities for socialization, it does not appear that the degree of social development that actually takes place simply as a function of being in a group is sufficient to justify the dilution of teaching that occurs. Social behaviors do not "develop" or emerge spontaneously in developmentally disabled persons simply through exposure to other persons beyond a very rudimentary level, if that. They must be taught systematically, initially in one-to-one and one-to-two situations. Furthermore, most social interactions require some language and cooperative play skills as prerequisites, and instruction in these behaviors proceeds best in one-to-one and small-group situations involving no more than three or four students.

Some ways of minimizing the dilution of instruction in classrooms are discussed below. It should be noted that the "problem" of group instruction is not inherent in the idea of classroom education for developmentally disabled students, but results from two factors, one obvious and one not so obvious. The obvious factor is the economics of educating large numbers of people, which generally dictates a group instruction model at all levels of education, whether or not it is in the best interests of the population being served. The second, less obvious, factor is the presupposition that the way to design educational programs for disabled persons is to extend traditional education for normal and more able special students downward, that is, to decrease the class size and simplify the curriculum. An alternative approach, which seems to have escaped consideration by education planners, would be to build upward from the one-to-one situation that has established its effectiveness since the early sixties. The idea here would be to use classrooms as settings for multiple one-to-one instructional activities that gradually changed to group instruction as it became increasingly necessary to teach "regular" classroom behaviors.

"Leverage" versus "Total Push" Curricula

The "curriculum" in the home treatment model is focused in the sense that during the initial stages of treatment it concentrates on language and the control of maladaptive behaviors. The majority of time is spent on teaching language because it is the quintessential "human" behavior that provides "leverage" in that it facilitates the acquisition of other kinds of behavior, especially social behaviors, which help the person to avoid institutionalization. Once language has begun to show steady progress and maladaptive behaviors are under control, behaviors in other domains are taught, including self-care skills, academic skills, play, and community-interaction skills. In contrast, most school curricula prescribe instruction in a number of areas simultaneously from the start in a "total push" approach. Language, academic, social, recreational, motor, self-care, and community-interaction behaviors receive about equal emphasis in terms of time allocation. This broad, total push approach results from the consideration of development in the normal person as a process of acquiring behaviors in multiple areas simultaneously. At the present time, there are no experimental data comparing the outcomes of persons treated according to the two approaches, but it might be noted that the total push model runs the risk of failing to provide a sufficient amount of language training to children who are known to need a great deal of it to make progress.

Strong versus Weak Punishers

In the home treatment model, relatively strong punishers can be used to reduce maladaptive behaviors if the parents consent, including isolation, time-out, and slaps. These punishers are either absolutely forbidden or dependent on administrative, as well as parental, consent in most schools. The classroom teacher may be limited to nonexclusionary time-out and extinction as behavior-reducing procedures. The result is that maladaptive behaviors which are eliminated in a matter of days or weeks in the home treatment model require months or years to be eliminated in school settings. Although it seems paradoxical that professional teachers who are expected to be able to teach a variety of complex adaptive behaviors are deemed unable to use aversive procedures appropriately, it must be noted that many have had no formal instruction in the use of aversives in their special education training and that schools live under the glare of uninformed public opinion. This "fishbowl" existence does much to prevent the use of known, rapidly effective treatments. Hopefully, it may provide impetus to the development of publicly acceptable, if less intense, treatment techniques.

Behavior Analysis versus Developmental Theoretical Orientations

The home treatment approach described in other chapters of this book is based on a theoretical framework known as "learning theory," which was formally introduced in the earlier chapters. The procedures which have been discussed are also known as *applied behavior analysis.* Essentially, the student is seen as having certain behavioral deficits and excesses which should be remediated directly through the provision of teaching procedures known to strengthen and weaken behavior. The teacher is seen as a direct "shaper" of behavior and knowledge. On the other hand, many classroom programs for developmentally disabled persons are based on developmental theories derived from Piaget, Werner, and Kephart. Such theories emphasize the emergence of behaviors resulting from maturation and the person's interactions with the environment. The role of the teacher of developmentally disabled students is to "stimulate" maturation indirectly by providing appropriate learning opportunities to help the person progress from one developmental level to the next.

Neither theoretical approach has all the answers at the present time, and few therapists or teachers rigidly adhere to either approach exclusively. They generally borrow concepts and techniques rather freely from both approaches, and sometimes invent procedures based on neither approach in their attempts to solve immediate practical problems. But it is important to recognize the differences between the two theoretical approaches because each is invoked to justify techniques and each involves certain risks that can be assumed to affect a student's progress. The behavioral approach runs the risk of failing to teach prerequisite behaviors in its concern with teaching age-appropriate skills as rapidly as possible. In defense of the behavioral approach, it may be argued that this problem is picked up when the data show the student's lack of progress; attempts are then made to determine what additional behaviors need to be taught and to teach them. The developmental approach involves a much more serious risk. In attempting to stimulate maturational changes indirectly through procedures of often dubious scientific validity, it runs the risk of spending so much time on prerequisite behaviors (or "readiness" skills) that age-appropriate behaviors are never taught, nor do they emerge spontaneously. "Developing," in the sense of acquiring new behaviors without direct instruction, is the thing that developmentally disabled students are least able to do, whether "stimulated" or not. Further, the lack of socially significant progress may not be noticed and addressed because the developmental position does not include a strong emphasis on data-based decision making.

CREATING EFFECTIVE BEHAVIORAL CLASSROOMS

No one who is not a teacher can fully appreciate the amount of effort that goes into creating a classroom that is effective in producing meaningful, positive changes in developmentally disabled persons. Some rather formidable problems of teaching, organization, scheduling, supervision, public relations, child advocacy, and personal motivation must be handled skillfully if both stagnation and chaos are to be avoided. All of these tasks cannot be addressed here, but some possible solutions and trouble-shooting considerations can be offered for a selection of commonly encountered problems.

Many of the features of a behavioral classroom have already been presented earlier in this book, and need only be briefly reviewed here:

1. Goals are explicitly stated in terms of overt behaviors and controlling stimuli. Such explicitness allows the teacher to better know whether she has been successful or not.
2. Food, social wants, and play are explicitly used as reinforcers.
3. Prompts are used extensively, and carefully faded.
4. Evaluation of student's progress is *objective* and *continuous,* sometimes hourly or daily, if need requires.
5. Classroom time is highly structured and centered on educational tasks, such as language building and self-care, with minimal time spent in free play, artistic activities, etc.
6. Parents are at the center of the educational process.
7. The teacher assumes responsibility for progress or lack thereof, which allows for elimination of ineffective procedures.

Let us now turn to a more detailed presentation of how one may optimize certain classroom features.

MAXIMIZING INDIVIDUAL INSTRUCTION

A number of steps can be taken to improve the amount of one-to-one instruction and to improve the productivity of group instruction. These include the use of volunteer assistants, optimizing the instructional configuration, shaping group instruction, and teaching independent work skills.

Using Volunteers

The most common way of maximizing one-to-one instruction is to include volunteers in the classroom. Students and parents can be trained in a relatively brief period of time to teach many of the tasks in a developmentally disabled person's curriculum. Including those parents who have the time to participate on a regular basis has the additional advantage of ensuring consistency of treatment across the school and home environments. A nearby college or university usually proves to be a very productive source of volunteers. Many psychology, education, and speech and hearing departments grant course credit to undergraduate students who do part-time work in the community. Graduate students can often be attracted by providing them with opportunities to satisfy internship or practicum requirements and to conduct research. Other sources of volunteers include high schools (through "career exploration" courses), women's groups, and foster grandparent programs.

In addition to extra sets of hands, volunteers bring enthusiasm and fresh perspectives on problems. Only rarely, however, will they bring relevant past experience. It is therefore essential that procedures for orienting, training, and supervising volunteers exist if they are to function effectively and not become a burden. Some very useful, practical guidelines for integrating volunteers into a classroom have been presented by Fredericks et al. (1977). These authors discuss training and supervision procedures, the matching of level of responsibility with level of teaching skill, and the scheduling of volunteers' time and assignments.

Optimizing The Instructional Configuration

Several possibilities exist for organizing the classroom configuration in ways designed to approximate one-to-one instruction. In essence, these amount to procedures for conducting one-to-one training in groups. For illustrative purposes let us assume a hypothetical class of eight students with one teacher and one assistant. One way of working with the students can be termed the *rotational model*. As the top part (Panel A) in Figure 37-1 shows, the teacher and the assistant each take half the students. Each adult then rotates from student to student conducting one trial with each in a predetermined order. For example, the teacher may start with the student on the left and present a command, a prompt if necessary, and a consequence for the child's response (Trial 1). Then the teacher presents Trial 2 to the second student, Trial 3 to the third student, and Trial 4 to the fourth student. The first student then receives his or her second trial (Trial 5), after which the second student receives his or her second trial (Trial 6), and so on. The students may all be working on the same task or each may have an individualized task. Each student is receiving the same sort of one-to-one training described earlier in this book, but in parallel with other students. The only essential difference from standard one-to-one training is that the intertrial intervals are longer in the rotational model, because the teacher is conducting trials with other students during the period between trials with a given student.

Variations of the rotational model are shown in Panels B and C of Figure 37-1. In Panel B, one adult works with four students at a table while the other adult works with the remaining students on other skills in a different area of the classroom (e.g., play, dressing, toileting). Panel C shows two adults using the rotational model with two students each. The other students, having previously acquired ap-

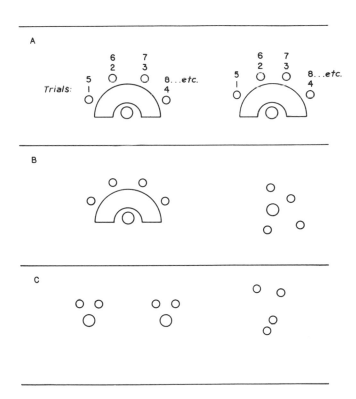

Figure 37-1. Rotational instruction configurations. Large circles indicate adults; small circles indicate students.

propriate play skills, occupy themselves in a nearby area where they can be loosely supervised. The two groups of students change places every 20 or 30 minutes.

Shaping Group Instruction

Chapters 33 and 35 provide some useful advice on how students could be helped to learn in group settings. Another approach to facilitate group instruction was developed by Koegel and Rincover (1974) in which students at about the same level of functioning work on the same task, responding in unison to the same command on each trial. The procedure involves a large number of assistants in the first stage. The program is diagrammed in Figure 37-2. In the first step, a one-to-one configuration is used, with an assistant behind each student, prompting and reinforcing correct responses to the teacher's commands. Over sessions, the students are weaned from a fixed-ratio (FR)-1 schedule of reinforcement to an FR-2 schedule (i.e., from reinforcement for every correct response to reinforcement for every second correct response). After four students are responding to criterion (90% of the responses or more are correct) without prompts, they are brought together to form a group with a teacher and two assistants in Step 2. Since each student has learned to respond twice for each reinforcement, each assistant is able to provide prompts and rewards for two students. The students are again brought to respond to criterion and the reinforcement schedule is thinned to FR-4. In Step 3, the two groups of four are brought together to form a class of eight and, after achieving the correct response criterion, are moved from an FR-4 schedule to a variable-ratio (VR)-8 schedule, in which each student is rewarded for every eighth correct response on the average. In Step 4, the assistants are faded out of the classroom and the teacher provides the reinforcers on a VR-8 schedule. Using this shaping program, Koegel and Rincover (1974) have shown that even a severely retarded autistic student can learn new verbal and basic academic behaviors in a group instructional format.

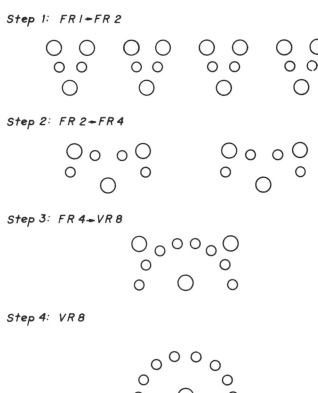

Figure 37-2. Simultaneous instruction training steps. Large and small circles represent adults and students, respectively. Based on Koegel and Rincover, 1977.

Expanding Your Child's World

Shaping Independent Work

After students have been taught basic classroom skills through procedures like those just described, their need to be able to work independently on individualized tasks will become increasingly apparent. A procedure for teaching developmentally disabled students to work independent of direct supervision for periods up to 45 minutes has been presented by Rincover and Koegel (1977). They conceptualized the problem of teaching children to work independently as one of chaining more and more of the student's responses to a single instruction from the teacher. Using worksheets like those shown in Figure 37-3, each student was initially rewarded for completing a familiar tracing task in one of the twelve squares after being instructed to "Trace the lines." Next, the student was required to complete two of the squares before receiving a reward, then three squares, and so on. Eventually, every student reliably completed all twelve squares in response to each instruction to "Trace the lines." Once these long chains of tracing

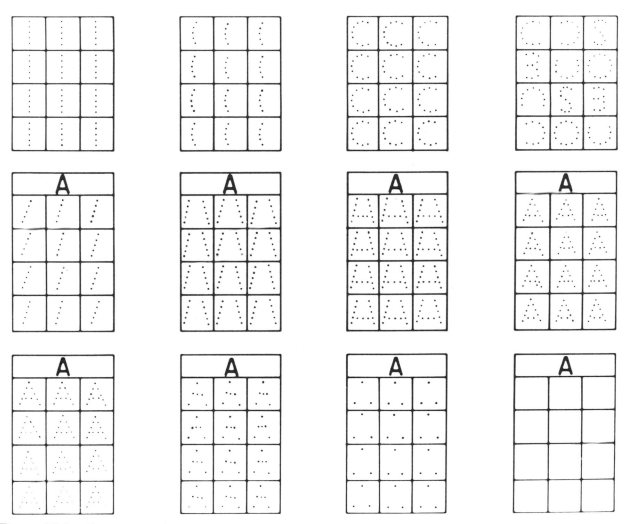

Figure 37-3. Sequences of worksheets used by Koegel and Rincover (1977) to shape independent work. The top row shows selected steps in shaping the tracing of curved lines; the bottom two rows show steps for shaping printing of the letter *A*. Reprinted by permission.

responses had been developed, the worksheets included tasks of gradually increasing levels of difficulty. One of the students was able to progress to commercial programmed workbooks. The teacher was able to move from student to student providing individualized help while the other students continued working productively. This procedure for teaching independent work is not restricted to paper and pencil tasks and could easily be extended to other tasks involving repetitive or sequential responding, such as dressing and undressing, workshop skills, appropriate play, and working with teaching machines.

MANAGING DISRUPTIVE BEHAVIORS

Note that education is basically a process of building appropriate behaviors under the control of relevant stimuli. The behaviors to be learned are often more difficult than we realize to a handicapped person. Also, the typical classroom is a situation that is quite rich in demands (instructions, commands, etc.) compared to the student's home or other residential environment. Adult demands and student's failure usually produce large increases in self-injurious, aggressive, and tantrum-like behaviors. The classroom may be the student's first experience in socialization, i.e., having to behave according to adult's rules instead of personal preferences, with all that socialization entails, including appropriate toileting, wearing clothes, delayed and absent rewards, sharing adult attention with others, and getting along with disruptive and aggressive peers. The "period of adjustment" is likely to be especially difficult and prolonged if a student's parents are overindulgent and have allowed self-centered and immature behaviors to continue too long. This brings us to our next point, which is that student's reinforcement histories at home, in other living environments, and in other classrooms will be largely unknown and must be guessed at as filtered through others. This means that the origins of the problem behaviors are likely to be impossible to discover, and, worse, current payoffs outside the classroom for problem behaviors may be very difficult to identify and control. Finally, most classrooms are not well equipped for dealing with problem behaviors, even where they are a daily occurrence. In the name of "normalization," most classrooms for developmentally disabled students are modeled after classrooms for normal children.

Given the preceding factors, which tend to be operating continuously in most classrooms, it is hardly surprising that disruptive behaviors occur. Some of these factors are subject to total or partial control; some are not. An awareness of them should at least minimize unproductive, wishful thinking that problem behaviors would disappear completely.

Diagnosing The Problem

The diagnosis of a problem behavior attempts to discover how the behavior is related to environmental events that precede and follow it. Think of diagnosis as the teacher's ABCs, where A is the antecedent, B the behavior, and C the consequence. It is generally useful to look first at the antecedent events: did anything happen just before the behavior that might have set it off? Was the student hit, teased, or interrupted? Did an adult present a demand or a difficult task? Did the student loose a valued object? Did the student see a person who was associated with restrictions or with rewards for disruptive behavior? On the consequence side, the question is: What happened right after the behavior? Here the aim is to discover what rewarded the behavior. Some of the common rewards for disruptive behavior include the teacher's attention in the form of redirecting the student after he has been disruptive, or reasoning with him, or reassuring him, or giving him mild punishment. Sometimes the emotional reactions from others, such as anger, pain, or surprise, may be sufficient to maintain disruptive behavior. Rewards for disruptive behavior can also occur when the behavior leads to escape from aversive events, especially work and adult demands.

If the foregoing investigation fails to turn up plausible causes, the scope of the analysis should be broadened to include less obvious and more remote factors. The child may be temporarily irritable or oversensitive to stimuli which would not ordinarily set off disruptive behavior because he is ill or injured, or has had a bad experience at home or on the bus before school. The presence of a new adult or a group of visitors may provide a fresh audience to test for the possible reinforcement they might provide for disruptive behaviors. There may have been a recent change in the daily routine, or disorganization, crowding, or high noise levels. There may be insufficient reinforcement for appropriate behavior. Transitional activities (moving from one location to another) may occasion problems, either because the teacher is distracted or because of the nature of what lies ahead (e.g., an aversive bus ride). The recent reduction or elimination of one problem behavior through extinction or punishment may result in the appearance of another, equally troublesome behavior if no appropriate alternative behavior has been established because these two procedures commonly increase the variability of behavior as a side effect. The reduction of a behavior in one environment may lead to an increase in that same behavior in a different environment, an effect known as *behavioral contrast*. Finally, there is the possibility of unknown or uncontrollable sources of reinforcement for the behavior outside of the classroom whose effects extend into the classroom. These examples do not exhaust the possible causes of behavior problems, but they should serve to indicate the variety of factors that might be considered.

The diagnosis of a problem behavior is greatly facilitated if each occurrence of the behavior is recorded, along with a brief description of antecedent and consequent events. When this is done over several days, two benefits accrue. First, patterns or classes of causal events may become apparent that have escaped casual observation. Second, the record will constitute baseline data against which to gauge the effects of subsequent treatments.

Often, doubts or disagreements about the critical causal factors occur. The most effective way of resolving such problems is to apply a little science and test the causal status of one of the factors under consideration. Once a steady baseline is evident, eliminate the factor for 2 weeks while keeping everything else unchanged, then reinstate it. If the factor is critical in the causation of the behavior, the behavior should show at least a decreasing trend, if not a large reduction, during the 2-week trial, unless it is being maintained by an exceptionally thin schedule of intermittent reinforcement. Furthermore, the behavior should increase again when the factor is reinstated. If the data show no change in the behavior, the factor being studied is probably not critical in causing the behavior. What we have just described, in an admittedly oversimplified way, is known as a *reversal experimental design,* which in various forms has contributed much to our knowledge of how to treat problem behaviors. The interested reader can learn more about its proper use and about additional procedures by consulting behavior modification textbooks, or Hersen and Barlow (1976). The important point is that a little objective data can go a long way toward resolving doubts and disputes in situations where everyone is an expert.

Implementing Treatments

Various treatment procedures for reducing undesirable behaviors and increasing desirable behaviors are discussed elsewhere in this book, as well as in behavior modification textbooks and books on the education of developmentally disabled persons. Therefore, instead of restating familiar material, we will emphasize some considerations in the use of treatment procedures that seem especially important in classroom settings.

Functional Analysis

A throughly-conducted diagnosis (a "functional analysis") generally suggests the correct treatment, unless the problem is unusually complex. For example, if it seems clear that a child's tantrums are positively reinforced by the attention they receive, consider extinction or time-out (withholding attention for tantrums) if it is practical and safe to use it (i.e., if the child's tantrums are not so severe as to be harmful to himself or others). If the tantrums allow the child to avoid unpleasant tasks, time-out would definitely be contraindicated. Time-out would only "help" the child avoid work and could therefore be expected to make the problem worse.

"Package" Treatment

Generally, a combination, or "package" of treatments will have to be implemented simultaneously to gain control over the behavior. Only in relatively mild, uncomplicated cases would the use of a single treatment procedure be effective. For example, in the case of a student who throws tantrums to get out of work, one could provide extinction for the tantrums while simultaneously requiring (prompting) the student to continue working, thus making the tantrums ineffective in avoiding the task. In most, if not all, cases involving an attempt to reduce behavior, the attempt will be much more likely to succeed and will succeed more quickly if an alternative, appropriate behavior is being strengthened through positive reinforcement at the same time. It would also be wise to see if the student's task could be made less aversive by simplifying it and/or presenting it in a "positive context" (Carr, Newsom & Binkoff, 1976) of increased adult attention or better tangible reinforcers. But be careful not to let attempts to simplify the task be the student's reward for having thrown a tantrum. Simplify the task at the *beginning* of a session (or trial) not *after* a tantrum.

Use of Time-out

Time-out in its various forms (including sitting in a corner or being ignored for a moment, as well as going to a designated room) is one of the more commonly used behavior-reduction procedures in classrooms. While it can be effective with a wide range of positively reinforced behaviors note that it is contraindicated in three circumstances: a) in the treatment of behaviors that avoid or escape demands (negatively reinforced behavior) for the reason mentioned above; b) in the treatment of most self-stimulatory behaviors, since the child generally controls the reinforcers for these behaviors and is usually free to indulge in them while in time-out; and c) in classrooms where there is an inadequate level of positive reinforcement, since time-out has to be time-out of an environment where positive reinforcement is frequently available to be effective. (This, by the way, is why time-out often has no effect in custodial, barren institutional settings—time-out from nothing is nothing, i.e., simply movement from one neutral environment to another.) If the teacher normally provides more criticisms and reprimands than praise, time-out would be expected to increase whatever behavior it follows, since it would provide a way of escaping the teacher's aversive behaviors.

Use of Physical Punishment

The use of physical punishment should be reserved for only very severe behavior problems that threaten serious harm to the child or to others, after other possible treatments have been either tried and been found ineffective or considered and rejected because they work too slowly or are likely to be ineffective or result in habituation. If it is decided to use physical punishment, it should be used only with the precautions we have mentioned in earlier chapters, that is with the parents' informed, written consent, only by designated, experienced staff, only with adequate data-recording procedures which track both the target behavior and the punishment applications, only if an intensive program to teach competing, appropriate behaviors is in place, and only under the direct supervision of a behavioral psychologist experienced in the use of the procedure. There are some important practical reasons, as well as the obvious ethical ones, for exercising such extreme caution in the use of physical punishment. First, the physical punishers that teachers sometimes use are often too mild or are applied too intermittently to effect more than a temporary suppression of behavior. Second, most administrators and professionals strongly disapprove of the use of physical punishment with handicapped persons, and may not be able to understand its occasional necessity. The teacher may lose her job, and the student his teacher. Thus, the cost of eliminating a behavior may be too high. In this regard it is important to emphasize what has been advocated in previous chapters, namely, that the parents of developmentally disabled students help the teacher with the student's unmanageable behaviors. Perhaps it would be best as matters now stand if the parents were expected (and taught if necessary) to help the teacher manage their children in class. That is, the parents should do the spanking (if necessary) and give the teacher more manageable students. (In defense of parents who have failed to do so, one need only point to the many special educators, clinical psychologists, and psychiatrists who have prescribed over the last several decades procedures which in all likelihood worsened the children's behaviors, and who made the parents feel guilty about being firmly nonaccepting of their children's inappropriate aggressions.)

Duration of Treatment

Any treatment procedure, with the exception of strong physical punishment, should be conducted for at least 2 weeks before it is abandoned as ineffective. Strong physical punishers are exempted from this guideline because when they are effective, they are usually effective very rapidly, producing a noticeable improvement within a day, and sometimes within five to ten applications. Other treatments should be expected to work more slowly, and should be given ample opportunity to demonstrate their efficacy, or lack of it, unless serious side effects emerge early in their use. Experience suggests that many more treatment attempts are abandoned prematurely than actually fail because they are ineffective.

FUTURE DIRECTIONS

Looking ahead, we expect to see education for developmentally disabled persons become progressively more effective than it is today. Several developments suggest this.

1. A blending of developmental and behavioral educational approaches, at least to some degree, seems likely, with the strengths of each approach contributing to an integrated curriculum.
2. There is an increasing tendency for schools to expand beyond their "core" classroom education programs into services meeting more of the needs of handicapped children and their families.
3. Finally, increasing numbers of schools are providing educational programs stressing early intervention, that is, educational programs for developmentally disabled infants, toddlers, and preschoolers. Early educational interventions no doubt will show major and dramatic positive effects. As these behavioral/educational procedures become more common in preschools, correspondingly greater numbers of children will be helped to a greater extent than at present.

CHAPTER 38

COMMON PROBLEMS AND PRECAUTIONS

This chapter summarizes some of the common problems that may be encountered in behavioral teaching programs for developmentally retarded children. Many of these problems or mistakes have already been presented in earlier chapters. This chapter brings together in one place the various precautions we have mentioned earlier.

The mistakes that do occur can be divided into two main groups. There is a general set of problems that cut across many teaching situations and are independent of the teacher's techniques, and there is a set of more specific problems that are most likely to occur within a behavior modification framework.

SPECIFIC PROBLEMS

This section points out some of the specific problems that may occur in a behaviorally designed teaching program. These problems are not always easy to detect, and you may need the help of a colleague or a peer group to point out errors in any teaching technique. Even though a teacher may start out quite perfect, it is not unusual that teachers "drift" from criterion performance over time (just as the children drift), and slow changes in teaching style are difficult to detect and difficult to self-eliminate. Peers can be very helpful in keeping one on the right track. The main problems that arise in behavioral teaching can be summarized below.

Rewards are Different From Punishments

One of the most common mistakes occurs when rewards begin to look like punishments and the child cannot discriminate between the two. If the teacher's "Good" is said in the same tone of voice and with the same enthusiasm as the "No," then in all likelihood the developmentally retarded child is getting inadequate feedback. (At certain advanced teaching levels "Good" and "No" may be stated with the same emotional quality because the *informational* value of these words will be sufficient to guide the child, but certainly during the early stages of learning for the developmentally retarded this is not the case.)

One possible reason why adults become less emphatic or enthusiastic about expressing "Good" and "No" may be because they extinguish their own feelings for these words over time. It is difficult to maintain the same kind of high-level emotional expression month after month, year after year. One needs reinforcement from peers in order to maintain such a discrimination.

Variety In Consequences

Many adults are restricted in the *kinds* of consequences they provide for their children. A good teacher is one who expresses approval (or disapproval) in a variety of ways: he or she verbally approves, kisses, hugs, strokes and tickles, and feeds the child, lets the child get out of the chair, plays with the child, and, in general, brings to him all the kinds of goodies a child can imagine. A teacher who is not as skillful may settle for a monotonous "Good," and the problem with such a stereotyped monotonous reward is that satiation is quickly reached for the reward and the child loses interest in the teaching situation.

Remember also that, in addition to rewarding the child with a variety of positive reinforcers, a good teacher may also manage to teach the child some uneasiness and tension when the child is faced with a problem to which he does not have a ready answer. Most normal children probably learn solutions to problems because the problem creates a certain state of tension or uneasiness in them. The reward for accomplishing a difficult task is not just to get the positive reinforcers, but to avoid or escape from the kinds of negative tensions and uneasiness that precede the problem solution. A good teacher is probably one who helps her children experience some of the same kind of tension or urgency before a problem is solved, and to experience relief over the solution.

Adult Is Boss

One of the main problems in teaching developmentally retarded children occurs when the adult fails to establish who is in control. Many adults have been advised to "walk on eggs" with their children, that is, to not present demands, to not upset or disturb them, and to watch out for their fragile egos, which is bad advice according to the principles we have outlined throughout this book. Let your children know you are the boss. Let them know that whatever privileges they enjoyed at earlier times are automatically revoked when they misbehave, and that, when privileges are earned back, it is the *adult* who decides how and when this occurs.

Also, once in a while the teacher has to be very strict. This may sound harsh but, if our data are correct, structured and "authoritative" environments may be best for developmentally retarded children during the early stages of their learning. Slowly, over time, the teacher's structure may be lessened, and replaced with more democratic procedures, but democracy has to be earned—it is not given. Keep in mind that it is possible to be firm and yet be friendly. You do want to become an important friend to your child, so that gaining and keeping your approval is significant for him.

Most teachers probably proceed too quickly into the curriculum and do not establish the kind of early control that is necessary for subsequent learning. The child who sits in a class rocking and flapping his arms, who screams or attacks himself or others when he is up against a frustrating situation, probably is not what most teachers would call an ideal student.

Much of the child's learning will depend on the type of adult who is selected to work with the child. It is best to select people who are assertive, confident, and outgoing, if our experience is a guide. People whose voices are very tender, who have difficulty asserting themselves, or who are obsessive about right and wrong just don't make good teachers of developmentally disabled children.

Be Careful In How You Reward

Most persons recognize that one has to be careful in one's use of punishment. It used to be thought that affection could do no harm, that developmentally disabled children could use all the loving one could give them. Increasingly, we are becoming aware of how one has to use love with caution. Love is powerful medicine; it can be used against the child as well as to his benefit. Many persons find it easier to love a sick child than a healthy one. Perhaps this attitude has contributed to conceptions of children as "mentally ill" and "damaged," and lowered our expectations of their future. More specifically, we are observing how showing affection (or withdrawing demands) contingent on self-injurious and other "psychotic" behaviors serves to shape and maintain such behaviors. The reason why many disabled persons are trapped by their behavioral deficiencies and sometimes even come close to killing themselves through self-injury is that they were loved at the wrong time. Teachers, psychologists, and psychiatrists can be the most dangerous of honorable and well-meaning persons.

Make The Trials Discrete

Another problem in technical execution of teaching relates to the succinct onset and spacing of trials. Koegel and associates (1977) at the University of California at Santa Barbara have discussed the importance of "discrete trials" (see Chapter 1). In order to make the instructions as distinct and discriminable as possible, it is critical that the teacher "pace" the trials. Sometimes one can observe an adult teaching a child in a situation that seems very "fluid," one in which no sooner is a trial ended and the reinforcement given than a new trial is presented with no pause or spacing between events. Or, if the child does not respond, the instructions are repeated with no pause in between. Such "fluidity" may work for normal children, but is too difficult for slower children. For such children, at least during the early stages of learning, it is critical that there is a spacing between the teacher's inputs so that the child can better discriminate what is said and "ready" himself for responding. Suppose a teacher says, "Johnny, look here, point to the red block, no, not the green block, I mean the red block," and presents this as a fluid and continuous statement. Such a teacher is probably becoming an ineffective person because her instructions begin to lose their communicative intent; she is being neutralized. Instead, as we have frequently argued throughout the book, the adult may say, "Johnny, look here," pausing at that time to allow the child to attend, and if the child does attend, then presenting a succinct instruction. The teacher then observes whether the child performed adequately or not, and, depending on the child's performance, rewards or not. Each step should be distinct and succinct.

Overselective Attention

One of the more significant problems that faces many developmentally retarded children concerns restrictions or overselectivity in their attention. As far as we can determine, developmentally retarded children restrict their attention and focus on fewer parts of a teaching situation than do normal, or average, children of the same chronological age. In other words, the children do not perceive all of the input the adult may want to provide. The problem is twofold: first, if the adult employs a lot of extra aids or cues, as in manually prompting or visually guiding the child through a task, the child may become "hooked" on the prompts or guidance cues and not perceive the other cues that the adult wants to associate with a particular performance. For example, if the adult helps a child by pointing out where the correct answer is, then the child may become unduly hooked on the adult's finger prompts and will visually track or otherwise follow the adult's hands in order to perform. The child's attention to the adult's hand may be so strong that he does not see or hear what else is going on. The children may carefully study the adult's face for those extra cues that give away the correct response, and be so intent on reading the adult's face that whatever else is happening passes them by. Have someone watch you to see if you use many such unintended prompts or extra cues.

Sensing versus Perceiving

Another problem in attention points out the difference between sensing and perceiving. For example, it is entirely possible for a child to look directly at the adult's face, and yet not see or hear anything that the adult is trying to communicate. The child may have no auditory deficit whatsoever and even shouting the instruction to him does not make him hear. Problems like that are probably universal. It is easy to remember how sometimes in school we entered a lecture hall, and left after 50 minutes with a total void as to what was said—the lecture seemed to have passed right by you. Many developmentally disabled children show such attentional peculiarities to the extreme. What this implies is that a child can be sitting nicely and looking at the teacher but not paying any attention at all to what is being said.

Paying "real" attention (seeing and hearing) probably comes about through differential use of rewards and punishment (or no reward). In short, attention is learned. In the various training steps outlined in this book, there always was a step that forced or enabled the child to pay meaningful attention to the teaching material. Most often this step involved *differential reinforcement*, that is, the child was rewarded for responding to the adult's cues, and *not* rewarded (or admonished) for responding when these cues were absent. For example, if the adult says "ah" and the child responds likewise, then he would be rewarded. If the child said "ah" and the adult had not spoken (or if the adult had said "mm") then the child would *not* be rewarded, and perhaps admonished! Through such a procedure the child will learn to respond at the right time, and he can only do so if he *attends*. He can learn to attend. Also, if your child learns to pay attention to one set of cues, this does not simultaneously mean that he has learned to attend to all other cues. For example, learning how to attend to consonants does not mean that he has learned to pay attention to vowels. Such attention has to be trained separately. The longer you work with a child, and the more progress he makes, the more clearly you will see this relationship between attention and reinforcement.

The child's problem in attention should be kept in mind in all learning situations. For example, developmentally disabled children probably learn relatively little by mere observation of other children or the teacher even though normal children learn that way. Particularly in the early stages of learning, developmentally disabled children learn mostly through direct one-to-one teacher-student shaping. It is a waste of time to place a severely retarded child among other children in a group, with the teacher verbally or visually instructing the children as passive observers.

Twenty Percent As Play

As one becomes successful in working with these children, the children become very reinforcing to the adult because they are actually learning something. Under these conditions it is a common mistake for adults to extend the teaching session beyond the child's capacity to learn, or at least to sit still. For example, it is not unusual to see teachers who have children sit still for an hour at a time. Be careful to program explicit breaks for the children every 5 or 10 minutes, where they can stand up and run around and otherwise exercise for a minute or two. Once every hour, have a somewhat longer break. Work hard for 2 hours, then have more informal school or teaching sessions for 2 hours, then return for 2 hours of hard work again. Try to set the day up to include 6 to 8 hours of hard work, with play or informal teaching interspersed throughout. Remember how reinforcing it was for you at recess to run around, scream, and act crazy. Perhaps 80% work, 20% play is the ideal. Also, remember to make such "getting out of chair" contingent upon correct behavior on the part of the child.

A related mistake is for the adult to make the teaching situation very academic and formal throughout. The adult may become so rewarded by the child's progress that the entire day is spent in academic tasks. Although it is hard to quote adequate data, it seems likely, particularly for small children, that the adult must schedule some time just for playing or rough-housing for no other reason than to facilitate the child's neurological development. It is possible to be strict and bossy for 5 minutes and then take a 1-minute break where everybody horses around, only to return to a structured situation for the next 5 minutes. The child should be able to learn to discriminate between play and work—all persons must learn that discrimination.

The Child Works Harder Than the Adult

Another problem that is a little more subtle and difficult to discern can be seen when an adult puts out a tremendous amount of effort and the child just passively sits back, enjoying himself while self-stimulating. Sometimes when a child moves very slowly, it is because the teacher tries too hard and the drill doesn't work at all. A child will not learn unless he works and puts out behaviors on his own. The ideal situation is one in which the child works very hard to come up with the right answer, and not the teacher.

If You Punish, Remember To Reward

One last problem we want to especially warn against concerns the use of discipline, or aversives, for "bad" behavior without also using lots of loving for "good" behavior. If one fails to reinforce good behavior then the effects of discipline or aversives will be very short lived, and the children will eventually begin to hate and fear their teacher. Whenever an adult disapproves of a child for unacceptable behavior, then that adult should prompt acceptable behavior that can be positively rewarded. For example, if the child has been told a loud "No!" for self-stimulating, then, as soon as the child sits still and does *not* self-stimulate, the adult must approve warmly "Good!" An adult who is strict must also be an adult who is very loving. If you find an adult who is strict and not loving, he probably would not be very good for your child.

GENERAL PROBLEMS

There are some general problems in teaching that we have referred to at various places in this manual. These problems are summarized below.

Working in Isolation

A very common mistake for parents and professional persons alike is to work in isolation, without regular feedback from a group of peers who can monitor one's performance. It is very difficult to work with developmentally disabled children, and the rules for teaching are inadequately described (it is still too much of an "art"), so that a person who works alone is likely to move astray and lose his skills. A peer group that meets weekly to observe each other's successes and failures is most important for any teacher or parent. It is too easy to make mistakes and not detect them, and one needs the encouragement of others to improve. To make such feedback instructive, work with your child in front of others; in such a situation one can be most explicit.

One related problem concerns the common and unfortunate separation between parents and teachers. To adequately teach the program discussed in this book, one has to engage all significant adults in the child's environment, and that includes both parents and teachers. Quite simply, the teacher has to know what the parent knows; the only way that will happen is if the parent informs the teacher. Similarly, the parent has to know what the teacher knows and the only way this will happen is if the teacher tells the parent. One can only do this in a group in which everybody is equal. It is rare to encounter such groups in most places where developmentally disabled children are taught. Instead, it is more common to see a school where the parents and the teachers meet together on a monthly basis or even less frequently and where the parents sit on one side of the room and the teachers on the other, each feeling uncomfortable about each other's presence. That is a poor working environment.

A similar mistake is to assume that if the child learns new behaviors in school that these behaviors will transfer to the home. We know now that it is very likely that school learning does *not* transfer to the home for developmentally retarded children. Historically, special education (as well as child psychiatry and clinical psychology) has isolated its educational efforts from the community at large. Somehow it was hoped that if the children would be taken from an "inadequate" home environment and placed within an "enriched" school (or clinic) environment, then the children would blossom forth everywhere. Most often, generalized change has to be programmed; it does not occur spontaneously.

Forgetting about After-Care

It is often the case that a teacher feels that the day is ended when school is over and the children are sent home. Thus, we think that school is over on Friday or it is ended in June when the child goes on vacation, or it ends with kindergarten when the child goes into first grade. Yet most teachers know that too many children with problems will regress and lose the gains they have made in school once school is over. Therefore, schools need more flexible programming to facilitate transfer of learning to nonschool environments. In the future, school for developmentally disabled children will become a 16-hour-a-day, 6-day-a-week, 12-month-a-year endeavor, connecting all environments. Perhaps only parents can provide such a service, but then the parents have to be trained and brought into the teaching staff. Teachers have to give their skills to the public.

Labeling

All too often terms such as "mental illness" or "brain damage" serve to segregate the child from other children, and to invite a set of interventions (or the absence of same) that work to the child's detriment. We are part of a profession where too often the mere diagnosis of a child's problem (not to mention the way it traditionally has been treated in state schools or mental hospitals), leads to the child's deterioration. In our work with autistic children, for example, we refrain from labeling the child *autistic* when introducing him to school or to other professionals. The mere label of autism scares many people. It is much less destructive to call the child "language delayed," or some such neutral descriptive term. Something is obviously very wrong in a profession when a child, after he has been diagnosed and treated, fails to improve or gets worse. If the concept of "mental illness" and related diagnostic labels are analyzed, it may be found that these terms bear no scientific and little moral value. In part, the concept "mental illness" survives because it serves to establish some acceptance for children who are different from others. That is, it may be better for the child to be called "mentally ill" than to be called "stupid" or "crazy." Although the concept of mental illness may have solved some immediate social problems some 80 or 90 years ago (when it was first coined), the long-range effect of the concept was detrimental because it failed to provide an adequate treatment.

At the present time, a term such as "mental illness" is not quite as popular as before (most persons recognize the danger associated with such labels), and is gradually being replaced with equally obscure labels, such as "brain damaged." There is no evidence that the newer term will help children more than the older term. The problem with both terms is that they do not lead to any scientific form of treatment. In fact, very often and perhaps much too often, these terms invite some hands-off approach that prevents effective treatment. It is possible that terms such as "mental illness" and "brain damage" were coined by professionals who were supposed to help such children but were faced with repeated failure, and who then put the responsibility for their failure on the child (the child is "too sick" or "too brain damaged"). Working with these children is difficult and the disappointments can be bitter indeed, and one has to survive somehow.

In any case, avoid a system where your child becomes trapped in obscure terminology, invented for someone else's benefit. Even if a child does have brain damage, he has to be taught, and that is an explicit process requiring him to take increasing responsibility for his life and to learn to face increasing maturity.

Spending Time on the Diagnosis

We have seen many parents who have spent an enormous amount of money and time trying to establish the "correct" diagnosis for their child. In general, these parents usually become more confused because the more places they visit, the more diagnoses they receive (retarded, autistic, aphasic, brain damaged, emotionally disturbed, schizophrenic, psychotic, atypical development). The more diagnoses a parent obtains, the more money a parent spends. It is rare that the diagnosis really alters the treatment anyway, so it is pointless to seek all these fine and often imaginary classifications.

There is, in our opinion, another danger behind extensive diagnostic work: it misdirects persons to look for answers to the child's problems "inside" the child, when today all we really can do to help the situation is to manipulate the child's external (educational) environment. As matters now stand, looking for problems inside the child too often implies a hands-off attitude and an acceptance of status quo. This is particularly true with terms referring to some (usually hypothetical) brain or "cognitive" damage, or mental illness construct.

This state of affairs may have come about because persons who diagnose are often not also good at teaching or giving therapy. Perhaps one cannot excell in both areas. It seems particularly true that theoreticians and diagnosticians in our field express opinions about the assessment and treatment of the developmentally disabled without themselves possessing skills or responsibility for treatment or education. In other words, all too many have lost touch with the data. If a professional does express diagnostic opinions about your child, ask if that person carries concrete responsibilities for treatment or education. If not, you should view his or her opinions with considerable reservation.

Although one may view diagnostic testing with a great deal of skepticism, behaviorally oriented teachers measure both behavior and its environment with a great deal of precision, and do so continuously. In any behavioral teaching effort one learns quite precisely what the strength of a particular response is, what exactly can be used from the environment to strengthen and weaken it, what the rate of change may be, and so on. These assessments are *directly* related to teaching and treatment, they are individualized for each student, and only persons with extensive treatment/teaching experience can perform such an assessment. It is also difficult to imagine a behaviorally oriented teacher who does not have a profound respect for his or her students' nervous systems. When working one-to-one with behaviorally disabled persons, one learns to observe, to wait, to "stalk," to stimulate, and to activate that extremely complex organic system, so as to quickly "slip in" an instruction when the system seems "open" and to soothe it with a stroking gesture for a reward. To teach with precision is to learn to use the most complex and delicate system available. In fact, many consider that behavioral teaching is to the nervous system what software programming is to a computer. One is defined in terms of the other, and both are essential for successful operation. It is nonfunctional diagnostic classifications and grossly ineffective hypotheses about the nervous system that many have problems accepting.

Teaching "Experienced" Professionals

For some unknown reason, most professionals, once they escape the stress of seeking an education and once they have received some monetary and community support for their professional efforts, are very resistant to change. This means that a parent who is trying to have an impact on the way in which a child is taught is more likely to succeed in working with students or young professionals. There are exceptions to this, and when one meets an older professional person who is curious about the profession and willing to change, one has the most effective liason a child can get. However, as a general rule, the longer a person has worked in the field, the less likely it is that such a person will acquire new ways of teaching or treating. We make this warning here because we have spent an enormous amount of time trying to teach well-established professionals (often at their request) to no avail. The main impact of new educational developments will center on students and the very young professionals.

Not Accepting Feedback

Since so little is known about teaching developmentally disabled children, and since so much has to be learned, every teacher or clinician has to be taught and continuously updated. An environment in which either the child's parents or teacher are not amenable to feedback or change is an environment in which the child may be "stored" for various periods of time, sometimes for a lifetime. One of the most common mistakes that people make in planning for developmentally disabled persons is to assume that a school or family environment, at any one time, is adequate. It is much more in the child's interest to assume that any one school or clinic is inadequate. Only an outside observer can fully help develop more adequate teaching and treatment. Therefore, try to avoid the "expert" teacher or clinician. There are no "expert" teachers or clinicians. Similarly, the sense of security that a pleasant teacher or doctor will give to a parent is false. Much too often, a parent will pay for this "security" a few years later when the child has failed to improve.

In giving feedback, try to construct a situation in which both the professional and the parent are likely to succeed at first, then heavily reward such a success. It is likely that if one starts with a simple task, like having the child sit on a chair and visually attend for a few seconds at a time, then one will succeed. Avoid the big tasks in the beginning, because the adults involved will be on extinction and will lose interest in the child. One can only learn to take criticism for failures when one also can experience successes. A full appreciation of what is involved in a good working relationship between adults and children, and between professionals and parents, is beyond the scope of this book, but it is of much importance.

Beware of Undesirable Changes in Yourself

If you work in a large institution, such as a state hospital, be aware that you may extinguish your idealism and good teaching techniques. By just being aware of such change, one can act to stop or at least delay it. There are many other changes to guard against. Be aware of the possibility that, if you do behavioral work with severely disabled children where you do employ a lot of "right" and "wrong," you may begin to turn into an extremely rigid, "black-and-white" person. Explicit "right and wrong" can help in the beginning of a child's curriculum, but such extensive and extreme control will inhibit spontaneity later. Also, be careful not to burn out too fast. Make your working environment reinforcing, have nice persons around you, and try to see the bigger picture. Even if progress is very slow, scare yourself once in a while with the awful prospect that if you don't do the work well, your child may end up in a state institution. Visit a state institution to see how bad it is. It will give you energy to carry on.

Avoid That "One" Program

Often a child will be placed in a classroom that is totally dominated by a particular approach, be it psychodynamic, behavioral, or sensorimotor. The problem with such a placement is that, at the present time, there are no data that can tell that any one approach is going to do all the work for the child. On the other hand, it is often difficult to add new, barely tested approaches because they are unlikely to have data to back them up. An experienced teacher or clinician, or a well-informed parent, is a person who is eclectic—he or she is familiar with several theoretical orientations, and can draw upon them when he wants. It is important to recognize the limitations of any one approach.

REFERENCES

Carr, E. G., Newsom, C. D., & Binkoff, J. A. Stimulus control of self-destructive behavior in a psychotic child. *Journal of Abnormal Child Psychology,* 1976, *4,* 139-153.

Fredericks, H. D. B., et al. *A data-based classroom for the moderately and severely handicapped* (2nd ed.). Monmouth, Ore.: Instructional Development Corp., 1977.

Koegel, R. L., & Rincover, A. Treatment of psychotic children in a classroom environment. I. Learning in a large group. *Journal of Applied Behavior Analysis,* 1974, *7,* 45-59.

Koegel, R. L., Russo, D. C., & Rincover, A. Assessing and training the generalized use of behavior modification with autistic children. *Journal of Applied Behavior Analysis,* 1977, *10,* 197-205.

Rincover, A., & Koegel, R. L. Classroom treatment of autistic children: II. Individualized instruction in a group. *Journal of Abnormal Child Psychology,* 1977, *5,* 113-126.

RECOMMENDED READINGS

Birnbrauer, J. S., Wolf, M. M., Kidder, J. D., & Tague, C. Classroom behavior of retarded pupils with token reinforcement. *Journal of Experimental Child Psychology,* 1965, *2,* 219-235.

Bricker, W. A., & Bricker, S. S. The infant, toddler, and preschool research and intervention project. In T. D. Tjossem (Ed.), *Intervention strategies for high risk infants and young children.* Baltimore: University Park Press, 1976.

Donnellan-Walsh, A. *Teaching makes a difference: Teacher's manual.* Santa Barbara, Calif.: Santa Barbara County Autism Project, 1976. (Available from NSAC Bookstore, 2808 Federal Lane, Bowie, Md. 20715.)

Kozloff, M. A. *Educating children with learning and behavior problems.* New York: John Wiley & Sons, 1974.

Kuypers, D. S., Wesley, C. B., & O'Leary, K. D. How to make a token system fail. In O. I. Lovaas & B. D. Bucher (Eds.), *Perspectives in behavior modification with deviant children.* Englewood Cliffs, N. J.: Prentice-Hall, 1974.

Lindsley, O. R. Direct measurement and prosthesis in retarded behavior. *Journal of Education,* 1964, *147,* 62-81.

Watson, L. S. *How to use behavior modification with mentally retarded and autistic children: Programs for administrators, teachers, parents and nurses.* Tuscaloosa, Ala.: Behavior Modification Technology, 1972.

INDEX

H

Hair, brushing or combing, teaching, 127-128
Hands
  clapping, imitation training for, 65-66
  quiet, teaching, 46-47
Home
  teacher at, 219
  treatment in, and classroom education, differences between, 223-225

I

Imagining, teaching, 199-202
Imitation training
  for facial expressions and gestures, 67-68
  for gross motor skills, 62-67
  making progress in, 68
  for pitch of speech, 98
  for simple actions, 61-69
  for speech sounds, 92-94
  for speed of speech, 98
  verbal, 89-98
  for volume of speech, 97-98
  for words, 94-97
Independent play, teaching, 105
Independent work, shaping, in maximizing individual instruction, 229-230
Instructional configuration, optimizing, in maximizing individual instruction, 227-228
Instructions
  giving of, in behavior shaping, 21, 22
  verbal, following, 81-88
Intrinsic rewards, building, 111
Intrinsically versus extrinsically controlled reinforcers, 211-212
Isolation, working in, as problem in behavioral teaching program, 239-240

L

Labeling
  of actions
    expressive, 147-148
    receptive, 143-146
  of feelings, 192-193
  of objects
    expressive, 139-142
    receptive, 135-138
  in sign language training, 156-157
  as problem in behavioral teaching program, 240-241
  of size
    expressive, 166
    receptive, 165-166
Language
  advanced, 163-183
  intermediate, teaching, 133-160
  receptive
    early, 82-84
    training in, 81-88
  sign, 153-160
  see also Sign language
Laziness, in receptive language training, 87
Learning
  discrimination, 64-65
  observational, 203-207
  teaching, 111
  preparation for, 43-56
  progress in, recording, 112-113
  with school friends, 219-220
Light, turning on, teaching, 85-86

M

Matching
  of colors, 78
  of objects in classes, 77
  of shapes, 78-79
  of three-dimensional objects, 77
    generalized, to generalized two-dimensional representations, 77-78
    identical, 72-76

  of two-dimensional objects
    generalized, 77
    identical, 76
  of visual stimuli, 71-79
Modeling
  for overcoming fears, 196
  in receptive object labeling, 137-138
Motivation
  and attention, relation between, 33-34
  problems of, in developmentally disabled children, 32-33
Mouth, opening of, teaching, 67
Multiple requests in early receptive language training, 84

N

"No!", working through task while using, for eliminating disruptive behaviors, 55-56
Nose, touching
  in early receptive language training, 85
  imitation training for, 63-64

O

Objects, labeling of
  expressive, 139-142
  receptive, 135-138
  in sign language training, 156-157
Observational learning, 203-207
Overcorrection as punishment, 17-19
Overselective attention, 34-35

P

Pants
  putting on, 125
  removing, 124
Parent
  at school, 218-219